WHAT IS ECONOMICS AND WHY DOES IT MATTER?

Through a series of contemporary cases, issues, and applications, this book provides an engaging initiation to the philosophy of economics.

The book explores the morality of economics, the role of the state, policies for well-being, and the methods applied by economists. To encourage the idea of debate, the book explores both the pro and contra arguments of key questions: Why can't economists predict future crises? Why do we pay taxes, and who should pay more? Should we open borders for economic immigrants? Why do we rely on GDP? Is economics an experimental science? By exploring these questions, and many more, the book provides an accessible and thought-provoking overview of current debates in philosophy of economics.

This book is an ideal introduction to contemporary issues and questions in the philosophy of economics for all academic readers.

Marcin Gorazda is an interdisciplinary scholar in the philosophy of economics, legal philosophy, and tax and commercial law of the Copernicus Center for Interdisciplinary Studies at Jagiellonian University in Krakow and a practising lawyer with a habilitation diploma in philosophy of law.

Tomasz Kwarciński is Associate Professor of Philosophy at the Krakow University of Economics, renowned for his interdisciplinary research and scholarly contributions in economics, ethics, social philosophy, and the philosophy of economics.

WHAT IS ECONOMICS AND WHY DOES IT MATTER?

Marcin Gorazda and Tomasz Kwarciński

Routledge
Taylor & Francis Group
LONDON AND NEW YORK

Designed cover image: Credit: Holger Kleine/Getty Images.

Illustrations by Katarzyna Kwarcińska

First published 2026
by Routledge
4 Park Square, Milton Park, Abingdon, Oxon OX14 4RN

and by Routledge
605 Third Avenue, New York, NY 10158

Routledge is an imprint of the Taylor & Francis Group, an informa business

British Library Cataloguing-in-Publication Data
A catalogue record for this book is available from the British Library

ISBN: 978-1-032-74477-3 (hbk)
ISBN: 978-1-032-74476-6 (pbk)
ISBN: 978-1-003-46938-4 (ebk)

DOI: 10.4324/9781003469384

Typeset in Times New Roman
by KnowledgeWorks Global Ltd.

CONTENTS

ABOUT THE AUTHORS

Marcin Gorazda

He was born in 1971 in Krakow, Poland, where he still lives. He graduated from Jagiellonian University in Krakow with an M.A. in Law (1995) and Pontifical University of John Paul II in Krakow (Postgraduate Studies in Philosophy, Ethics and Culture 2007). He qualified State Judge (1997) and Attorney at Law (2001). He was a practising lawyer specialising in tax and commercial law. He earned a PhD in Philosophy (2011) and a habilitation diploma in Philosophy of Law (2018). He is a member of the Copernicus Center for Interdisciplinary Studies at Jagiellonian University in Krakow, Poland (2008–present), the Polish Academy of Art and Science (2018–present), Polish Philosophy of Economics Network (2014–present). He is a member of various Polish and international commercial companies' boards of directors (non-executive), supervisory boards, and charity organisations.

He is the author of numerous papers on philosophy, philosophy of economics, law, tax law and legal philosophy published in Polish, English, and German. He is also the author of *Filozofia ekonomii* (*Philosophy of Economics*), Copernicus Center Press, Krakow 2013; *Granice naturalizacji prawa* (*Limits of the Naturalisation of Law*), Wolters Kluwer, Warszawa 2017; *Między dobrobytem a szczęściem. Eseje z filozofii ekonomii* (*Between Well-being and Happiness. Essays on the Philosophy of Economics*) Copernicus Center Press, Krakow 2020.

Tomasz Kwarciński

He is Associate Professor in the Faculty of Public Economy and Administration at the Krakow University of Economics (Department of Philosophy), with extensive experience in academic research, business ethics, social philosophy, and philosophy of economics. Born in 1979 in Krynica-Zdrój, Poland, he lives in Kraków. He graduated from the Catholic University of Lublin with an M.A. in Philosophy (2003), an M.A. in Economics (2005), and a Ph.D. in Philosophy (2008). In 2022, he obtained a habilitation diploma in Economics, and in 2021 he completed Postgraduate Studies in Methods of Statistical Data Analysis at the AGH University of Science and Technology.

He is a member of the Polish Economic Society, the European Network for the Philosophy of the Social Sciences, and the Polish Philosophy of Economics Network. He has published numerous papers on economics and the philosophy of economics in both Polish and English. His book-length works include *Równość i korzyść: Amartyi Kumar Sena koncepcja sprawiedliwości dystrybutywnej* (*Equality and Justice: Amartya Kumar Sen's Concept of Distributive Justice*), published by the University of Economics in Kraków Press in 2011, and *Między dobrobytem a szczęściem. Eseje z filozofii ekonomii* (*Between Well-being and Happiness: Essays on the Philosophy of Economics*), published by Copernicus Center Press in Kraków in 2020.

ACKNOWLEDGEMENTS

We would like to thank our colleagues from the Polish Philosophy of Economics Network, whose research has largely inspired the individual chapters of this book. In particular, we extend our gratitude to Łukasz Hardt, who has widely published his research on economic models from a realistic standpoint; Mariusz Maziarz, who has thoroughly investigated all aspects of causality in economics; Krzysztof Nowak-Posadzy, whose work on reflexivity and the cultural dimensions of economic phenomena has been truly inspiring; Agnieszka Wincewicz-Price and Joanna Dzionek-Kozłowska, who have explored the analysis of moral behaviours of economic man; and, last but not least, Bartosz Scheuer, who represents the constructivist and instrumentalist approaches to economics.

INTRODUCTION

Economics is a peculiar science. It has ambitions to be treated as any other natural science. It uses extensively advanced mathematics and models. It suffers from the so-called physics envy. On the other hand, it is deeply rooted in our folk psychology. It simplifies human emotions and reduces intentions. It assumes that all economic agents' actions are subordinated to predefined goals, primarily getting wealthier. It believes that agents are driven by a sort of logic that can be either assumed or deconstructed by thorough observation or experimentation. Once deconstructed, it can be extrapolated into sophisticated models that provide an understanding or predictions with respect to economic facts. It is also rooted in inductive reasoning. Like post-Hegelian historians, macroeconomists seem to believe in an objective spirit of history, which can be revealed in relations between collected or constructed macroeconomic variables which are stable over time.

Those strong ambitions do not go hand in hand with the common reception. Although economics is an indispensable element of governmental policy and to name a politician an economic ignorant is still one the heaviest insults, and although economists usually enjoy high social status followed by decent salaries, lay-people and politicians quite often perceive the science as ineffective, unable to predict economic turbulences and improve citizens well-being. Thus, we deal with science full of tensions and contradictions, full of different schools and approaches whose proponents are in a never-ending dispute with each other. We deal with the science that enjoys an incomprehensibly high social status, without which any management or governance could hardly be imagined.

The reflection on the science subject matter, scientific methods, the way in which scientists undergo their research and their ontological, epistemic, and ethical assumptions is a traditional domain (at least since the beginning of the

DOI: 10.4324/9781003469384-1

20th century) of the philosophy of science – in this case – philosophy of economics. The book the reader has just got is on the philosophy of economics.

To explain what this is, we start from the example. Would you agree that handing cash to homeless people is an effective and efficient instrument for struggling with homelessness? Most of the readers would likely not agree. Our moral intuitions speak against such a solution. We quite often perceive homelessness as deserved due to someone's irresponsible decisions, addictions, or laziness. Folk common sense supports the policy of giving a fishing rod and teaching how to fish instead of a fish. However, is such a policy successful?

In 2009, a research team in London conducted an intriguing social experiment. They provided 13 homeless individuals with £3000 each without specifying how they should spend it. The only question posed to the recipients was as follows: "What do you think would be good for you?". One year later, 11 of them had found accommodation, some had begun education courses, learnt to cook, or sought to overcome their addictions. The editors of *The Economist* (2010) even remarked that "the most efficient way to spend money on the homeless might be to give it to them".

Could this anti-poverty strategy be applied on a broader scale, for instance, across an entire country? Would such actions stand a chance of succeeding not only in London but also in Poland, Germany, France, or the United States? If we are to be honest, we simply do not know. Indeed, one or even several successful experiments are insufficient to answer such a question definitively. But what if different economists, relying on their own research, arrive at opposing conclusions? What if some claim that we should give money to the poor, while others insist that this must never be done? How do we decide who truly has the right?

Through research, experiments, and economic analyses, we can often call into question deeply entrenched intuitions, such as the notion that one should never give money to people in need. Like all scientists, economists pose bold questions, formulate daring hypotheses, and then endeavour to test them against reality. Yet, the conclusions they reach are only as robust as the methods they employ and the reasoning they adopt. It is precisely these aspects of economists' work – namely their methods and modes of reasoning – that capture the attention of philosophers of economics. Philosophers of economics examine the nature of economic reasoning, as well as the explicit or implicit assumptions that underlie economic theories and models. They reflect on the certainty of economists' conclusions and the extent to which proposed solutions can be applied in varying contexts. These are exactly the issues we aim to discuss in our book an engaging introduction to the often spirited philosophical debates about economics.

The title reveals the fundamental conviction we share, namely that economic research development is vital to both individuals and communities. In explaining why this is so, we emphasise that economic research contributes to human and social well-being and that a crucial aspect of such well-being is what people consider to be "happiness". Finally, we suggest that achieving this objective might benefit from taking a step back to observe how economists operate, much as philosophers usually do. This belief runs counter to many widespread intuitions. Economists are often seen as bookkeepers whose principal task is to cut spending and rein in politicians' fanciful ideas, ostensibly because there is never enough money. We, however, hold that, regardless of differing worldviews and methodologies, almost all economists, from Karl Marx to Milton Friedman, share (or at least shared) an overarching goal: the enhancement of human well-being; however, they may have defined it.

This is perhaps where economics differs from other sciences, particularly the natural sciences. Copernicus' heliocentric theory is rightly called a scientific revolution; it undoubtedly captured imaginations and fundamentally reshaped humanity's understanding of the universe. Yet, its influence on the average person's daily life seems relatively modest. Political-economic decisions, or lack thereof, have a far more tangible impact on our everyday affairs. Will we be able to afford a holiday this year? Will we be granted a mortgage? Will we lose our jobs? It can be challenging to discern the actual factors that make our lives better or worse, especially when they are obscured by government propaganda. While our essays may not provide direct answers to these questions, we hope they will help readers adopt a more critical approach to public statements made by politicians and economists and shed light on some of the hidden mechanisms of that subterranean current which quietly shapes our material lives.

Economics and philosophy in examples

We begin by discussing how the paths of philosophy and economics have intersected. Were ancient sages and philosophers interested in trade? What exactly do economists do? Why did they fail to anticipate the crisis that ravaged the global economy at the turn of the 21st century? These questions are addressed in the first part of the book, *Philosophy and Economics*.

One of the key assumptions that still sparks controversy among some economists is the conviction that economic theories do not merely describe and explain reality but also rest upon particular ethical assumptions and value judgements. For example, an economist studying the relationship between public debt and economic growth assumes, presumably for specific reasons that the latter is desirable; that is greater prosperity is seen as beneficial because it enables people to fulfil their desires more fully and that, after all, is what life is about. We examine these issues in the second part, *Ethics and Economics*. In particular, we ask what it means to say that economics is a moral science. Should we tax robots? How much would we need to earn to achieve happiness? Is admitting economic migrants a moral duty? To what extent can the state treat adults like children, nudging them to act in their own best interest?

A distinctive feature of the economic approach to analysing economic realities is its heavy reliance on models. The book's third part, *Methodology and Economics*, focuses on this issue, among others. Why do economic models resemble children's fairy tales? In what ways do modern economic measures differ from medieval methods of measuring phenomena? Why do handsome men tend to be less intelligent? Can we tackle poverty through experimentation?

In this section, we also explore the new insights gained by incorporating knowledge from other disciplines into economics and the significance of economists offering alternative explanations for phenomena traditionally investigated by other social sciences. Is a family really just a small factory? Why must the Tribble tribe become extinct? Does joining the Episcopal Church make one wealthier? These are but a few of the questions we address. Wherever possible, we illustrate these issues with examples to enhance accessibility for the reader.

The book has been conceived as a cohesive whole. Thus, individual chapters contain cross-references and, when read in the order suggested by the table of contents, form a coherent narrative about the origin, growth, and controversies of a discipline whose primary purpose is to make people prosperous and happy. Nonetheless, there are other ways of approaching the text. Although each chapter references other sections, it is also designed to stand alone, allowing readers to engage with them in any sequence they find most convenient. The short essay format also enables us to draw from a wide range of sources, not only scholarly monographs and academic articles but also more journalistic materials.

This book is exceptional in another respect. Readers will not only encounter graphs, tables, or diagrams of the sort typically found in academic works; in fact, for the sake of readability, we have endeavoured to minimise the use of such graphical aids. Instead, we have included illustrations whose intended ambiguity prompts further reflection on economics, its aims, and its limitations.

Last but not least, we wish to highlight that this work is an improved and expanded translation of the original Polish version. We have introduced new sources and citations and added an entire Chapter 6. In some examples, we have chosen to refer to local events (e.g., the introduction of Employee Capital Plans in Poland) to demonstrate that universal theories can have local instantiations. We hope these additions will enrich readers' journey into the philosophy of economics.

Reference

The Economist (2010, November 4). Cutting out the middle men. *The Economist*.

PART I

Philosophy and Economics

100

1

HOW DID ECONOMICS GET TO THIS POINT?

The great escape

Whoever is reading these words is probably a resident of one of the developed countries and is perhaps not fully aware of what a benign time and place he or she has come to live in. For many millennia of the existence of their species, humanity has been balancing on the brink of misery and death – at least when viewed in our modern terms. About 200 years ago, the liberation march towards a better existence began. Despite the numerous armed conflicts sweeping the world during this period, including two world wars, the Holocaust, the Great Famine in Ukraine, and the "great leap forward" in China, so far, this march has continued unabated. This view is shared by economists as well as sociologists, and social psychologists of both conservative-liberal views, such as Deirdre McCloskey (McCloskey, 2016) or Steven Pinker (Pinker, 2011) as well as those on the left, such as Angus Deaton (Deaton, 2013). Some call the march the "great betterment" and others the "great escape" but agreeably claim that this escape (betterment) occurred in three key dimensions of human existence: wealth, health, and security. Let's look at some figures. Before 1800, the average daily consumption of a person on the planet was USD 3, calculated in terms of their real purchasing power. This is a level found today in the poorest countries in the world, such as Afghanistan or Haiti. Today, the average consumption is more than ten times higher at USD 33, which corresponds to the standard of living in Brazil. In the most developed countries such as France, Japan, or Finland, consumption exceeds USD 100 per day. Before 1800, the world was in permanent economic stagnation if we compare it with today's growth. During the best periods of economic growth at the time, consumption levels could reach USD 6–8 per day in the best places in the world. A meagre 2% annual economic growth means that we are doubling our wealth every 35 years.

DOI: 10.4324/9781003469384-3

This consumption or global production can be calculated and averaged in different ways, bringing it down to comparable figures, but the results of these calculations almost always show the same pattern: stagnation for hundreds of years and rapid growth beginning in the 19th century (Figure 1.1).

It is a fact that even in countries that were not at the centre of world industrial development, like Poland, where the authors come from, economic growth was tremendous, although interrupted by wars and crises. Figure 1.2 clearly shows the gross domestic product (GDP) *per capita* growth on Polish lands from 1850. We can read from it an eightfold increase between 1850 and 2000.

This can also be seen from the data on workers' wages in the Polish lands, which is not easy to collect and compare. Real wages increased 2.6 times between 1921 and 1938, 2.5 times between 1960 and 1990, and about 1.5 times between 2001 and 2016 (Leszczyńska, 2018). Even assuming corrections for the Great Depression and the collapse of the war, we can confidently say that today's wage earner is many times richer than the one at the beginning of Polish independence (1918). He is also definitely healthier and likely to live longer. In 1920, the average life expectancy for women was around 50 years and for men 48. In 2015, it was almost 82 and 74, respectively. These figures look striking if we go back another half-century. In the Grand Duchy of Posen between 1850 and 1852, the average life

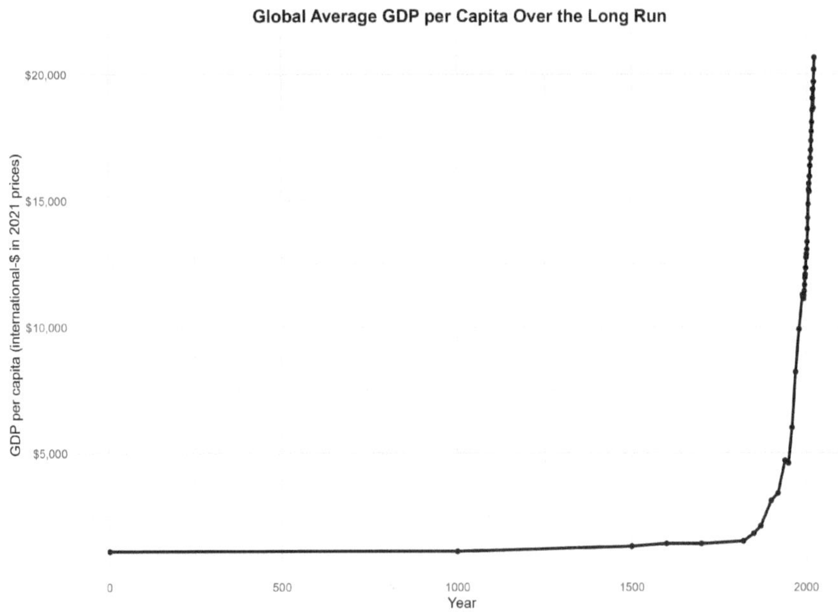

FIGURE 1.1 Global average GDP per capita over the long run

Source: World Bank (2023). Bolt and van Zanden – Maddison Project Database 2023. Maddison Data Base 2010. https://ourworldindata.org/grapher/global-average-gdp-per-capita-over-the-long-run (Accessed: December 2024)

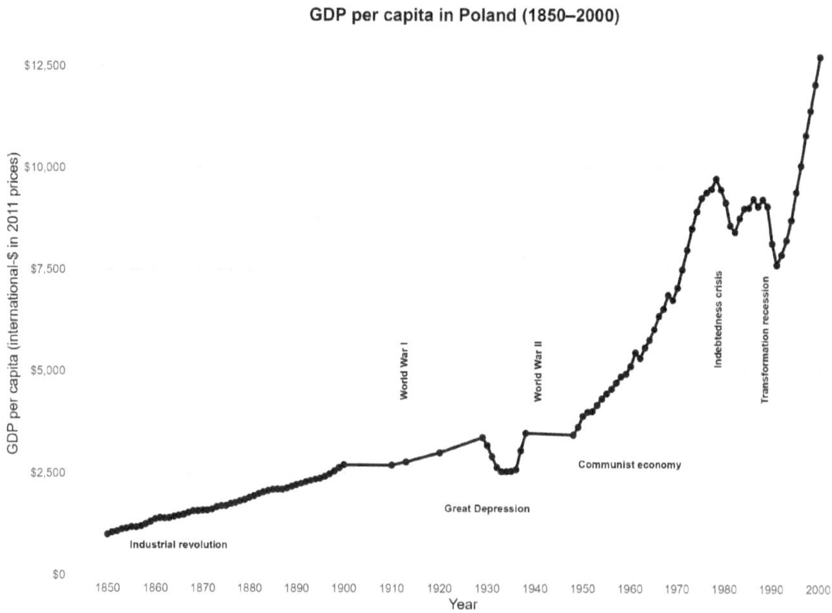

FIGURE 1.2 GDP per capita in Poland (1850–2000)

Source: Orłowski, Rozwój i załamania: gospodarka polska w ostatnim tysiącleciu (Development and breakdown: The Polish economy in the last millennium), http://www.nobe.pl/gospodarka-pol-1000.htm (Accessed: December 2024)

expectancy for men and women was just 28 and 27 years. Of course, the average was decisively influenced by the gigantic child mortality rate. In 1870, in Galicia, one in four newborns did not live past the first year of life (Kubiczek, 1994). Today, even in the poorest countries in the world, life expectancy exceeds 45 years (Deaton, 2013, p. 29).

Today, the average person on Earth lives in an environment that is far more secure than 200 years ago, including the risk of armed conflict and crime-related deaths. Relative to the population, we experience far fewer wars and aggressions. And we are talking about the world as a whole, not just developed countries. Extensive data on this subject are provided by Steven Pinker (Pinker, 2011). However, it is enough to compare basic statistics, also from Polish lands. In 1880, Poznań had a population of 65,000, and between 1877 and 1879 there were 175 deaths from unnatural causes (homicides, suicides, and unfortunate accidents, which at the time often covered up unexplained homicides). This gives about nine cases per 10,000 inhabitants per year. In 2021, there were 69 such fatal accidents in the entire Wielkopolska region (population 3,489,000), which gives about 0.2 accidents per 10,000 inhabitants per year.[1] The risk of death due to accidents or homicides has decreased by almost 50 times in 150 years (Urząd Statystyczny w Poznaniu, 2008)!

To what should this increase in wealth, security, and life expectancy be attributed? Counter-intuitively, the answer to this question is not easy and is a bit like arguing about which came first – the egg or the chicken. We know that this success is positively correlated with a number of socio-economic factors since trade, industrial production, population, education, science, new ideas, and new technologies all increase during the same period. But, as will be discussed in later chapters, correlation does not determine causality. We do not know what came first – the technology or the idea. In some simplification, two hypotheses can be formulated. One, which we do not hesitate to call "Marxist" and according to which "social being determines consciousness", means that we first have technological and economic transformations, and only ideological transformations adapt to them. Despite the reference to Karl Marx, many thinkers who do not admit to Marxism still share this view today. On the other hand, however, is the "ideological" hypothesis that there must have been a re-evaluation of the social belief system, the value system, which was a prerequisite for economic and technological change. When Max Weber writes about the Protestant ethic as allegedly the source of the economic success of selected German states in the 19th century, he supports this hypothesis (Weber, 2002). Similarly, some sociologists do the same by recognising that a fundamental condition for the development of entrepreneurship is social capital expressed, inter alia, in the level of mutual trust. Both Marxist and ideological hypotheses do not exclude feedback but undoubtedly distribute the accents differently. The most prominent representative of the ideological hypothesis is the American economist Deidre McCloskey, already mentioned. She argues that this "great improvement" was initiated by the development of a set of previously undervalued bourgeois virtues, first in the 17th century in the Netherlands and then in the 18th century in England. In the simplest terms, in both of these countries, which were bourgeois and living off overseas trade, wealth became a symptom of desirable entrepreneurship and resourcefulness, which was also followed by beliefs in the natural dignity and equality of all people. Dutch and British merchants became role models, and their ideas began to spread throughout Europe, North America, and the rest of the world, bringing, as a consequence, a radical increase in wealth. According to McCloskey, this "great improvement" was "tested by trade". Only those merchants who achieved actual financial success had a real impact on the ideological transformation of the countries in which they lived. Trade and the new bourgeois ideas went step by step. But not without obstacles. For centuries, in the way of the "great improvement" has stood the *clerisy*, for whom the basis of the functioning of human societies is a compact and powerful state organisation, for whom commercial freedom, individual dignity, freedom, and equality are a threat. The clerisy, however, does not so much include the paid functionaries of the state, but rather their ideological supporters, somewhat perversely referred to in this chapter as philosophers, who confidently adhere to such views.

Since ancient times, at least, the great rulers of this world have loved the great theorists and philosophers and willingly supported them with much reciprocity.

For among the latter, *economics*, i.e. the art of managing a farm, and *chrematistics*, i.e. the art of getting rich, were not held in high esteem and for a long time broke through the glass ceiling of strongly idealistic, or even theological, concepts of state, law, and society.[2] This is hard to believe from today's perspective, in which there is straightforward talk about the unique role of economists in the creation of public policy or the imperialism of economics invading other social sciences with its methods, but this dominance of economics is a story that only began in the second half of the last century. When the great British economist, John Maynard Keynes, warned against imposing contributions on defeated Germany after the First World War, prophesying an economic and social crisis, no one particularly listened to him. One did not have to wait long for the consequences. The remarkable social position of economists (although this also varies) does not necessarily translate into the social position of merchants (or, in modern terms, entrepreneurs). It could be said that society has strongly mixed feelings towards parvenus: mild envy with regard to their usually above-average income, anger with regard to the growing wealth stratification resulting (at least in part) from tax avoidance, respect for the ideological and investment courage of some, but also contempt for ostentatious consumption (also of some). In this contempt, also lined with pejorative moral evaluations (probably sometimes justified), the so-called humanists, philosophers, and people of science are leading the way.[3] The two worlds of business and science, merchants and philosophers, have a long-standing, historically based aversion to each other, although both intermingle. Both use similar methods (theoretical models and their empirical testing) to solve the problems posed to them, and they experience failures and successes. However, we will venture the unpopular hypothesis that merchants better manage this problem-solving. So first, we will talk about methods and then the historical background.

Are scientific ideas dying for us?

Karl Popper, one of the most influential philosophers of science, is considered to be the founder of the naturalistic conception of knowledge (Popper, 1972). In its modern variant and in a certain simplification, it can be said that science is an element of culture and is a highly adaptive product in evolutionary terms. As a species, we are not only subject to biological evolution, but certain patterns of our individual and collective behaviour also evolve. Some of these turn out to be adaptive (i.e. better adapted to a given environment), and others are not. The former spread, and the latter "die out". Science is an example of a cultural variant that has successfully spread. Popper noted, however, that in the world of intersubjective ideas that people create and exchange, there is also an evolutionary competition. Before a particular scientific idea is applied, it is subject to a test of scientific discourse as to its scientificity, plausibility by a particular empirical test, consistency with existing knowledge, internal integrity etc. Some scientific ideas (or perhaps even most) fall away already at this stage and never get their chance for practical application.

And maybe that's a good thing because a significant proportion of them would probably lead to lamentable results in practice. Our ideas die for us. Thanks to science, we don't have to test them on ourselves, putting ourselves at risk of losing life, health, or property. In scientific discourse, we kill the wrong idea. However, this vision of science turns out to be a bit too optimistic. Like biological evolution, it constructs haphazardly from whatever it can find, producing a plethora of falsely adaptive solutions that can last for years as long as environmental pressures are weak at any given time. *It's the environment, stupid!*[4] The key to whether the selection mechanism of ideas is working well is this environmental pressure. In the world of ideas, we can, to a certain extent, create the selection mechanism ourselves, for example, through specific financial incentives that make certain ideas funded and others not, or through a "diffuse sanction" created by the scientific community that eliminates ideas that are too subversive. So, how does the environment deal with the selection of scientific ideas? Generally speaking, moderately.

Throughout history, this environmental pressure has been more subordinate to the demands of the courts and their tastes than to the relevance or usefulness of scientific ideas, especially for broader sections of society. This in itself does not devalue bespoke achievements. In addition to developing the heliocentric theory, Nicolaus Copernicus left behind a little-known work written to the order of the bishop of Warmia, the *Treatise on the Minting of Coin*, with very practical conclusions on monetary reform in Prussia. The precursors of modern science, the Greek philosophers, remained in a relatively comfortable position. Being members of the Greek aristocracy and owners of extensive farms, which were mainly run by slaves, they could afford to concern themselves with anything. The selection pressure on their ideas was thus weak, which in the field of social sciences resulted in rather exotic concepts, unfortunately still inspiring some today. The breakthrough came with the emergence of the modern idea of the university, which, whether funded by students or by local rulers, was intended by design to be relatively egalitarian and to ensure freedom of scientific thought. How does this concept work today? Not too badly, but ....

In 2013, the British weekly magazine *The Economist* published a report with the remarkable title, *How Science Goes Wrong*. The authors pointed out that contemporary *mass media has created* counter-effective selection pressures on scientific research. In simple terms, the choice of research area, as well as the specific issues that scientists deal with, is more subordinated to the aesthetics of public expectations than to their usefulness or relevance. Scientists, like celebrities, seek recognition and the funding that follows it. They find it in popular innovations rather than in painstaking replications of research already done and its eventual critique. The overproduction of new (or novel) ideas, combined with the lack of their critique, based on sound empirical testing, leads to an overproduction of ideas that are not correct, *false positives*, and an overhasty rejection of ideas that are correct (*false negatives*). The problem applies particularly to the social sciences, including psychology and economics. Contrary to Popper's optimism, false ideas refuse to die, and true ideas disappear in the flood of unverified research.

Businesses are dying of bankruptcy

And how do merchants relate to this? When they set up a company, they also have their own theory as to how it should operate: what it should produce or sell, how it should be organised to keep so-called transaction costs as low as possible, who it should employ and how much it should pay them, who will buy its products and at what price. Leaving aside rarely carried out marketing or pilot studies, every company is a kind of experiment. Even if it has a model idea that can be discussed in advance, it will sooner or later have to be tested on the market anyway. If the "theory of the company" fails, instead of the expected profits, there is an unexpected loss, which consequently forces an adaptation of the strategy to the existing environment. When the adaptation is not accurate or fast enough, the theory dies with the company through bankruptcy. In the modern world, thousands of micro-theories of companies are created and die every day. Their test is radical. The key to survival is the multiplicity of these micro-theories, or rather ephemeral hypotheses, acting as genetic mutations (i.e. innovation) and the speed of adaptation. This mechanism has worked quite well for several thousand years, that is, since we have been able to ascertain the existence of organised trade in human societies. Perhaps in a primordial version, it has worked even longer, being responsible for reinforcing extensive cooperation in the species *Homo sapiens* and enabling it to survive periods of successive glaciations. Its radical expansion, however, came in the modern period and was initiated in 17th-century Netherlands and 18th-century England. This is because a friendly environment was developed there. According to McCloskey, this mechanism is also responsible for the aforementioned radical enrichment of people all over the world, a definite improvement in their well-being, and it is despite the fact that during this period (since the 18th century), the population has increased tenfold. Its evolutionary and ruthless nature explains why the "great improvement" is "tested through trade".

On the sources of mutual resentment

Before they became philosophers (i.e. the few who could afford it), the ancient Greeks were primarily sailors and merchants. And a significant proportion of them did not live in Greece. Thales was from Miletus (today's Turkish coast), not far from Ephesus, where Heraclitus came from. Pythagoras was probably born in Sidon (today's Lebanon) and died in Metaponto (today's Italy). Archimedes, on the other hand, came from Syracuse (Sicily). They lived where the expansion of the Greek *polis* reached and where they established their trading colonies, above all in the so-called Classical period (480–323 BC). Apart from navigational skills, what distinguished the Greeks from other civilisations was an economy based on free entrepreneurs and private property, with a limited role for state power. The latter tended to focus on maintaining economic equilibrium and protecting it (law, dispute resolution, protection of property rights). The basis of the economy was the household (about which Aristotle wrote), but alongside it, it was increasingly the specialised, depersonalised profit-oriented enterprise (about which, among the philosophers, hardly anyone wrote). In 431 BC, one in four inhabitants of Athens did not own land – they were engaged in crafts and trade. This specific organisation ensured Greek supremacy in the Mediterranean for many centuries (with the possible exception of Sparta, adored by the philosophers, which followed a very different, militarised path of development). It also provided the free Greeks with the wealth by which philosophers, living off the work of others, could afford to philosophise unfettered. They remained, however, astonishingly impregnated to see the sources of civilisational success of which they were (and are) the most spectacular manifestation. Despite the separation of specific scientific disciplines (physics, metaphysics, ethics, natural science, astronomy, mathematics, logic etc.) in antiquity, there was no isolated, relatively coherent reflection on the market, the economy, and the regularities occurring there. Wealth was not regarded as desirable in itself. Instead, the pursuit of happiness was possibly desirable. Even traditionally anthropocentric orientations (Epicureanism, Sophists) were suspicious of wealth and money. The experience of evolutionary change (without human intervention) in a direction that would be judged as good was alien to ancient thinkers. The social world (as well as the inanimate world) was seen as either stable or degenerating. Socrates, Plato, and Aristotle – three of the most prominent philosophers of ancient Greece – were unable to understand the nature of the process of burgeoning commercial links between the various Greek cities. Plato developed an organicist theory of state and society, for which the model was the commercially backward Sparta. The existence of the state was an end in itself. The happiness of individuals was realised "by the way". The criterion of morality was the interest of the state, and the controllers, its officials. The ruling classes, the philosophers and the military, lived essentially in an economic commune. Private property was possible at the level of the producers (people of profit). Their activities, however, were subordinated to the objectives of the state. There was a strict division of labour and specialisation. Economically, it was an agricultural and manufacturing community – self-sufficient (*autarchy*). Trade was not needed for anything. The law was to prevent the growth of wealth from trade. Travel abroad was only possible with the permission of the state and after the age of 40. There was a strict class division and constant censorship regarding intellectual activity (sic!). Aristotle was somewhat more gracious, for he did deign to note the existence of commerce and its certain importance for society. In essence, however, he despised chrematistics, the art of acquiring money, which included wage labour, usury, and trade. Significant in this respect is his division of the ways of getting rich into "natural", which includes the accumulation of things needed for life (pastoralism, hunting, agriculture), "indirect", i.e. barter, where the thing being exchanged is used independently of its "proper use", and "unnatural", consisting in the use of money as a means of exchanging goods. According to this division, as in Plato, the ideal was a self-sufficient order – the *autarkos*. Similarly, social order was also established, i.e. taxis, which are the result of the deliberate organisation of individual, intentional actions. Any evolutionary spontaneity of this order did not fit into these categories (de Soto, 2018; Hayek, 1991).

These philosophers, who to this day represent a symbol and point of reference for the whole of Western civilisation and who imposed their conceptual grid and style of thinking in science and philosophy for centuries, at the same time initiated the opposition of intellectuals to anything that had to do with trade, industry, or economic profit. The "anti-capitalist mentality" of humanists and men of science becomes their emblem. There is also the anti-egalitarian belief in the elitism of certain social strata and the fear of excessive political freedom, which the despised masses would certainly not be able to use rationally. These ideas have not died and have made themselves known in different historical periods in varying degrees of intensity. This is how the philosophy of the state of Thomas Aquinas, or the philosophy of the German Romantics and Hegel in particular, is structured. This was also the path Karl Marx took, who, although he did not despise the working masses, saw no chance for social understanding, saw conflicts everywhere, and foresaw the inevitable dictatorship of one social class over another. Nowadays, existentialism, in particular that of the communist Jean-Paul Sartre, and postmodernism, with Zygmunt Bauman's anti-consumerism at the forefront, are steeped in these ideas.

On attempts to overcome mutual resentment

Economics is also made up of philosophers. Although the first serious thinkers about the economy, the mercantilists, tended to be merchants or came from that background, the first economists were undoubtedly philosophers. In addition to considering the wealth of nations, Adam Smith wrote about moral sentiments; John Stuart Mill was primarily a social philosopher, logician, and ethicist. Friedrich August von Hayek, Nobel laureate in economics, wrote that "nobody can be a great economist who is only an economist (…) the economist who is only an economist is likely to become a nuisance if not a positive danger" (Hayek, 1969). These are, however, somewhat different philosophers compared to those described above. What they have in common are several characteristics that resonate with these bourgeois virtues. Taking man as he is (or appeared to them to be) – with all his vices: greed, thirst for fame, and herd instincts – they want above all, according to their limited resources, to make him richer and thus somewhat happier, searching and wandering, like merchants, to see what works and what does not. A merchant who takes offence at his customer's reluctance to buy his goods, or who, worse still, tries to educate these customers according to his own value system and vision of the world, will soon go bankrupt, opening the path to the development of those businesses that simply try to provide people with what they want and need. For the merchant, any customer who pays for his goods is good, regardless of his nationality, race, or social class. Likewise for "worldly philosophers",[5] economists. If, on the other hand, the interests of the people are in some apparent or actual conflict, then they consider how to reconcile or resolve them at the least possible cost.

An economy that seeks prosperity for as many people as possible is founded on doubts about proposed solutions and on constant compromises between divergent human interests. And while we are convinced, following McCloskey, that the key to the prosperity that humanity has already achieved so far lies in certain mercantile patterns of thought and virtue, we cannot be certain on this point either, and we share these doubts in the following chapters.

Notes

1. https://stat.gov.pl/obszary-tematyczne/ludnosc/statystyka-przyczyn-zgonow/zgony-wedlug-przyczyn-okreslanych-jako-garbage-codes,3,6.html (accessed, December 2024).
2. Both terms, economics and chrematistics, come from classical Greek and were used in this sense by Xenophon and Aristotle.
3. Literature seems to be traditionally averse to the bourgeoisie and capitalism. Suffice it to recall the caricatured personification of homo oeconomicus that Dickens' Ebenezer Scrooge became.
4. "It's the environment, stupid!" – This was the title of one of the chapters of his book by evolutionary economist Andrew W. Lo (2004).
5. The term "worldly philosopher" is used in English to refer to philosophers concerned with temporal goods, i.e. most often classical (Heilbroner, 2000).

References

Deaton, A. (2013). *The great escape. Health, wealth and the origin of inequality*. Princeton University Press.

de Soto, J. H. (2018). *Economic thought in ancient Greece*. Retrieved 05 19.2025, from Mises Institute. Mises Daily: https://mises.org/mises-daily/economic-thought-ancient-greece

Hayek, F. A. (1969). The dilemma of specialization. In *Studies in philosophy, politics and economics*. Touchstone.

Hayek, F. A. (1991). *The fatal conceit (the errors of socialism)*. University of Chicago Press.

Heilbroner, R. L. (2000). *The worldly philosophers: The lives, times and ideas of the great economic thinkers*. Penguin Books.

Kubiczek, F. (Ed.). (1994). *Historia Polski w Liczbach. Ludność. Terytorium*. Zakład Wydawnictw Statystycznych. Retrieved from http://mbc.cyfrowemazowsze.pl/Content/18436/Historia%20Polski%20w%20Liczbach_1994%20198147.pdf

Leszczyńska, C. (2018). *Historia Polski w LIczbach. Tom 5. Polska 1918-2018*. Zakład Wydawnictw Statystycznych. Retrieved from https://stat.gov.pl/obszary-tematyczne/inne-opracowania/inne-opracowania-zbiorcze/historia-polski-w-liczbach-tom-v-polska-19182018,34,1.html

Lo, A. W. (2004). The adaptive markets hypothesis. Market efficiency from an evolutionary perspective. *The Journal of Portfolio Management* 30, 15–29. https://doi.org/10.3905/jpm.2004.442611

McCloskey, D. (2016). *Bourgeois equality. How ideas not capital or institutions, enriched the world*. The University of Chicago Press.

Pinker, S. (2011). *The better angels of our nature: Why violence has declined*. Viking Books.
Popper, K. R. (1972). *Objective knowledge: An evolutionary approach*. Oxford University Press.
Urząd Statystyczny w Poznaniu. (2008). *Statystyczna karta historii Poznania*. (K. Kruszka, Ed.). Poznań: Urząd Statystyczny w Poznaniu. Retrieved from https://poznan.stat.gov.pl/publikacje-i-foldery/inne-opracowania/statystyczna-karta-historii-poznania,6,1.html
Weber, M. (2002). *The protestant ethic and the spirit of capitalism: And other writings* (P. Baehr & G. C. Wells, Trans.). Penguin.

2

WHAT IS ECONOMICS ABOUT?

As discussed in the previous chapter, the "great betterment" – the unprecedented increase in wealth of an ever-growing world population – began in the 17th century in the Netherlands and continued into the 18th century in England. The developing economy inspired the search for answers to questions about the causes of this development, what conditions were necessary for a country to become rich, what reforms had to be introduced to achieve economic success. Thus, it is no coincidence that the first systematic treatise laying the foundations for the new field of knowledge known today as economics bears the title *An Inquiry into the Nature and Causes of the Wealth of Nations* (1776) – authored by Adam Smith, a professor of moral philosophy from Glasgow. Certainly, this does not suggest that debates on economic matters were non-existent prior to this period. Smith's work drew profusely on the work of the Physiocrats, who saw the source of wealth as agriculture and was a critique of the mercantilist beliefs, which held that a country could only grow rich at the expense of other nations. Thanks to Smith, however, in the late 18th and early 19th centuries, first in England and Scotland, then in other European countries, discussions of economic issues began to take an increasingly systematic form. They were conducted under the common banner of "political economy" and, from the late 19th century onwards, "economics". This process is well illustrated by the relative frequency of the words "economy", "political economy" and "economics" in English-language books over the last 200 years (see Figure 2.1).

Assuming that the relative frequency of certain words in publications reflects interest in a given issue, it can confidently be said that interest in the economy significantly exceeded interest in economics throughout the study period. The exception seems to be the 1930s, when almost as much was written about economics as about the economy. This graph also demonstrates how, in the early 20th century, the term

DOI: 10.4324/9781003469384-4

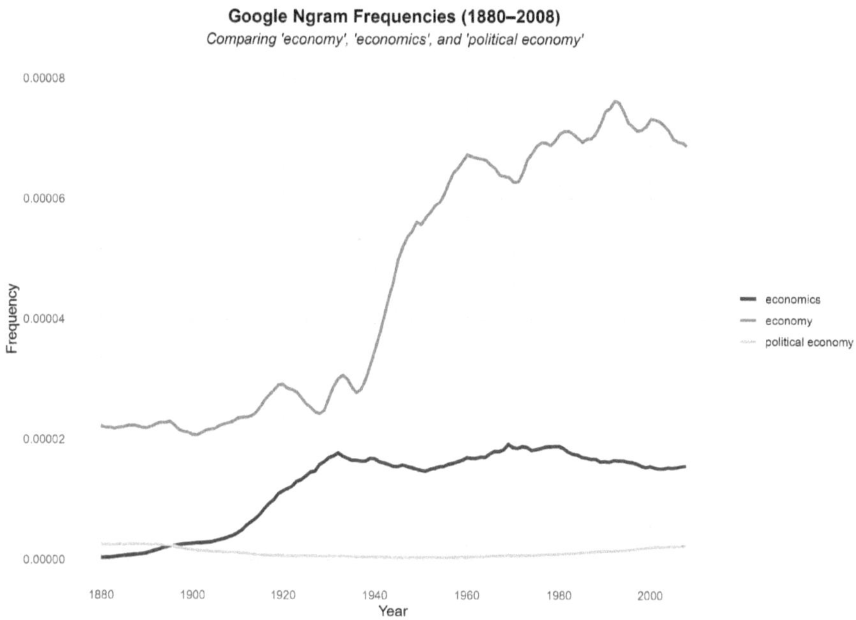

FIGURE 2.1 Frequency of the words "economy", "political economy" and "economics"
Source: Google Ngram

"political economy" lost its meaning, and the field of knowledge pioneered by Smith came to be commonly referred to as economics.

The science of wealth

Why did Smith and other classical economists refer to their field of research as "political economy"? The answer to this question is simple: the term "economics" was already in use. First used by the Greek philosopher Xenophon in the 4th century BC, it referred to household management, that is, efficient management within the family. By describing his field as political economy, Smith wanted to emphasise that its object of study was the wealth of a nation, not of an individual. What does this wealth consist of? How is it achieved? How can the state be managed effectively? These were the fundamental questions of political economy during Smith's era. "But the great object of the political economy of every country", Smith wrote, "is to increase the riches and power of that country" (Smith, 1776). How does this great task relate to the actions of individuals? According to Smith, the division of labour, the accumulation of capital by entrepreneurs, which is then productively invested, and mutually beneficial market exchanges form the basis of national wealth. The analysis of such actions by individuals is what political economy addresses. This perspective was even more emphatically expressed by

John Stuart Mill, a prominent logician, political philosopher, and economist who continued Smith's thought. He stated that "Political Economy considers mankind as occupied solely in acquiring and consuming wealth (…)" (Mill, 2009).

Mill acknowledged that people are driven by a variety of motivations. Parents nurture their children out of love, friends offer each other selfless support, and a person consumed by hatred might bring about their own financial downfall just to harm those they view as enemies. Life is undoubtedly more complex than what is captured from an economic perspective. However, to provide concrete insights about the economy, to draw conclusions about its workings, and to make predictions, we must simplify the picture significantly. By assuming that in the economic realm, individuals are primarily motivated by the pursuit of wealth, their actions become both understandable and predictable. The concept of a person solely focussed on acquiring wealth was later termed by commentators as "economic man" or *homo oeconomicus*. However, it's important to emphasise that economists do not believe every human being is always motivated in their actions by the desire to increase wealth. Rather, when an individual engages in economic activities – such as producing, selling, or buying goods or providing services – their actions can be interpreted as being primarily driven by this dominant motive of wealth pursuit.

For Mill, the pursuit of wealth is a fundamental economic principle. Alongside this, there are several self-evident economic laws. One such law is that each successive increment of labour or investment in fertiliser on the same plot of land yields progressively smaller increases (the law of diminishing returns). Another is the principle that population growth outpaces food production (Pastor Malthus' population law). National wealth accumulation depends on these laws, and the economist's role is to identify them and derive logical conclusions, which then inform suitable state economic policies.

Two undeniable facts characterise the early development of economics. Firstly, economics was viewed as the science of wealth from a social perspective, focussing on the wealth of nations. The multiplication of wealth was deemed possible and predictable because economic actions were believed to follow certain scientific laws recognised by economists. Secondly, economics was considered an empirical science. For instance, Adam Smith's work provided a detailed overview of interest rates in England, France, and the Netherlands, as well as changes in workers' wages, and the prices of gold, silver, and wheat over four centuries. John Stuart Mill also grounded his analyses in empirical reality. Although he primarily employed a deductive method, basing conclusions on predefined assumptions, he regarded the initial point of economics – the introspective understanding of one's motives for action – as fundamentally empirical.

From wealth science to human science

The late 19th century brought revolutionary views formulated by three great economists: the English logician and economist William Stanley Jevons, the founder of the Austrian School of economics, Carl Menger, and the French economist Léon Walras. They recognised that the prices of goods and services depend not on the costs of production – as argued by Smith, Mill, and other classicists – but on the benefits (utility) they bring to consumers. It is not because a pearl is valuable that someone spent a few hours fishing for it (putting in the labour); rather, it is valued by consumers (useful to them) that the pearl catcher has an incentive to provide it, and thus the labour he invests becomes valuable (Colander & Landreth, 2002). This shift in emphasis from the cost of production to the satisfaction of consumption of goods and services in determining their market value also represents a shift in how we think about the object of economics. This was perfectly expressed by Alfred Marshall, the British economist who combined these revolutionary marginalist views with the analyses of the classical school to form the foundations of neoclassical economics. For Marshall, "Political Economy or Economics is a study of mankind in the ordinary business of life; it examines that part of individual and social action which is most closely connected with the attainment and with the use of the material requisites of wellbeing. Thus it is on the one side a study of wealth; and on the other, and more important side, a part of the study of man" (Marshall, 1890).

Economics thus ceases to be solely a science of wealth and begins to be seen as a science of people. Its scope is determined by the actions of individuals in the economic realm, particularly those concerning the material things necessary for achieving wealth. For the first time in the history of economics, human well-being is being placed so clearly at the centre of economists' interests. When we buy a new car, we don't do so to enrich the nation but to derive satisfaction from the purchase and improve our lives. In Marshall's view, an understanding of economic interdependence should provide the basis for action that will increase prosperity and make it possible to eradicate poverty.

Marshall is also credited with shifting from the term "political economy" to "economics". This change emphasised that *economics,* like *physics,* had evolved into a mature science capable of generating specialised knowledge. Additionally, there was a desire to exclude ideological, value-laden beliefs associated with the political dimension from the scope of economics. This concern – that economics might be "polluted" by ideology, politics, or ethics – supported the trend of narrowing the focus of economics in successive periods of its development.

The science of action under conditions of limited resources and unlimited desires

The most influential definition for modern economists was proposed by the British economist Lionel Robbins. He stated, "Economics is the science which studies human behaviour as a relationship between [a given hierarchy of] ends and scarce means which have alternative uses" (Robbins, 1932, p. 15).

Each of us has once longed to purchase something beyond our means. It could be the latest smartphone, a high-performance gaming computer, a luxury limousine, or a seaside apartment. Human desires and the urge to own are boundless. Unfortunately, the resources available to satisfy these desires are finite. If I were to spend my annual income on my dream car, I wouldn't have enough left for essentials like food, clothing, or rent. So, what remains for me to do? I must prioritise my goals and only pursue those that are achievable with my available resources. Similarly, entrepreneurs must decide which ventures are worth investing their funds in. According to Robbins, economics studies human behaviour under the constraint of limited resources to achieve a potentially unlimited array of goals. In a world of universal abundance where everyone could satisfy all their desires, economists would have no concerns. However, as long as we must make choices constrained by limited means, economics remains relevant.

Defining economics as the science of making choices under conditions of scarce resources to achieve goals has significant implications for economists' responsibilities and the analysis of human actions. The primary task of economics becomes solving the optimisation problem – that is determining how to achieve set goals in the most efficient manner with the available resources. Economists often find that market exchange is the best tool for this purpose. Through market exchanges, the diverse offerings of entrepreneurs meet the demands expressed by consumers. Ultimately, this allows everyone to choose the products or services they can afford at any given time.

But how do economists discern what individuals truly desire? They assume that the choices people make in the market provide insights into their preferences. Economists recognise that people generally can – and do – rank their preferences from least to most important. Therefore, they conclude that fulfilling these preferences or satisfying the underlying desires benefits individuals. Consequently, behaviour based on an ordered set of preferences is considered rational action. Thus, welfare and rationality are linked to people's preferences, and, in turn, to the market choices they make. But does this mean that people are only rational when engaging in commercial transactions?

The science of rational choice

The focus of economists on rational decision-making has expanded the scope of economic research into territories traditionally associated with sociology, psychology, and law. For instance, why does a criminal decide to commit a crime? According to Gary S. Becker, winner of the 1992 Nobel Prize in economics, the answer lies in profitability: the criminal, like an entrepreneur or consumer, aims to realise his preferences with the resources available to him. So, how can crime be reduced? Economically, the answer is straightforward: increase the penalties or the likelihood of punishment – essentially raising the cost of committing crimes.

Becker also pioneered the economic theory of the family. Decisions regarding marriage or the number of children, which he treats as durable goods – similar to cars or appliances – are analysed through their cost-effectiveness. If someone decides to start a family, it implies that sharing child-raising responsibilities is seen as more profitable. Similarly, many couples find that buying a flat together through a joint mortgage is more feasible (Becker, 1976).

These topics will be explored further in Chapter 15. Here, it's crucial to note that, in Becker's view, what defines economics is not the subject matter – people's everyday economic activities – but the unique economic approach of minimising costs in actions. This method can be applied to any decision by evaluating what is most profitable, what resources are available, and what is lost by choosing one option over another. However, this raises a critical question: Is economising actions truly the essence of economics?

The science of mutually advantageous exchange

Robbins' view of economics as the science of rational choice, which inspired Becker's radical conclusions, has faced criticism despite its popularity among economists. Critics argue that it fosters a controversial vision of society and the market, clashing with traditional liberal values. According to this critique, not only should individual choices be rational, but the collective choices of a society should be as well. Kenneth Arrow, awarded the Nobel Prize in economics in 1972, demonstrated a conflict between individual and social rationality, suggesting that societal decisions might not align with the aggregate of individual preferences.

This conflict could be resolved by conceptualising society similarly to an individual – with its own set of collective preferences and rational decisions made through its representatives. However, equating social rationality with individual rationality implies that societal choices are made by an entity that both knows and decides what is best for its citizens, possessing the necessary tools to implement these decisions. Robert Sugden (2018) criticised this approach, comparing it to economic policy recommendations made as if advising a "benevolent autocrat". These themes will be further explored in Chapter 9.

Emphasising that the domain of economics is rational choices also presents a distinct vision of market exchange. It is viewed as a tool for the realisation of preferences. For example, if I want to drive a new car, I can buy it at a price that another person is willing to accept, thereby achieving an optimal fulfilment of our preferences. In this manner, the resources needed to produce certain goods are allocated where they can be most useful. With consumer and producer preferences known, calculating the price at which goods will find their buyers becomes a purely mathematical problem that economists solve.

However, some economists argue that the most important aspect of market exchange is not the fact that it leads to an optimal allocation of scarce resources. Rather, the significance lies in the market as an institution that enables people to engage in a process of mutually advantageous exchange. People who may not interact in their daily lives, who may hold different political views, value systems, live in different parts of the world, and speak different languages, can achieve mutual benefits through market exchange. A deeply religious person can buy a Bible produced by an atheist in a bookstore, and both parties will be satisfied with this exchange.

According to the liberal tradition, associated with thinkers like David Hume, Adam Smith, John Stuart Mill, Friedrich Hayek, and James Buchanan, society is a community of people engaging in mutually advantageous exchanges, and the market facilitates this participation. Therefore, the process of market exchange itself, in which people engage responsibly, holds particular interest for economists, rather than merely the conditions that achieve the end state once the exchange has occurred.

Economics is what economists do

Given the lack of consensus on the definition of economics, perhaps the American economist Jacob Viner was correct when he suggested that economics is simply what economists do. To understand what contemporary economists focus on in their research, one can examine the distribution of publications across different fields within economics, based on articles that have appeared in leading economic journals. A study analysing over 130,000 articles published in 80 economics journals from 1980 to 2015 reveals that microeconomics is the most popular area of research. This field concentrates on the behaviours of households and businesses, as well as the dynamics of individual markets for goods, services, and production factors such as land, labour, and capital. Following microeconomics, the broad category labelled "other research" ranks second. This category encompasses a variety of topics, including economic history, environmental economics, experimental economics, law and economics, political economy, and urban economics. Macroeconomics, which focusses on the determinants of national income, ranks third in popularity. Other areas, such as econometrics, public finance, labour economics, international economics, industrial organisation theory, and development economics, also receive significant attention but to a lesser extent (Angrist et al., 2017).

Significant variation is evident not only in the research areas favoured by economists but also in the methods they employ. According to data from major economic journals for the years 1994 and 1995, experiments in economics constitute 6% of all empirical research, matching the proportion of purely theoretical studies based on textual analysis. In contrast, statistical data analysis (45%) and survey research (39%) dominate the field (Saris & Gallhofer, 2014, p. 3). We will discuss the economics method and the use of experimental approaches in greater detail in the chapters of the third part of this book. At this juncture, it is worth noting that the specialisation in research fields and the employment of specific economic approaches demonstrate the methodological maturity and professionalisation of the discipline. The ongoing debates regarding the subject of economics, however, underscore that the central focus of this science is humanity and its pursuit of a better life.

References

Angrist, J., Azoulay, P., Ellison, G., Hill, R., & Lu, S. F. (2017). Economic research evolves: Fields and styles. *American Economic Review*, *107*(5), 293–297. https://doi.org/10.1257/aer.p20171117

Becker, G. S. (1976). *The economic approach to human behavior*. University of Chicago Press.

Colander, D. C., & Landreth, H. (2002). *History of economic thought*. Houghton Mifflin.

Marshall, A. (1890). *Principles of economics*. Econlib. https://www.econlib.org/library/Marshall/marP.html?chapter_num=2#book-reader

Mill, J. S. (2009). *A system of logic, ratiocinative and inductive*. Project Gutenberg. https://www.gutenberg.org/ebooks/27942

Robbins, L. (1932). *An essay on the nature and significance of economic science*. Macmillan and Co.

Saris, W. E., & Gallhofer, I. N. (2014). *Design, evaluation, and analysis of questionnaires for survey research* (2nd ed.). Wiley.

Smith, A. (1776). *An inquiry into the nature and causes of the wealth of nations* (Edwin Cannan, Ed., Vol. 1). Methuen. https://oll.libertyfund.org/titles/smith-an-inquiry-into-the-nature-and-causes-of-the-wealth-of-nations-cannan-ed-vol-1

Sugden, R. (2018). *The community of advantage: A behavioural economist's defence of the market*. Oxford University Press.

3

WHY CAN'T ECONOMISTS PREDICT FUTURE CRISES?

Is it really so bad with these predictions in economics?

Economics is perceived as a science that suffers from its weakness in the field of predicting certain economic events. This includes both seemingly simple questions: Will sugar prices rise or fall in the near future? Will a particular company be profitable or not? Is it worth investing in governmental bonds? However, there are also more complex ones: What will the exchange rate of the Swiss franc to the euro be at the end of 2026, or how much will the EU's GDP change? In each of these cases, if one compares the forecasts to the actual recorded values, it appears that the economists who got the forecasts right were probably just lucky. Why, then, do we need a science whose predictions have the value of a bet in roulette, or even less (because there, at least, the results can be accurately estimated with a sufficiently large number of bets, which in turn allows the casino always to win)? If we were to estimate the accuracy of bullets fired from handguns with equal accuracy, the odds would be stacked against us.

This circulating and arguably somewhat wrong-headed view of the science of economics (as we will try to demonstrate below) is historically grounded. Classical economists of the 19th century felt confident enough in their analyses at some stage to decide to publish their gloomy predictions. Thomas Malthus (1766–1834) presented a scenario of economic developments based on limited land resources (agriculture was the dominant form of economy at the time) and the link between the wages of wage earners and their fertility rate. The higher the wages, the higher the standard of living and the greater the incentive to start a family and have children. In turn, the more children, the more wage earners in the next generation, and the greater the labour supply, which, with constant land resources and constant demand for that labour, leads to a reduction in

DOI: 10.4324/9781003469384-5

wages and pauperisation of workers (Malthus, 2011).[1] The repetitive cycle is slowly moving towards a growing impoverishment of wage workers. David Ricardo, starting from similar assumptions (a limited stock of arable land), took Malthus' reasoning further. He recognised that rising demand for food would lead to rising profits for landowners in the first period but, in the longer term, would translate into rising food prices, rising labour costs (they have to earn at least enough to feed themselves) and thus falling profits for businesses (Ricardo, 1821). Karl Marx, on the other hand, a little later, recognised that the progressive impoverishment of the working class and the enrichment of the class owning the means of production (i.e. unlike Ricardo had predicted, they were getting richer, however) would necessarily lead to an inevitable crisis of overproduction, the only solution to which could be the revolution of the proletariat and the nationalisation of the means of production (Marx & Engels, 1848). As it is not difficult to see, none of these predictions came true. The workers' revolution indeed broke out in one country in the world, but to this day, there is still debate as to why it was there and to what extent it was linked to Marxist theories. In those countries where radical economic change should have taken place because of their advanced industrialisation, nothing of the sort happened. There was neither mass pauperisation of the workers, although, in fact, in the second half of the 19th century, the population in the countries of Europe and North America began to grow markedly. However, instead of growing poverty, the quality of life improved.[2] Nor did the decline in business profitability predicted by Ricard take place.

Much could be written about why these predictions failed to materialise. Given that each was slightly different and some contradictory, the explanation for their failure will be somewhat different each time. From the point of view of the subject of this chapter, however, this is not so important. What does matters are the different reactions to these failures, especially those that ended up with different explanations and different predictions, ultimately more accurate. To the surprise of many, the latter are not lacking either. After all, it is somewhat the other way around with economics (along with other social sciences) than with the natural sciences (like physics or chemistry). Thanks to a well-chosen school curriculum, we are convinced of the sheer success of the sciences, from Newton's principles of dynamics to the theory of relativity, the Mendeleev system or the theory of chemical bonds. The possible failures of the sciences, flawed theories, and thus predictions have such a small impact on our daily lives that they rarely break through into our consciousness, although there is no shortage of them. In our daily lives, we are constantly experiencing economic surprises too: the drastic appreciation of the Swiss franc endured painfully by those who had contracted mortgage loans in that currency, the fall in the value of investment funds due to the COVID-19 pandemic or inflation which came soon after, or the interest rate on bank deposits. From school, we have not acquired a similar conviction about the successes of economic science, and the general enrichment of the world, as we wrote in Chapter 1, has been going on long enough to escape our attention. For this, it seems to us that experts, i.e. economists, should warn us about these adverse developments.

So, has this science had any success so far? We will try to cite some examples.

1 The British economist Alfred Marshall in 1873 formulated a prediction quite different from Marx's about the development of the working class (Marshall, 1925). He was undoubtedly more knowledgeable than Marx about the conclusions of government reports, which showed that the situation in Britain had been steadily improving over the previous few decades. This included increases in workers' wages, improvements in their living conditions and more extensive education and participation in society. Marshall concluded from his own observations that this was a sustainable trend. Workers' wages will increase in line with their increasing skills, which in turn will lead to increased productivity and demand for their labour. An element reinforcing this trend is their rising standard of living, which necessitates an increase in their qualifications to increase their income so that this standard is at least maintained or increased. Unlike Malthus and Ricardo, Marshall also predicted a decline in fertility in working-class families linked to increased investment in education (Opocher, 2010). Readers of the first chapter of the book already know how accurate these predictions turned out to be. And for most of us, Marshall's predictions seem obvious: the better our qualifications, the greater the chance of a well-paid job. But they were not obvious in 1873.
2 In 1919, the then 35-year-old father of modern macroeconomics, John Maynard Keynes, opposing the peace terms imposed by the Allies on Germany in the Treaty of Versailles, wrote a short treatise that proved prophetic (Keynes, 2012). Keynes objected first and foremost to the huge contributions imposed on Germany because, in his view, the war-weary economy could not bear them and, if it nevertheless repaid them under the threat of military intervention, this would lead to gigantic inflation, economic crisis, and the impoverishment of large sections of the population. Consequently, it will result in resentment and revanchist sentiment, culminating in another, much more severe armed conflict. It did not take long for these gloomy predictions to be realised. Keynes advocated the opposite, i.e. loans to rebuild infrastructure and the economy. His ideas were only put to use after 1945 and developed into a general theory, which is today the basis for the monetary policy of most central banks (Keynes, 2009).
3 In 2000, the UK government held a tender for 3G telephony operator licences. The estimated proceeds from this auction were expected to be around £3–4 billion. In the end, 22.5 billion was obtained, which was considered an enormous success by, among others, the economists who worked out the details of how the tender was conducted (Backhouse, 2010, p. 27). Its organisation was based on auction theories developed since the 1980s by, among others, economists such as William Vickrey (1914–1996), John McMillan (1951–2007), and Paul Milgrom. These theories aimed to design the auction in such a way that a particular

good would go to those bidders for whom it represented the highest value and who were able to manage it most efficiently and thus offer the highest price to the seller while at the same time ensuring fair competition and a chance of winning for all interested participants and protecting against the possible overvaluation of the good. These theories still form the basis for many other successful tenders today.[3]

4 Anyone who has ever dealt with investments must have come across the *discounted cash flow* (DCF) model. This model, consisting of a series of mathematical equations, allows us to answer the question: What is the present value of a specific asset that has the capacity to generate future profits? To the untrained, the model gives the impression of being complicated. This is because it allows individual preferences, alternative investments, the risk of generating specific profits in the future, etc., to be taken into account. It can be used to determine both the value of a fixed-rate bond and the value of an entire company. Its application has undoubtedly changed the investment market for many years. Most of those who use it do not know that the foundations for this model were laid by the American economist Irving Fisher in 1930 (Fisher, 1930).

What is the science of economics all about? Between realism and scientific constructivism

It is clear from the above somewhat subjectively selected examples that economics is a science that, apart from its apparent failures, has several successes. The latter affect our daily lives, as it were, in the background. They contribute to the fact that, as a rule, we are better educated than our grandparents and earn more, that we live in a relatively safer and more affluent world, that governments manage their resources more efficiently, increasing redistribution to their citizens, and that we have relatively widespread access to bank credit, which, regardless of how one judges it, increases the level of daily satisfaction of our preferences. However, in order to properly weigh up this balance between the successes and failures of economics and to come closer to answering the question of why it often fails and whether this will ever change, it is worth considering at the outset what science, in general, and the science of economics especially is all about. The most intuitive answer is as follows: about truth! Science should describe the studied reality in the most truthful, accurate way possible. Such an answer is an expression of one of the stances in the philosophy of science, which we call scientific realism. It assumes that scientific theories indeed describe some investigated fragments of reality in their essential aspects. The specific entities postulated by these theories and, more importantly, the relations indicated therein (generalisations, which we sometimes call scientific laws) actually exist. This position in the philosophy of economics is presented, among others, by the Finnish philosopher Uskali Mäki, whom we will discuss further in the third part of the book, in Chapter 11. Scientific realism does not claim to reflect the reality under study accurately. It only claims that scientific theories (or models) accurately reflect this reality in some selected, relevant aspects. Even if we cannot predict the course of economic events on the basis of a given model, according to the realist, this does not depreciate the model itself. There are a number of circumstances that interfere with the "operation" of the model, which are related to the complex nature of economic reality. The foundations for such an understanding of economics were laid by John Stuart Mill (1806–1873), who believed that it could be practised as an abstract and theoretical science along the lines of geometry (Mill, 2008). Economics deals with one selected aspect of human nature, which is our propensity to get rich, treats this propensity like axioms in geometry, and deductively derives theorems from it. These are true and enable us to understand economic phenomena, but they do not provide an accurate prediction of their consequences. For realists, therefore, the "truthfulness" of the model is guaranteed by the "truthfulness" of the axioms and the correctness of the inferences. Hence, in modern economics, there is a well-developed dispute about the so-called realism of the assumptions of economic models. The more realistic these assumptions are, the more "true" the model is supposed to be. Realists, however, do not expect economic models to make accurate predictions in the first place; or, in other words, their occurrence or absence is not an essential criterion for evaluating a model. The problem of predicting economic crises is solved by negating it.

A counterweight to this understanding are the scientific constructivists or instrumentalists. They have in common the conviction that our scientific theories are not necessarily a picture of some reality independent of us but instead are mental constructs of our cognitive apparatus and a way of ordering the multiple sensations of this apparatus. The selection between better and worse theories is made on the basis of a criterion other than their presumed truthfulness, understood as conformity to this reality. This is because we do not have any tools that would allow us to assess this conformity. On the other hand, we can assess, based on our experience, whether a given theory accurately predicted certain economic events, regardless of how true its assumptions were (Friedman, 2008) or whether it proved useful in solving a specific problem (Reiss, 2012), or whether it was rhetorically persuasive enough to a particular audience to persuade them to implement a specific public policy (McCloskey, 1998).

Let us return for a moment to the examples given above. The first two refer directly to specific predictions made by Marshall or Keynes. On the basis of these, however, either they or their successors devised a series of socio-political solutions to increase workers' productivity and full employment policies or stimulate economic growth through appropriate monetary policies. The next two examples are already instruments in their own right, serving specific purposes (to carry out an efficient tender or to make a profitable investment). Neither of these theories will answer the question of what the final price will be set in a tender or what the "true" current value of a given financial instrument is. This points to their instrumental rather than realistic nature. But will these examples, indicated as successes of economics, always ensure that we achieve our objectives? Of course not. Over the last few decades, the demand for upskilling in the United States has led to a drastic increase in the cost of education, students' indebtedness, an oversupply of university graduates in the labour market and a decline in their real wages. Economic history, also in recent periods, knows a number of cases that revealed so-called non-Keynesian effects (Rzońca, 2007), meaning that Keynes' assumptions that underpinned his criticism of the Treaty of Versailles and later became the core of his *magnum opus* (Keynes, 2009) do not always work as Keynes himself imagined. The UK auction was a success for the organisers but not necessarily for the participants, who apparently over-invested. Indeed, the positioning effect of the licence was underestimated, which meant that none of the major operators could, in terms of image, afford not to bid for the licence, regardless of the relationship between the value of the investment and the expected rate of return. This brings us back to the problem of complexity in the social sciences identified by the realists.

Complexity. Is economics a social meteorology?

Auguste Comte (1798–1857) was one of the first thinkers to draw attention to the complexity of the social sciences. He classified all the then-known sciences according to their generality and complexity. There was no economics, but there was sociology (or social physics as he called it), which was identified as the least general and most complex. At the other end were astronomy and physics, as the most general and least complex. However, this reasoning was based largely on an intuitive understanding of complexity. A more mathematised approach was pioneered by the French mathematician Henri Poincaré (1854–1912), who dealt with the so-called three-body motion problem. Classical Newtonian mechanics dealt well with two-body interactions. However, the introduction of a third body into the system made calculations extremely complicated. Moreover, small changes in the initial values of the system led to radically different results. Such a system was, therefore, structurally unstable. Poincaré's research initiated a new direction (or rather, new directions) in mathematics, which he refers to today as complexity theory or, somewhat colloquially, chaos theory, and whose literary expression is the movement of a butterfly's wings in one hemisphere that causes a hurricane in the other. Meteorology has become an emblematic example of complexity. Our inability to predict the weather in the long term is explained precisely by this complexity and the structural instability of the system. There is no shortage of those who justify the failures of economics in this way. If having relatively well-recognised equations describing particle dynamics, we are unable to apply them to weather forecasting; we are even less able to do so in the case of the social sciences, where, at various levels (individual and group), we are confronted with an incalculably large number of interdependent variables (Mainzer, 1994). This approach treats economics like physics and market participants (i.e. us) like atoms to which certain laws that determine our behaviour apply. Even if this is the case, it would be difficult to say at present that, as with atoms, we have these laws well recognised. This does not prevent economists from looking for all sorts of regularities in market activities, using mathematical concepts for describing complexity, ranging from advanced statistical tools, quantitative analysis, regression equations, game theory, cellular automata, attractors and fractal patterns.

On the other side of this physicalist approach to the social sciences are those thinkers who, from the outset, point to an essential qualitative difference between the physical world and the human-made social or economic world. This difference lies precisely in the impossibility of comparing human behaviour to that of particles. A particle does not make an independent choice as to the direction of its movement, and even less does it condition this direction by the behaviour of other particles. The movement of molecules in the atmosphere is chaotic and random. According to the physics of gases, the principles of statistics can be fully applied to them. On the other hand, man's actions appear to be directed towards the realisation of some goal, in other words, intentional. This is how successive generations of economists have treated them. This is because human intentional action is at the heart of how markets work (Frydman & Goldberg, 2007; Hayek, 1945; Knight, 2008). However, this action is not only intentional but also reflexive. Indeed, when we analyse the behaviour of individuals in the market, it is easy to see that they not only subordinate their actions to their stated goals but also modify these goals and actions in accordance with external circumstances and, in particular, in accordance with the goals and actions of other individuals. This characteristic is what some have called reflexivity (Soros, 2013). It produces a rather peculiar effect at the macro level. Let us assume that I have a perfect economic theory describing the behaviour of share prices on the London Stock Exchange. This theory is perfect, which means that it allows me to predict the share price of AstraZeneca plc (a British-Swedish multinational pharmaceutical and biotechnology company) in a month. Knowing this share price and that it will rise or fall by a given percentage during this period, I have a unique opportunity to make an appropriate investment which will provide me with a profit (either by purchasing shares and selling them later or by purchasing appropriate derivative financial instruments[4]). However, by pursuing such an opportunity, I am simultaneously increasing the demand for the financial instrument in question and influencing its anticipated price. My theory is no longer perfect, or it never was. However, suppose I know that other investors use the same theory and have similarly predicted the share price by adjusting their investment portfolio accordingly. In that case, I can incorporate this expected behaviour of theirs into my investment. This kind of thinking secured an economic Nobel Prize for Robert Lucas, who in 1972 pointed out that people adjust their behaviour not to actual changes in monetary policy but to anticipated changes. This observation became the basis of the theory of rational expectations.

But is it possible for economic theory to take into account the anticipated expectations of market participants and the expectations of expectations and the expectations of anticipated expectations, etc.? In other words, despite reflexivity, is it possible to create a perfect theory that considers the impact of its results on itself?

Leaving aside the apparent regression to infinity here, the impossibility of constructing such a theory was pointed out by the Austrian philosopher and economist Friedrich Hayek. His argument, however, is more from the realm of cognitive psychology and mathematical computational undecidability than economics. In a nutshell, we can put it as follows:

1 The basis of any economic model is the decisions made by individuals in the market. Aggregate decisions determine how the whole economy will behave.[5]
2 Each individual makes decisions according to a specific model of reality that he creates in his mind.
3 A model of reality is created by discriminating stimuli received by our cognitive apparatus. This apparatus assigns them to appropriate sets according to their attributes. Creating a model of reality at the individual level, therefore, consists of discriminating stimuli.
4 Such a mental model has at least two limitations: only stimuli with a certain level of repetition will be included (due to the characteristics of neuronal functioning), and there will be as many sets or classes as the "neuronal computational order" allows.
5 A perfect theory to explain the functioning of the market would first require a perfect theory of decisions, which would require a perfect theory of agent modelling of reality (i.e. discriminating sensory stimuli). Therefore, we would have to construct a model of the cognitive apparatus, which would require a classification ability at least one level higher than that of the modelled mind. Obviously, we do not and will not have such a capacity (Hayek, 1992).

Adaptation and evolution

The problem of undecidability can also be approached from another angle. Can we develop a universal vaccine for all varieties of flu viruses? Unfortunately, no. The reason is prosaic. Viruses mutate at a rate that makes new strains appear every year, and vaccines are ineffective, at least for these new strains. Can we predict mutations? So far, no. They are completely random. So, a constant race is going on, and biologists and pharmacists are always one step behind. This biological metaphor has its justification. Already in the 19th century, alongside classical economists, there were those who believed that the social sciences should be constructed not along the lines of geometry or physics but rather of biology, in particular, taking into account the then-just-published theory of evolution.[6] Among the forerunners of such thinking was Thorstein Veblen (1857–1929), an American economist of Norwegian origin whose biological and evolutionary metaphors outraged readers of the time. He initiated a current in economics called institutionalism, which is still an important part of the study of economics today.[7] Contemporary institutionalists are also often evolutionists. However, it is not about mutations in our genetic code and biological evolution but about our behavioural patterns and cultural evolution. Let us try to introduce this mode of analysis in economics briefly.

The basis of modern evolutionary psychology is the assumption that if we observe a characteristic, repetitive pattern of behaviour, e.g., a tendency to care for offspring or heterosexual monogamous relationships, we can suspect that this pattern is or, at some stage in the development of the species was evolutionarily adaptive, i.e. that it favoured the expansion of the population that followed it. Behavioural patterns arise like genetic mutations, randomly and chaotically. Those that are not adaptive at any given time disappear. The selection mechanism at the individual level works in such a way that the individual makes various decisions by trial and error, evaluates the results, and modifies his or her behaviour for the future accordingly. One would, therefore, expect this to lead, over a certain time horizon, to perfectly rational patterns of behaviour geared to the greatest possible individual benefit. In such a context, however, how can one explain, for example, the tendency to purchase luxury products at a price many times higher than products of comparable quality without the relevant emblem?[8] How does one explain acts of heroism and sacrificing one's own life to save the lives of others? Both these behaviours seem irrational from the point of view of the economic man. This is where the concept of group selection or multilevel selection comes to our aid.[9] Its essence lies in the fact that the adaptability of a given trait is not assessed from the perspective of the individual but from that of the "selfish gene".[10] Building a high social position by acquiring and displaying expensive positional goods increases the attractiveness of the holder and thus his chances of procreating with the most attractive female partners. Since the bearers of similar genes are family members and even entire communities, the sacrifice or altruistic (non-egoistic) behaviour of individual group members will be adaptive insofar as it promotes the survival and expansion of the group. In this way, behaviour patterns spread not only as individual strategy decisions but even more as so-called cultural variables, copied between members of a collectivity, giving them an advantage over other collectivities. Of the two tribes, the one that uses language rather than hooting in communication will gain the upper hand, and the one that can communicate and accumulate its experiences in writing will dominate over them. Thus, from the 18th century onwards, as we wrote in Chapter 1, those societies whose organisation was based on political and economic liberalism began to take primacy in the world.

Similar analyses are also conducted at a much higher level of detail. The American economist Andrew W. Lo, among others, presented a behavioural-evolutionary explanation of the recent financial crisis. It is based on the evolutionary spread of patterns, which are investment strategies developed by trial and error by hedge funds. As soon as these strategies prove successful (where the measure of effectiveness is the return on invested capital), other funds copy them. At a certain stage, everyone starts investing the same way and in the same financial instruments, leading to a speculative bubble and eventual collapse (Lo, 2017).

Economists and cultural anthropologists who carry out such analyses often use computer simulation models (*ABM – agent-based models*). These are usually very simplified models of the development of a population with defined attributes in a given environment. They make it possible to trace how defined attributes (e.g., investment strategies or specific cultural artefacts) affect the development or degradation of a population. The path through simulation models is unavoidable because, although some mathematical equations are used in the theory of evolution, their use does not directly lead to a shortcut from assumptions to the outcome. However, this method reveals two characteristic weaknesses. One we already know from meteorology. Evolutionary models are even more complex and structurally unstable than weather models. Very slight changes in the initial values of variables lead to a completely different picture of the final population. The second enters the field of computer science. Increasing the number of variables, or, colloquially speaking, making the model more realistic, leads us to mathematical incomputability, or computability, in which the simulation takes as long as the actual development of the population and is thus useless from the point of view of predicting future results.

Dismal science

The eponymous term has clung to economics firstly because of its gloomy predictions of economic developments (declining corporate profits, impoverishment of the working class, etc.) but then because of its inability to accurately describe the market and predict economic events and the consequent counter-productive prescriptions put forward by economists to improve the situation supposedly.[11] Despite some optimistic examples at the beginning of the chapter, the argumentation presented above actually sounds bleak. We have at least three fundamental reasons why we are doomed to a perpetual inability to create efficient models that accurately predict economic events.

1 Firstly, at the root, we have chaotic and random patterns of behaviour. Even understanding the mechanism of evolutionary pressure, we do not know to which patterns it will apply. Their possible number is infinite.
2 Secondly, due to a different degree of complexity, we are not able to model our decision-making model (Hayek's argument).
3 Thirdly, even if we were able to do this, the complexity of the model could be comparable to the complexity of the reality being modelled and would be computationally inaccessible, or we would get results at a time when the effects we wanted to predict would become apparent.

So why the initial optimism? There are many ways of attacking complexity and many mathematical techniques to deal with it with greater or lesser approximation. At this point, however, two are worth mentioning.

1 Even very complex systems evolving on the basis of a genetic algorithm enter transitional equilibrium states. Using elements of game theories for this purpose, one speaks of evolutionarily stable strategies that lead to the emergence of repeatable patterns of behaviour over a definable time horizon. Economics is able to identify these and incorporate them into its models. For example, the concept of positional goods has already found a permanent place in microeconomics textbooks. We know roughly what they may include and how markets for such goods function (Frank, 1985).
2 The author of the evolutionary analysis of financial markets himself, Andrew W. Lo points out that even with the rapid evolution of investment strategies, some of which may prove dangerous to the stability of the market as a whole, we still have the opportunity to act. The proposed strategy is reminiscent of the aforementioned race between virus mutations and vaccines, although Lo uses a different comparison and points to the committees that investigate the causes of aeroplane accidents. Indeed, based on a specific case, their primary task is to come up with recommendations on how to avoid a similar accident in the future. This system works quite well. Why, then, could a similar early warning system not work in the financial markets?

Finally, let us return to the dispute between realists and instrumentalists. In the interpretation presented above, the expectation that a given economic theory or model is supposed to represent some kind of economic reality could only apply to those evolutionarily stable areas where, over a defined time horizon, repetitive patterns of behaviour operate, forming the basis for economic regularities suitable for modelling, as the realists would wish. All the rest is a dynamically and adaptively changing reality to which, at most, we can react according to our objectives, as Lo proposes. This last solution has nothing to do with scientific realism any more but is purely instrumental.

Notes

1 We also write about Malthus' demographic predictions in the third part of the book, in Chapter 16.
2 We write about this in more detail in Chapter 1.
3 We also refer to this example in Chapter 14.
4 It is also possible to make money on falling share prices on the stock market, through so-called *short selling*. In economic terms, this involves "borrowing" a certain number of shares, with an obligation to return them within a certain period of time. If the borrower sells the shares shortly after "borrowing" them and buys them back just before they are returned, the borrower will make a profit when the price falls. In practice, the execution

of a short sale is done not by transferring ownership of the shares, but by entering into a corresponding futures contract, which itself can also be traded on an exchange.

5 It is worth mentioning that while there is a consensus in mainstream economics for such an analysis, also referred to as micro-level macroeconomics, there is no shortage of dissenting voices that believe that in order to establish certain relationships at the macro level; we do not need to analyse individual decisions (Osiatyński, 2019).

6 The publication of Charles Darwin's work, *On the Origin of Species*, took place in 1859.

7 We write a little more about institutionalism in the third part of the book, in Chapter 10.

8 We write about Veblen's concept of positional goods in Part III in Chapter 16.

9 More on the subject of group selection and its implications can be found in Part III, in Chapter 17. The concept of group selection was already hinted at by Darwin. Its development into the mathematical formula of multilevel selection is due to the American geneticist George Price (Harman, 2010).

10 The concept of the "*selfish gene*" was introduced to the literature by the American biologist and science populariser, Richard Dawkins (Dawkins, 1976).

11 The term "dismal science" was first used by the British historian Thomas Carlyle referring to the situation of former slaves in the West Indies, whose existence, in his view, had not improved at all after the abolition of slavery and the introduction of wage labour (Carlyle, 1853).

References

Backhouse, R. E. (2010). *The puzzle of modern economics: Science or ideology?* Cambridge University Press.

Carlyle, T. (1853). *Occasional discourse on the nigger question*. Thomas Bosworth.

Dawkins, R. (1976). *The selfish gene*. Oxford University Press.

Fisher, I. (1930). *The theory of interest, as determined by impatience to spend income and opportunity to invest it*. Macmillan.

Frank, R. H. (1985). *Choosing the right pond: Human behavior and the quest for status*. Oxford University Press.

Friedman, M. (2008). The methodology of positive economics. In D. M. Hausman (Ed.), *The philosophy of economics. An anthology* (pp. 145–178). Cambridge University Press.

Frydman, R., & Goldberg, M. D. (2007). *Imperfect knowledge economics. Exchange rate and risk*. Princeton University Press.

Harman, O. (2010). *The price of altruism: George price and the search for the origins of kindness*. W.W. Norton & Company.

Hayek, F. A., 1945. The use of knowledge in society. *American Economic Review*, *35*(4), 519–530.

Hayek, F. A. (1992). *The sensory order. An inquiry into the foundation of theoretical psychology*. The University of Chicago Press.

Keynes, J. M. (2009). *The general theory of employment, interest, and money*. Classic Books America.

Keynes, J. M. (2012). *The economic consequences of the peace*. CreateSpace Independent Publishing Platform.

Knight, F. (2008). Economics and human action. In D. M. Hausman (Ed.), *The philosophy of economics. An antology* (pp. 100–107). Cambridge University Press.

Lo, A. W. (2017). *Adaptive market. Financial evolution at the speed of thought*. Princeton University Press.

Mainzer, K., 1994. *Thinking in complexity. The computational dynamics of matter, mind, and mankind*. Berlin/Heidelberg/New York: Springer.

Malthus, T. R., 2011. *An essay on the principle of population*. [Online] Available at: http://www.econlib.org/library/Malthus/malPop3.html#VII.20 [Accessed 18.02.2011].

Marshall, A. (1925). The future of the working classes. In A. C. Pigou (Ed.), *Memorials of Alfred Marshall* (pp. 101–118). Macmillan and Co.
Marx, K., & Engels, F., 1848. *Manifesto of the Communist Party.* [Online] Available at: https://www.marxists.org/archive/marx/works/1848/communist-manifesto/ [Accessed 05.08.2024].
McCloskey, D. N. (1998). *The rhetoric of economics*. The University of Wisconsin Press.
Mill, J. S., 2008. On the definition and method of political economy. In *The philosophy of economics. An anthology* (pp. 41–58). Cambridge University Press.
Opocher, A. (2010). The future of the working classes: A comparison between J.S. Mill and A. Marshall. *The European Journal of the History of Economic Thought*, *17*, 229–253.
Osiatyński, J. (2019). Spory o mikroekonomicne podstawy makroekonomii po Kaleckim i Keynesie. In T. Kwarciński & A. Wincewicz-Price (Eds.), *Metaekonomia tom II. Zagadnienia z filozofii makroekonomii* (pp. 36–80). Copernicus Center Press.
Reiss, J. (2012, November). Idealization and the aims of economics. Three cheers for instrumentalism, *Economics and Philosophy*, *28*, pp. 363–383. https://doi.org/10.1017/S0266267112000284
Ricardo, D., 1821. *On the principles of political economy and taxation.* [Online] Available at: http://www.econlib.org/library/Ricardo/ricP1.html [Accessed 03.06.2013].
Rzońca, A. (2007). *Czy Keynes się pomylił? Skutki redukcji deficytu w Europie Środkowej.* Wydawnictwo Naukowe Scholar.
Soros, G. (2013). Fallibility, reflexivity, and the human uncertainty principle. *Journal of Economic Methodology*, *20*(4), 309–329. https://doi.org/10.1080/1350178X.2013.859415

PART II
Ethics and Economics

100

4

IS ECONOMICS A MORAL SCIENCE?

Imagine a situation that could happen to any of us. On your way to work or university, you notice your wallet lying on the street. Inside, there is a significant sum of money, say £200, and a business card with the owner's name and address. Faced with this scenario, most people would pause to consider what to do next. Should they return the wallet with the money intact or keep the cash and discard the rest? This kind of moral dilemma can reveal much about human behaviour, and one might wonder: What would most people actually do?

This very question was posed to students at Cornell University as part of a study examining how educational background influences ethical decision-making. Specifically, researchers asked this question to students enrolled in an introductory microeconomics course and compared their responses with those of students taking an introductory astronomy course. The results revealed a striking difference: by the end of the semester, a significantly higher percentage of economics students were "less honest", meaning their willingness to return the money decreased compared to the beginning of the course (Frank et al., 1993).

These findings suggest that the assimilation of economic models and theories – which often assume that individuals act in their own self-interest, rationally seeking to maximise personal benefits – has a notable impact on students' moral attitudes. The attempt to capture the difference in the views of students before and after their economics education was to eliminate the competing hypothesis that studying economics attracts people who are more selfish and less cooperative with others. Even if this type of preselection does indeed occur, economic education further exacerbates the selfish attitudes of its participants.

To some extent, this supports the idea that economic theories don't just describe human behaviour – they shape it. At the same time, the inverse is also true: the moral beliefs and behaviours of individuals within a market must be considered

DOI: 10.4324/9781003469384-7

when building economic models. These reciprocal influences between education, moral attitudes, and economic theory suggest that our understanding of self-interest in economics is deeply intertwined with ethical considerations.

The moral dilemma of organ markets

An interesting case study in the intersection of economic realities, moral beliefs, and economic models is the issue of organ distribution for transplantation. According to Poltransplant statistics, 1193 people in Poland were waiting for a kidney transplant as of December 2023. During that same month, 81 kidney transplants were performed using organs from deceased donors and 9 from living donors.[1] In the absence of a transplant, patients with kidney failure must endure arduous dialysis treatments, which often result in exclusion from professional life and, ultimately, premature death.

Economists argue that the insufficient number of kidney transplants from living donors could be increased if economic incentives were introduced. In essence, a legal market for organs could save many lives by encouraging more donations.[2] However, what stands in the way of such a solution? The answer is largely moral conviction. Most people strongly believe that the human body should not be commodified. But why? The justification generally falls into three main arguments.

Firstly, many contend that trading organs reduces the human body to an object, akin to a commodity. For them, the human body is sacred and of far greater value than any tradable goods such as mobile phones, laptops, or cars. Secondly, there are concerns that a market for organs would unfairly exploit the poor, who might feel forced to sell their organs due to financial pressure. Finally, a more extreme worry is that legalising organ trade could lead to a slippery slope where people are harmed or even killed for their organs, purely for profit.

While each of these arguments can be debatable – indeed, some economists have called for these moral concerns to be set aside and suggested actions to modify people's beliefs in this area (Brennan & Jaworski, 2016) – a practical economist proposing solutions to the organ shortage must still account for these beliefs. A flawless economic model showing mutual benefit between the donor and recipient of a transplanted organ is irrelevant if public outraged prevents such exchange. Alvin Roth, the 2012 Nobel Prize winner in economics, understood this when he compared people's outrage at the possibility of organ trade to a technological or budget constraint. Just as businesses are limited by their available technology, and consumers are bound by income restrictions, moral outrage serves as a constraint for the kind of solutions that can be implemented. Roth argued that it might be easier to transcend technological constraints, such as developing artificial organs for transplantation, than to change deeply held moral objections to organ trade (Roth, 2007).

That said, acknowledging public discomfort with organ trafficking does not mean giving up on modelling this type of social reality or finding ways to improve the efficiency of organ distribution. Roth's proposed chain transplantation algorithm is a perfect example of an innovative solution that respects moral concerns. In this system, an altruistic donor gives a kidney to a person in need, setting off a chain reaction of transplants. In the next step, the relative of the recipient (typically a spouse) donates a kidney to another patient waiting for a transplant. This pattern repeats, forming a chain of several transplants. Crucially, these surgeries do not need to be simultaneous, and since the chain begins with an altruistic donor, there is no risk of someone backing out and leaving the patient without a kidney. This eliminates the scenario where one person gives an organ expecting their loved one to receive one in return, while the person who was supposed to donate an organ intended for their spouse backs out at the last minute. The algorithm proposed by Roth ensures that the person in need receives the organ first, and only then does their loved one donate their kidney to another person. This market-design model, based on *matching market* algorithms, significantly increases the number of life-saving transplants without relying on a price mechanism, which many find morally objectionable (Rees et al., 2009).

Of course, not all economic models need to explicitly account for the moral beliefs of participants. In models like perfect competition, the key assumption is that there are many buyers and sellers, none of whom can individually affect the market price. In a duopoly, we assume two dominant actors control market volumes and prices. Even here, though, there is a tacit assumption that participants in the market follow certain social rules. Entrepreneurs aim to maximise profits but should not do so by killing competition. Consumers can increase their income by trading leisure for work, but they should not resort to theft (Hardt, 2019).

Even Milton Friedman (1970), who famously argued that the primary responsibility of business is to increase profits, acknowledged that it must be done "(…) while conforming to the basic rules of the society, both those embodied in law and those embodied in ethical custom". Thus, economic life does not operate in a moral vacuum. Trust between market participants, grounded in shared moral norms, is essential for any successful market exchange.

Values can only be fought for

Acknowledging the value judgements of the subjects under study does not necessarily imply that the economic model itself is value-laden. Beliefs such as "people have a moral outrage against the possibility of organ trafficking" or "traders recognise that trade should respect basic moral standards" merely describe the attitudes of market participants. Economists are not required to decide whether holding such beliefs is better or worse.

Influenced by the neo-positivist ideal of science, which sees moral disputes as inconclusive and meaningless because, due to their emotional basis, 20th-century economists placed great emphasis on removing value judgements from economics. One prominent advocate of this approach was Milton Friedman. In his essay

The Methodology of Positive Economics, Friedman argued that economics, like physics, should be objective, asserting that "fundamental differences in basic values (…) men can ultimately only fight". According to him, rational debate on values is not possible (Friedman, 2008 [1953]; Mäki, 2009b).

Although Friedman was one of the most eminent economists of the 20th century, earning a Nobel Prize for his works on macroeconomics; his view on purging value judgements from economics was, in our opinion, flawed on two counts.

Firstly, a rational argument about values is possible. We often debate value judgements, and these judgements can be influenced by factual information. For example, if I argue that GDP growth is inherently good, I might reconsider this belief if I learn that such growth has led to increased social inequality. The fact the poor are becoming poorer while the wealthy are becoming richer would likely affect my positive valuation of economic growth. Amartya Sen (1967), also a Nobel laureate in economics, referred to these kinds of judgements – those subject to revision based on facts – as *non-basic judgements*.

But what about judgements we refuse to change in light of facts – *base judgements*? When it comes to these types of judgements, there is often more consensus than we might think. If you ask someone whether it is right to kill an innocent person or torture a child, you will likely find widespread agreement that these actions are wrong. In contrast, if you ask economists what caused the 2008–2009 financial crisis, a fact that took place, you will encounter a range of conflicting opinions and a heated debate. Even Friedman himself, in the passage on entrepreneurs' expectations of increasing profits, noted that they seek to do so while respecting social rules and moral customs. This suggests at least some level of shared understanding among businesspeople regarding which moral standards should be upheld.

Friedman's second mistake is the belief that positive economics can be entirely free of value judgements. This is impossible, in part because economists formulate their theories using natural language – the language of everyday communication. And natural language, by its nature, is infused with values.

Voluntary or involuntary unemployment?

For almost every person, securing a job – ideally a well-paid one – is a job crucial goal. Over the years, economists have debated whether unemployment can always be considered voluntary, or there is such a thing as involuntary unemployment. The distinction is key: voluntary unemployment occurs when a person has the opportunity to work but chooses not to, whereas involuntary unemployment refers to the situation in which a person loses their job and cannot find another suitable one. Economists who favour a liberal perspective argue that a flexible labour market should allow almost everyone who wants to work to find employment. In their view, the only individuals who remain unemployed are either those in transition between jobs (known as frictional unemployment) or those who, when faced with the choice between work or leisure, consciously choose the latter. In such cases, unemployment is classified as voluntary.

However, the concept of "voluntary" unemployment carries both a technical and a moral dimension. From a purely economic standpoint, choosing not to work may seem voluntary, but the term "voluntary" also implies a degree of freedom and absence of coercion. Historically, moral philosophy has emphasised that voluntary actions are not inherently problematic, as the legal maxim *volenti non fit iniuria* suggest "no harm is done to the willing". If someone willingly chooses a course of action and suffers as a result, they cannot claim injury, and by extensions, others are under no obligation to remedy that harm. According to this principle, if the unemployed person refuses to take a job at a lower wage, they are responsible for their own situation and should not expect benefits or compensation.

Yet, this strict interpretation overlooks the crucial element: the conditions under which choices are made. As Daniel Hausman, a leading scholar in the philosophy of economics, points out, economists often fail to distinguish between voluntary action and rational behaviour. While the decision may be rational, it is not necessarily voluntary if the circumstances are coercive. For instance, if a person is confronted by a robber who demands "your money or your life", choosing to hand over money is a rational decision, but hardly a voluntary one. The individual's choice is dictated by the threat of violence, not by a genuine desire to relinquish their property. The robber's demand, though it presents a choice, is based on an unlawful exercise of power.

In a similar vein, Keynesian economists argue that involuntary unemployment can occur in certain economic conditions, particularly in periods of crisis. They contend that if a worker agrees to take a low-paid job far below his qualifications, skills, or aspirations – one that significantly limits the contribution they could make to society – this decision is rational but not truly voluntary. It is akin to the person handing over their wallet under duress. While accepting the job may seem like the best available option – all things considered – it is not a fully voluntary one. The worker may have no real alternative, faced with the stark prospect with economic hardship and an inability to provide for their family. Under such constrained circumstances, employment becomes a rational but involuntary response to external pressures.

This understanding complicates the simplistic binary of voluntary versus involuntary unemployment. If the job opportunities available are so limited that individuals are forced into roles significantly below their potential, can we still classify them as voluntary unemployment? According to this interpretation, even those who are technically employed might be considered involuntary unemployed if their work does not align with their skills and capabilities. Determining whether workers have access to sufficiently good job opportunities involves value judgements. Thus, economists who argue that involuntary unemployment is possible, especially during a major economic crisis, challenge the idea that all unemployment is voluntary, integrating value judgements into what should be a purely positive economic theory (Hausman et al., 2016, pp. 39–52).

If economics, which seeks to explain reality and predict market behaviours (positive economics), cannot be fully free of value judgements, this is even more true for normative economics, which is explicitly concerned with evaluating alternative states of the world. A clear example of this can be seen in a memorandum from one of today's leading economists, whose bold recommendations we shall examine in more detail.

Why should Africa bear more pollution?

In the 1990s, Lawrence Summers, then serving as a Chief Economist of the World Bank, allegedly circulated an internal memo in which he wondered, "… shouldn't the World Bank be encouraging more migration of the dirty industries to the LDCs [Least Developed Countries]?" He put forward three primary arguments to support this idea. Firstly, Summers posited that the economic costs of pollution are largely measured by lost wages – those that individuals could have earned were they not suffering from pollution-induced diseases or premature death. By this logic, since wages in developing countries are significantly lower, the economic cost of pollution is proportionally less. For instance, while the average monthly income in the United States is over $6000, in the Democratic Republic of Congo (DRC), it is merely $55.[3] Thus, transferring pollution from the United States to the DRC would, in Summers' view, make economic sense; the loss in wages due to pollution-induced mortality in the DRC would be relatively small. As Summers put it, "(…) the economic logic behind dumping a load of toxic waste in the lowest wage country is impeccable and we should face up to that".

Secondly, Summers argued that the harmful effect of pollution accumulates non-linearly over time. Initially, the environmental impact of placing the factory or waste dump in a relatively unspoiled area is minimal, but as pollution increases, its detrimental effects compound. It is only after the accumulation of pollution over time that people begin to experience its impact more clearly, leading to more frequent illness and shorter life span. As Summers expressed it: "I've always thought that under-populated countries in Africa are vastly under-polluted, their air quality is probably vastly inefficiently low compared to Los Angeles or Mexico City".

Thirdly, Summers noted that many of the diseases impacted even slightly by environmental pollution, such as prostate cancer, tend to manifest later in life. Therefore, he argued clean air and healthy environment are particularly important for those who are likely to live long enough to develop such diseases, namely the wealthy residents of developed nations. In contrast, the demand for environmental quality is less pronounced among poorer populations in developing countries, as they face more immediate survival concerns and have lower life expectancy. Economically speaking, the demand for environmental quality exhibits high income elasticity.

In light of these arguments, should African nations be compelled to accept pollution from industrialised countries? Summers' memo does not advocate such coercion. Rather, he suggests that because pollution inflicts greater economic costs on wealthy, developed countries and poses a comparatively lower burden to developing nations, a mutually beneficial transaction could emerge. Develop countries would be willing to pay to transfer their pollution, and developing nations might accept it in exchange for appropriate compensation. In Summers' view, both parties could potentially benefit from such an agreement.

A key assumption underlying this argument is that harm from pollution is viewed as a reversible and compensable loss of well-being (DeMartino, 2022; Kwarciński, 2022). From this perspective, as long as the damage to individuals or the environment can be compensated – whether through financial means or other forms of compensation – the harm is seen as acceptable and the overall well-being of both parties can still improve. However, despite this "irresistible" economic logic, many people would likely find the idea of transferring toxic waste to Africa morally unacceptable for various reasons – ranging from the belief that we should not harm the more vulnerable population, to the argument that wealthier nations have better technology to manage pollution, to the conviction that we should care for the environment as a global good, irrespective of whether it is in wealthy or poor countries.

These critics may also reject the assumption that harm can be easily reversed or fully compensated, especially when considering long-term environmental damage or the health impacts that persist across generations. They would judge such an action to be morally reprehensible and unfair to the people of developing nations. This raises the question: Why do the intuitions of ordinary people seem to conflict with the reasoning of economists? Is there a fundamental tension between the value-laden perspective of the public and the value-laden logic employed by economists?

At its core, Summers' argument is grounded in the value-laden framework. Like much of welfare economics, his reasoning assesses competing states of the world based on normative judgements. In this case, the two scenarios under consideration are as follows: (1) leaving toxic waste in developed countries or (2) relocating it to developing countries. If both perspectives are rooted in value judgements, why should economic rationale take precedence over the moral intuitions of laypeople? Economists' response is typically grounded in the Pareto principle, after the eminent Italian mathematician and economist Vilfredo Pareto, which asserts that the state of the world is better if it improves one party's position without simultaneously worsening another's. According to this criterion, if the transaction satisfies the preferences of all parties involved, it represents an improvement in overall welfare (well-being). Economists argue that they do not dictate what individual preferences should be; instead they claim to leave the definition of well-being to those actions reflect their own desires.

Thus, it seems that while welfare economics may involve normative judgements about specific outcomes, its foundation lies not in the value judgements of economists themselves, but in the preferences of the market participants. By this logic, transferring pollution from developed countries to developing countries could enhance global welfare – not because economists' moral intuitions override those of laypeople but because the transaction satisfies the preferences of both parties involved. In this way, normative economics bears a close resemblance to positive economics, which seeks to describe, explain, and predict the behaviour of market participants without imposing value judgements of its own.

However, upon closer examination, the situation is not so straightforward. Firstly, as has been demonstrated in the analysis of involuntary unemployment, value judgements do appear in positive economics as well. Secondly, the logic underpinning Summers' arguments does not fully remove the role value judgements. Equating the improvement of a person's well-being with the fulfilment of their preferences is itself a value-laden assumption. Why should well-being be measured by preferences alone? Why not consider alternative metrics, such as life satisfaction or sense of happiness? As we shall see in Chapter 7, increasing income and fulfilling a wider range of preferences do not necessarily translate into greater happiness. Furthermore, as behavioural economists have shown, individuals are not perfectly rational; they are often subject to cognitive biases, meaning that what they prefer may not always be in their best interest.

Consequently, it might be worthwhile to consider the formulation of a list of universal goods – such as health, a decent income, mobility, social interaction, or play – that contribute to human well-being regardless of whether individuals consciously choose them. For example, smoking is harmful to health, even if it aligns with an individual's current preferences. The British philosopher Derek Parfit (1986) called this a list of objective goods, suggesting that some things are inherently good for people, irrespective of their subjective preferences.

Why, then, do economists prioritise the fulfilment of preferences over other potential measures of well-being, such as happiness or a list of objective goods? This choice fundamentally shapes the logic of economic reasoning. Even if transferring pollution appears mutually beneficial in the short term, we might assess it negatively if we measure well-being in terms of health outcomes or happiness. Another critical consideration is how well-being is measured. Calculating the costs and benefits of pollution based on lost wages has a profound impact on the conclusions drawn about pollution transfer.[4] Why, then, do economists insist on linking well-being to the fulfilment of preferences? The answer lies in one of economics' most famous metaphors: the invisible hand of the market.

The invisible hand of the market

The concept of the "invisible hand", formulated in the works of Adam Smith, remains an enduring metaphor for the market's seemingly magical ability to align individual self-interest with the general good. More precisely, the vague metaphor of the invisible hand finds formal expression in the first theorem of welfare economics. This theorem posits that any economy characterised by market competition is Pareto efficient, meaning that no individual's situation can be improved without worsening the situation of someone else. In this context, the decisions of consumers and producers, driven by their preferences, lead to the best possible outcomes when judged by the Pareto efficiency criterion.

Market competition, therefore, is seen as a mechanism that maximises preference satisfaction. Since the well-being of individuals is often equated with the fulfilment of their preferences, the market is considered an effective tool for enhancing overall welfare. Through market choices, individuals reveal their preferences, and by extension, their preferences are linked to their well-being. This connection ties the functioning of the market directly to the general good.

The importance of this dynamic became particularly evident during the COVID-19 pandemic. Long queues at shops, a looming global economic crisis, and the prospect of widespread unemployment underscore the critical role of markets in sustaining livelihood. Yet, the pandemic also highlighted that economic activity is not the sole determinant of well-being. When cinema or, a restaurant, and other social spaces were closed, it became clear that these activities did more than merely fulfil preferences – they provided opportunities for social interaction, happiness, and emotional well-being. These dimensions of well-being, often overlooked in mainstream economics, suggest that satisfaction of preferences is not the only measure of a good life.

Economists tend to favour a preference-based concept of well-being because it aligns with their valuation of the market as a tool for satisfying individual choices. The market offers people the freedom to engage in transactions they believe are beneficial to themselves. Some economists explicitly acknowledge that this freedom constitutes the "moral heart" of economics.[5]

Putting the cards on the table: Transparency and discursivity

Economics is inherently a moral science because human beings are moral agents. They evaluate actions – both their own and others' – not only in terms of effectiveness but also in terms of rightness. Their life choices are shaped by the value system they recognise. As a discipline concerned with human behaviour, economics, too, is shaped by these moral considerations. Economists, when developing models, must account for the moral beliefs of the individuals whose behaviour they study. Furthermore, economic theories themselves have the capacity to shape the moral outlook of their audience. Most significantly, both positive and normative economics are, to varying degrees, influenced by the moral beliefs of the economists who develop them.

Given the value-laden nature of economics, how should economists respond to this reality? The neo-positivist view suggests that economics, if it is to be considered a science, must be free from moral considerations; value-ladenness, according to this perspective, is unscientific and, therefore, meaningless. Alternatively, some economists might seek to sidestep the issue altogether, ignoring the role of moral values in economic analyses. However, a third and more compelling approach acknowledges that eliminating value-ladenness in economics is impossible and seeks to manage this normative burden in constructive ways.

Philosopher of economics Julian Reiss proposes two strategies to address this challenge: transparency and discursivity. Transparency requires economists to clearly state their moral beliefs and disclose any personal or institutional interests that might influence their theoretical preferences or research outcomes. This methodological openness ensures that the audience is fully aware of the values and assumptions embedded in the analysis. Discursivity, on the other hand, involves embracing the possibility of disagreement, both in terms of empirical facts and moral values (Reiss, 2014). This approach involves revealing all the theoretical "cards" that an economist holds, allowing the audience to fully understand the value assumptions embedded in economic models and analyses.

Notes

1 https://www.poltransplant.org.pl/statystyka_2023.html (Accessed: December 2024).
2 http://bostonreview.net/welch-morals-markets (Accessed: December 2024).
3 https://www.worlddata.info/average-income.php (Accessed: November 2024).
4 We write more about the controversy over economic measures in the third part of the book in Chapter 13.
5 https://economix.blogs.nytimes.com/2011/01/25/the-moral-heart-of-economics/ (Accessed: December 2024).

References

Brennan, J., & Jaworski, P. M. (2016). *Markets without limits: Moral virtues and commercial interests*. Routledge.
DeMartino, G. F. (2022). *The tragic science: How economists cause harm (even as they aspire to do good)*. University of Chicago Press.
Frank, R. H., Gilovich, T., & Regan, D. T. (1993). Does studying economics inhibit cooperation? *The Journal of Economic Perspectives*, *7*(2), 159–171. https://doi.org/10.1257/jep.7.2.159
Friedman, M. (1970, September 13). A Friedman doctrine: The social responsibility of business is to increase its profits. *The New York Times Magazine*. https://www.nytimes.com/1970/09/13/archives/a-friedman-doctrine-the-social-responsibility-of-business-is-to.html
Friedman, M. (2008). The methodology of positive economics. In D. M. Hausman (Ed.), *The philosophy of economics. An anthology* (pp. 145–178). Cambridge University Press.
Hardt, Ł. (2019). Utylitaryzm, deontologia i etyka cnót: zbieżne czy przeciwstawne fundamenty etyczne ekonomii? *Biuletyn Polskiego Towarzystwa Ekonomicznego*, *4*, 20–35.
Hausman, D., McPherson, M., & Satz, D. (2016). *Economic analysis, moral philosophy, and public policy*. Cambridge University Press.

Kwarciński, T. (2022). The tragic science: How economists cause harm (even as they aspire to do good) by George F. DeMartino. *Social Entrepreneurship Review*, *2*, 102–106. https://doi.org/10.15678/SER.2022.2.001
Mäki, U. (Ed.). (2009b). *The methodology of positive economics: Reflections on the Milton Friedman legacy*. Cambridge University Press.
Parfit, D. (1986). *Reasons and persons*. Oxford University Press. https://doi.org/10.1093/019824908X.001.0001
Rees, M. A., Kopke, J. E., Pelletier, R. P., Segev, D. L., Rutter, M. E., Fabrega, A. J., Rogers, J., Pankewycz, O. G., Hiller, J., Roth, A. E., Sandholm, T., Ünver, M. U., & Montgomery, R. A. (2009). A nonsimultaneous, extended, altruistic-donor chain. *New England Journal of Medicine*, *360*(11), 1096–1101. https://doi.org/10.1056/NEJMoa0803645
Reiss, J. (2014). Struggling over the soul of economics: Objectivity versus expertise. In *Experts and consensus in social science* (pp. 131–152). Springer. https://doi.org/10.1007/978-3-319-08551-7_7
Roth, A. E. (2007). Repugnance as a constraint on markets. *Journal of Economic Perspectives*, *21*(3), 37–58. https://doi.org/10.1257/jep.21.3.37
Sen, A. K. (1967). The nature and classes of prescriptive judgements. *The Philosophical Quarterly (1950-)*, *17*(66), 46–62. https://doi.org/10.2307/2218365

5

WHAT IS MORE IMPORTANT

The size of the pie or the way it is divided?

Taxing robots

We are witnessing an unprecedented advancement in technology. Routine tasks, such as booking airline tickets or hotel rooms, are increasingly handled by automated systems. In some cases, human interaction is almost entirely eliminated – automated check-ins, for example, allow travellers to access hotel rooms using a PIN code generated during booking. This signals a future where automation and robotics will increasingly replace human labour. Automated production lines, Amazon's highly efficient warehouses run by a minimal workforce, and the testing of autonomous vehicles – bolstered by recent developments in artificial intelligence (AI) – are all driving this transformation. As these technologies evolved, concerns about job displacement are growing among workers in various industries, who fear that advances in hardware and software will deprive them of employment.

These concerns are not unfounded. Even advocates of technology have recognised the potential negative impact of automation on the labour market. Bill Gates, founder of Microsoft and a prominent supporter of technological innovation, has proposed a robot tax, sparkling widespread debate.[1] Gates argues that, just as human labour is taxed – through income tax, health contributions, and pension funds – robotic labour should be subject to similar taxation. Revenue from such a tax, he suggests, could be used to support workers' displacement by automation, funding social benefits, retraining programmes, and education.

However, critics have raised objections to this proposal, questioning both its practicality and its impact on economic efficiency. Lawrence Summers, former chief economist of the World Bank and economic advisor to President Barack Obama, offers a fundamental critique. According to Summers, taxing robot labour

DOI: 10.4324/9781003469384-8

could reduce productivity by discouraging technological innovation. For instance, if 50 workers can build robots capable of performing the tasks of 100 workers, a high tax on robot labour might disincentivise the production of these robots altogether. Summers contends that there are two possible approaches: either restrict automation to protect jobs by taxing robots or encourage technological development to boost productivity, thereby expending the economy's overall output. In his view, only by enlarging the "economic pie" – the total goods and services produced – can society hope to share its benefits equitably through taxation and redistribution.[2] Prioritising distribution, he argues, would limit growth and reduce overall wealth available to society.

This sentiment is shared by Robert Lucas, the 1995 Nobel Prize winner in economics. Lucas cautions against an overemphasis on redistribution, asserting that it distracts from the more important goal of increasing production. He wrote in his *2003 Annual Report Essay* for Federal Reserve Bank "Of the tendencies that are harmful to sound economics, the most seductive, and in my opinion the most poisonous, is to focus on questions of distribution (...). The potential for improving the lives of poor people by finding different ways of distributing current production is nothing compared to the apparently limitless potential of increasing production" (Lucas, 2004).

There is undeniable merit to Lucas' point. The past two centuries have seen unprecedented economic growth – what has been referred to as the "great betterment" – leading to significant increases in life expectancy and living standards in many parts of the world. As explored in Chapter 1, this area of global growth has resulted in an enormous rise in GDP *per capita*, contributing to an overall increase in wealth. However, this process has also been accompanied by a steady rise in inequality, particularly in terms of income and wealth distribution.

Consider the findings from Oxfam's "Time to Care" report: 2153 of billionaires control more wealth than 4.5 billion people, or 60% of the global population.[3] While there has been a slight decline in global inequality in recent years – largely due to economic growth in China and India – inequality within countries has grown. According to the World Bank Group (2016), the global Gini index, which measures income inequality (it takes the value 0 when all members of a society have equal income and the value 100 in the case of extreme inequality, when one person has all of society's income), fell from 66.8 in 2008 to 62.5 in 2013. However, within individual nations, disparities in income have increased. For example, China's Gini index rose from 32.2 points in 1990 to 43.7 points in 2010, and in Poland, the index increased from 25.5 in 1987 to 38.0 in 2004.[4]

This brings us to a critical question: Are economists Summers and Lucas correct in suggesting that the distribution of wealth matters less than the opportunities to increase it? Is economic life fundamentally defined by an unavoidable tension between growth efficiency and fair distribution?

Equal sharing of the pie increases social welfare

The potential conflict between efficiency and equity has not always been a central focus in economic discourse. There is, however, a long-standing argument in favour of an egalitarian distribution of income within society. If billionaire Bill Gates were to receive an additional dollar, it would likely bring him little satisfaction; he might not even notice it. By contrast, if the same dollar were given to someone subsisting on less than $2 per day, it would not only be put to immediate use but would likely bring significant utility and joy. Thus, transferring income from the wealthy to the poor is considered socially beneficial, as the loss in utility for the rich is smaller than the gain for the poor, given the diminishing marginal utility of income. Following this line of reasoning, the greatest social welfare would be achieved when all members of a community receive the same income: perfect equality, maximum efficiency.

However, despite the apparent appeal of this reasoning, the argument for income equality rests on several contentious assumptions that warrant closer examination. Firstly, can the utility derived from income genuinely be measured by the satisfaction or pleasure it provides? Is it indeed that, as a person's income rises, the additional satisfaction form each successive dollar diminishes? Finally, is it possible to meaningfully compare the utility derived by different individuals? Many economists express scepticism about positive answers to these questions. Since we have no method of directly "seeing" into the minds of individuals, there is no way to precisely determine the utility they derive from a particular income level. More importantly, comparing one person's utility to another's is even more problematic. For instance, if we observe that Adam prefers coffee while Eva prefers tea, we can infer each person's preference hierarchy. However, we cannot determine if Adam prefers coffee twice as much as he does tea, or if Eve derives five times the satisfaction from tea that Adam does. Any claims about these subjective experiences remain speculative at best. Without a robust basis for making interpersonal utility comparisons, the argument for income egalitarianism becomes tenuous.

Even if one were persuaded by the initial argument in favour of income inequality, it is crucial to recognise that this reasoning only applies to a scenario in which the total of economic "pie" remains constant. In reality, inequality can serve as an incentive, motivating individuals to exert greater effort, accumulate wealth, and expand the overall availability of goods and services.

The market rewards according to merit

In 2019, Robert Lewandowski, the celebrated Polish footballer, signed a lucrative contract with Bayern Munich, under which he would earn 20 million euros per year – amounting to a daily salary of approximately PLN 240,000.[5] This figure is vastly disproportionate when compared to the average income of Polish citizens, or even the residents of wealthier European Union countries. Does this stark income inequality suggest an inherent unfairness? Not necessarily.

Lewandowski's exceptional skills as a striker make him an asset to his team, and fans demonstrate their appreciation by attending matches and paying for tickets. From this perspective, his high salary can be seen as deserved; the market rewards him for his unique abilities. If many players possessed Lewandowski's level of talent, or if reaching his calibre were easily achievable, then it's unlikely he would command such a fee. However, his combination of skills and rarity in the football world elevates his market value. Additionally, his success serves as an inspiration to young people striving to attain similar levels of achievement. Though market awards are distributed unevenly, one could argue that they are merited and thus fair. Furthermore, the inequality generated by these rewards often act as a motivator, ultimately increasing the size of the "economic pie".

However, the notion that economic efficiency and fair distribution are inherently compatible is not without complications. On the one hand, individuals often attribute their successes to personal talent and effort, downplaying the role of luck. Conversely, when faced with failure, people are inclined to attribute it to bad luck rather than a lack of ability. This psychological tendency complicates our understanding of merit and reward. To be clear, this is not to suggest that high achievers like Lewandowski do not deserve substantial compensation for their hard work; such a claim would be unjust. Rather, it highlights that people who are very talented and put enormous effort into their work are often outnumbered by those whose achievements owe as much to luck as to talent and perseverance (Frank, 2016). In other words, market success is not purely a merit award. Even if Lewandowski's talent and effort justify a high salary, the market compensates him not solely for his merit but because few players reach his level, and of those who do, he has been luckier. Market dynamics place a premium on scarcity and desirability rather than on social importance.

This distinction becomes evident when comparing Lewandowski's work to other essential services. His performances, while entertaining, are not critical to societal survival; essential functions such as food production or waste collection hold far greater importance. Yet, despite the fundamental nature of these roles, they are compensated far less generously than professional footballers. Meanwhile, although rubbish collection is extremely important to people, the work of those in this profession is valued incomparably lower than that of professional footballers. This discrepancy underscores a key point: the market does not reward services based on their contribution to meeting important human needs but on consumers' willingness to pay.

Consider, for example, the case of eflornithine, a drug used to treat African sleeping sickness – a life-threatening disease affecting approximately 65 million people in Sub-Saharan Africa. Left untreated, this disease can be fatal.[6] However, because those affected are typically impoverished, the market for eflornithine as a life-saving medication is limited. Pharmaceutical companies were eventually persuaded by the World Health Organization (WHO) to produce the drug, but only because they discovered its profitable application in developed countries as a facial hair removal cream. In market terms, eflornithine is deemed more valuable as a dermatological agent than as a life-saving medicine (Hausman et al., 2016).

The market, therefore, operates as an efficient mechanism for allocating scarce resources, directing them to those willing to pay the most. However, this system does not inherently fulfil the criteria of fairness, particularly if fairness is understood as rewarding individuals based on merit. Thus, while the market may create economic inequality, it cannot be justified solely on the basis of a fair distribution of market rewards. One possible justification for this inequality, however, is that the market's mechanisms can expand the overall "economic pie", potentially benefiting even the least advantaged members of society.

The poorest will also get something

One of the best-known standards of social justice was formulated by the American political philosopher John Rawls. In his influential work, *A Theory of Justice* (2005 [1971]), Rawls proposed the rule – known as the difference principle – that social inequality is acceptable only when it contributes to improving the situation of the least advantaged members of society. In other words, as a society, we can accept that some people will earn more than others, provided that this disparity ultimately benefits the poorest members. However, if the rich continue to grow richer while the circumstances of the poor remain stagnant, this indicates that the benefits of economic growth are being distributed unfairly.

In the 1980s, Rawls' criterion appeared relatively straightforward to fulfil. Policymakers believed that liberalising trade, reducing the role of the state, and lowering the tax burden on business would create prosperity that would "tickle down" to all levels of society. For example, Ronald Reagan's policy of reducing taxes on the wealthiest individuals in the United States was based on the assumption that the benefits of increased wealth among investors, businessmen, and entrepreneurs would translate into job creation and, eventually, improved standards of living for poorer citizens. However, over time, the premise that prosperity among the wealthiest would generate widespread economic benefits has not been supported by empirical evidence. A report by the International Monetary Fund (IMF) openly acknowledged this shortcoming, indicating that a 1% increase in the income share of the richest 20% of society leads to a 0.08 percentage point reduction in GDP. Conversely, a one per cent increase in the income share of the poorest 20% of citizens results in a 0.38 percentage points increase in GDP (Dabla-Norris et al., 2015, p. 7). This data suggests that an increase in the wealth of the richest segments of society does not contribute meaningfully to the "economic pie" available to poorer segments.

This trend of wealth accumulation among the rich – typically capital owners, whether in the form of land, machinery, real estate, corporate shares, or other financial assets – while the poor, who rely primarily on wages, remain disadvantaged, is further illustrated by the work of French economist Thomas Piketty. In his best-selling book *Capital in the 21st Century,* Piketty highlights the significant imbalance between the return on invested capital, which has historically hovered around 5–7% per annum, and the rate of economic growth, which has remained around 0–2% per annum over centuries. This disparity means that wealth inherited from previous generations grows much faster than the economy as a whole. For instance, if economic growth is 1% (g = 1%) and the return on capital is 5% (r = 5%), then reinvesting merely one-fifth of the income generated from inherited capital allows this wealth to grow at the same rate as the economy. If the capital owners save a larger portion of their profits, their wealth accumulates even faster, capturing an increasing share of the "economic pie" without significantly improving the quality of life for society's poorest members (Piketty, 2014).

Recent economic research indicates that rising levels of inequality within societies are concerning not only because they challenge standards of justice (such as Rawls' difference principle, which only justifies inequality when it benefits the least advantaged) but also due to their adverse impact on economic growth and stability. High levels of income and wealth inequality are often correlated with low levels of human capital, as measured by education levels, life expectancy, and various social issues such as substance abuse, the obesity epidemic, and increased crime (Wilkinson & Pickett, 2009). These factors can significantly hinder both the amount and sustainability of economic growth in affected societies (Ostry et al., 2019). If unequal distribution of the "economic pie" negatively impacts the size of the pie, a pressing question arises: Does it make sense to address this issue through redistributive measures? In other words, is income redistribution the right remedy?

The dripping bucket of redistribution

The second fundamental theorem of welfare economics (we discussed the first theorem in the previous chapter, examining whether economics can be considered a moral science) suggests that any efficient allocation of resources, in the Pareto sense, can be achieved through an initial redistribution of resources followed by market competition (Stiglitz & Rosengard, 2015, p. 66). An efficient allocation, in this context, is one where no reallocation can improve the welfare of one individual without worsening the welfare of at least one other. For example, consider a world of extreme inequality in which a single person owns all resources. This situation, despite its stark inequality, would qualify as efficient in the Pareto sense because improving the position of those with nothing would require taking resources from the one who has everything, thereby making that person worse off.

The second theorem of welfare economics, however, offers hope. It suggests that if we start from redistributing resources from the wealthiest individual to others and then allow market forces to operate, the resulting allocation can once again be Pareto efficient. In this new scenario, any improvement in one person's position could only occur at the expense of another, meeting the criterion for efficiency. But is this new state – achieved after redistribution – better than the initial condition of extreme inequality? From the perspective of social justice, the answer seems to be an unequivocal yes. However, in terms of economic efficiency, both scenarios are considered equally optimal in the Pareto sense. Thus, according to the second theorem of welfare economics, it appears possible to create a fairer society without sacrificing efficiency. But is this really the case?

In the 1970s, this optimistic interpretation of the second theorem was challenged by American economist Arthur Okun. In his influential book *Equality and Efficiency: The Big Tradeoff*, Okun (1975) presented a thought experiment to illustrate the costs of redistribution. He invited readers to imagine that transferring resources from the rich to the poor was like pouring water from one vessel to another using a bucket riddled with holes. Each time we attempt to redistribute, some of the water leaks out. If the state, through taxation, seeks to transfer an extra dollar from the rich to the poor, it often ends up taking more than a dollar from the wealthy due to "leakage" effects. This occurs because higher taxes can reduce the motivation of the wealthy to work or invest, leading to lower overall productivity. Additionally, the administrative costs of tax collection and social transfers mean that the poor ultimately receive less than a full dollar for every dollar taken from the rich. Okun's conclusion was that striving for greater equality through redistribution necessarily involves a trade-off: the "economic pie" shrinks as we attempt to slice it more equitably.

For decades, this idea of an inherent conflict between equality and efficiency, or more broadly, between social justice and market efficiency, has become an accepted dogma in economic though. However, like many widely held economic beliefs, this trade-off does not entirely hold up under scrutiny from empirical research. Recent analyses by Jonathan Ostry, Deputy Director of the Research Department of the International Monetary Fund, challenge Okun's conclusion. Ostry's research, for example, demonstrates that an increase in net income inequality (referring to income earned after taxes and social transfers) – as measured by a rise in the Gini index from 37 to 42 – can reduce economic growth by 0.5 percentage points. Redistribution, by contrast, has been found to have little to no adverse effect on economic growth.

The relationship between inequality, economic growth, and redistribution is thus more complex than Okun's simple trade-off suggests. While it is true, as Okun argued, that redistribution may discourage the wealthy from working and investing as vigorously due to higher taxes, excessive inequality itself can be detrimental to growth. Inequality can motivate competition, innovation, and entrepreneurship, but only to a point. Beyond that point, high inequality weakens human capital by depriving many individuals of adequate access to education, healthcare, and financial stability – factors crucial for a productive and innovative workforce.

Moreover, redistribution efforts that invest in public goods, such as education, healthcare, and infrastructure, not only reduce social inequalities but also contribute to more dynamic and sustainable economic growth. Healthier, better-educated, and financially secure individuals are more likely to become skilled workers, entrepreneurs, and consumers of high-quality goods. High inequality, by contrast, can undermine growth by eroding human capital and reducing the capacity of larger population segments to participate fully in the economy. As a result, greater equality in the distribution of economic resources is not only compatible with economic efficiency; it may also promote a more dynamic and resilient economy. In this way, Ostry and his collaborators present a more optimistic view: a "win-win" scenario where redistribution supports both equality and economic growth (Ostry et al., 2019).

Fairness and efficiency

There is, therefore, no basis for claiming that only economic growth (the more spectacular, the better) or only the way resources are distributed (the more equal, the better) matters. The economy is a system of multiple interdependencies, so both the concern for the size of the "economic pie" and the way it is distributed are important. Simply stating that the goal of a just society with a strong market economy is not a utopia is not enough, however; we need concrete tools to realise this goal. One of the most important tools is an efficient and fair tax system.

Taxes and other public levies are generally coercive and non-equivalent; citizens have to pay them without the right to demand specific returns from the state. However, the willingness to pay taxes also depends on factors like tax morale, which is influenced by the perceived fairness of the tax system and the quality of public services provided. It is difficult, for example, to consider a fair system in which, as in Poland, a significant part of social transfers is financed by relatively less well-off groups of taxpayers (Gorazda, 2019). Similarly, it is hard to expect citizens to willingly pay taxes if they perceive public services – such as public transport, education, and healthcare – as low quality.

In addressing these challenges, is the solution to impose additional taxes on the richest, to exempt the poorest, or perhaps to tax new forms of capital, like robots that tend to replace human labour? Should luxury consumption be taxed more heavily? These questions deserve careful analysis based on the specific circumstances of individual societies. However, two points seem certain. Firstly, empirical data suggest that focusing solely on economic growth – i.e. the size of the "economic pie" – is insufficient. Secondly, any attempt at equitable redistribution must consider its costs and its impact on overall economic output, as illustrated by Okun's "leaky bucket" metaphor.

The tension between fairness and efficiency in taxation will be examined in much greater detail in the next chapter, with a specific focus on tax burdens and collection strategies.

Notes

1 https://qz.com/911968/bill-gates-the-robot-that-takes-your-job-should-pay-taxes/ (Accessed: December 2024).
2 https://www.washingtonpost.com/opinions/picking-on-robots-wont-deal-with-job-destruction/2017/03/05/32091f08-004b-11e7-8ebe-6e0dbe4f2bca_story.html?postshare=4531488791793643 (Accessed: December 2024).
3 https://www.oxfam.org/en/press-releases/worlds-billionaires-have-more-wealth-46-billion-people (Accessed: December 2024).
4 https://data.worldbank.org/indicator/SI.POV.GINI?locations=PL-CN&name_desc=false (Accessed: December 2024).
5 https://www.money.pl/gospodarka/robert-lewandowski-dostal-podwyzke-bayern-monachium-bedzie-mu-placil-240-tys-zl-dziennie-6419381957675137a.html (Accessed: December 2024).
6 https://www.who.int/news-room/fact-sheets/detail/trypanosomiasis-human-african-(sleeping-sickness) (Accessed: December 2024).

References

Dabla-Norris, E., Kochhar, K., Suphaphiphat, N., Ricka, F., & Tsounta, E. (2015). Causes and consequences of income inequality: A global perspective. IMF Staff Discussion Note 15/13. Washington, DC: International Monetary Fund. https://www.imf.org/external/pubs/ft/sdn/2015/sdn1513.pdf

Frank, R. H. (2016). *Success and luck: Good fortune and the myth of meritocracy*. Princeton University Press.

Gorazda, M. (2019). Sprawiedliwość podatkowa. In T. Kwarciński & A. Wincewicz-Price (Eds.), *Metaekonomia II. Zagadnienia z filozofii makroekonomii* (pp. 316–347). Copernicus Center Press.

Hausman, D., McPherson, M., & Satz, D. (2016). *Economic analysis, moral philosophy, and public policy*. Cambridge University Press.

Lucas, R. E., Jr. (2004). The industrial revolution: Past and future. *The Region*, *18*(1), 5–20. https://www.minneapolisfed.org/article/2004/the-industrial-revolution-past-and-future

Okun, A. M. (1975). *Equality and efficiency: The big tradeoff*. Brookings Institution Press.

Ostry, J. D., Loungani, P., & Berg, A. (2019). *Confronting inequality: How societies can choose inclusive growth*. Columbia University Press.

Piketty, T. (2014). *Capital in the twenty-first century* (A. Goldhammer, Trans.). The Belknap Press of Harvard University Press.

Rawls, J. (2005). *The theory of justice* (reissue edition ed.). Harvard: Belknap Press. Harvard University Press.

Stiglitz, J. E., & Rosengard, J. K. (2015). *Economics of the public sector*. W.W. Norton.

Wilkinson, R., & Pickett, K. (2009). *The spirit level: Why greater equality makes societies stronger*. Bloomsbury Press.

World Bank Group (2016). *Poverty and shared prosperity 2016: Taking on inequality*. Washington, DC: World Bank. https://hdl.handle.net/10986/25078

6

WHY DO WE PAY TAXES, AND WHO SHOULD PAY MORE?

The origins of taxation

In the 1998 movie *Meet Joe Black*, Brad Pitt plays "Death", concealing his true identity under the guise of a tax inspector. He adopts this cover after hearing the common adage that nothing in life is certain except death and taxes. This saying reflects our firm conviction that both are inevitable and somewhat unpleasant. Death, as a biological phenomenon, is indisputably unavoidable beyond religious beliefs. But why do we pay taxes? Are they an ontological necessity? It would seem not.

Historically, there were at least two main reasons for taxation: the threat of plunder and "voluntary" submission to a sovereign. Invaders, such as the Normans in Europe, invented the method of "blackmail". Instead of pillaging a village, they would threaten to do so and, in exchange, receive an agreed-upon tribute. Voluntary submission, on the other hand, occurred whenever a tribe or society sought protection or aimed to achieve a common good requiring resources and coordination, willingly paying for it (Keen & Slemrod, 2021).

Let's be honest. This second origin of taxes – the notion of voluntary submission – sounds promising and aligns well with the modern narrative of a social contract. However, it has little to do with historical facts. Taxes are fundamentally linked to the state, and although the idea of a spontaneously emerging hierarchical, state-like organisation is appealing, in most cases, both the state and its levies were imposed from the outside. At least until the early modern period, when rebels of various kinds began to rise, and enlightened philosophers advanced ideas of civil society, taxes were enforced tribute to a king, supported by military power. Gradually, taxes shifted – at least in theory – from mandatory tribute for the monarch to "voluntary" contributions towards a common good.

DOI: 10.4324/9781003469384-9

The story of *Meet Joe Black* reminds us that, for ordinary taxpayers, taxation has always been – and most likely will continue to be – an oppressive and inescapable form of expropriation. These two seemingly opposing origins of taxes have shaped our thinking about this unpleasant duty and carry implications for perceptions of tax fairness. While a king's tribute requires little in terms of fairness, focusing instead on efficiency, a "voluntary" contribution immediately raises questions about the fair distribution of burdens and benefits.

Civilising taxes

Efforts to "civilize" taxes – to justify them within a framework of fairness – have a long history in political theory. One of the first to attempt this was Adam Smith. Being a keen observer of contemporary governance, in his *opus magnum*, Smith formulated the so-called four canons of taxation (Smith, 1776): equity, certainty, convenience, and efficiency.

Equity suggests that all taxpayers should be treated equally and fairly, with equality as the foundation of fairness. Any breach of this equality requires strong justification in terms of other respected rights, privileges, or values. Certainty means that tax obligations should be clearly defined by law so that taxpayers can understand their liabilities, free from the obscure discretion of officials. Convenience posits that fulfilling tax obligations should be easy for taxpayers, both economically and procedurally. Lastly, efficiency advocates for minimising tax collection costs and avoiding interference with market resource allocation.

Smith's insights on fair taxation sparked a long-standing debate. His successors sometimes approached the issue from vastly different perspectives. Some emphasised the economic freedoms of taxpayers (von Justi, 1762), while others highlighted economic efficiency, administrative costs, flexibility, and political responsibility (Stiglitz & Rosengard, 2015, p. 511). Economists often see taxes as a mechanism for transferring assets among economic agents. They, therefore, advocate for neutrality, meaning taxes should minimally interfere with economic relations in the market. The state's power to impose levies makes it a formidable market player capable of disrupting free competition between companies. Liberally minded thinkers argue that such interventions in the free market are harmful. However, these interventions may also serve beneficial purposes, such as stabilising economic cycles or reducing income and wealth inequalities (Strayer, 1958).

Legal and political philosophers often view taxes as an expression of the state's coercive power, one that must be constitutionally constrained (Brzeziński, 2017). This dichotomy between enforced tribute and voluntary (or at least consensual) contributions reflects economic and political perspectives on tax fairness.

Traditionally, public finance distinguishes between horizontal and vertical tax justice, which mirror two fundamental intuitions of fairness (Musgrave, 1959): equals should be treated equally, and unequals should be treated unequally. The roots of this approach lie in utilitarian doctrine, with Bentham's saying that "everybody counts for one, nobody for more than one" (Mill, 2013, loc. 47413). However, in vertical tax justice – where distinctions are made among "unequals" – utilitarian doctrine focuses solely on income and wealth inequalities. In an ideal state, everyone would have the same wealth and income. Consequently, the more one earns, the more one pays – a concept often called the "ability to pay principle".

When considering fairness in other respects, libertarian doctrine plays a role. It assumes natural inequality among people, but equal fundamental rights, which serve as a "no-trespassing fence" against sovereign interventions, including taxation. These fences may protect taxpayers' economic interests (von Justi, 1762) or procedural rights (Rawls, 2005; Stiglitz & Rosengard, 2015). Although there are numerous principles in both legal and financial literature, here we illustrate just a few key examples.

1 **Economic Principles**

- **Non-confiscatoriness:** Taxes should not amount to confiscation of property. For example, in a 1995 ruling, the German Constitutional Court (BVG – Bundesverfassungsgericht) found that capital gains tax exceeding 50% placed an excessive burden on taxpayers, violating property rights protections.[1] Taxes should also not lead to the so-called excess burdens, which means burdens deterring taxpayers from taking up the taxed actions and thus undermining the tax base.
- **Efficiency and pragmatism with respect to tax procedure:** The costs of tax collection should be proportionate to the revenue collected, with streamlined procedures for minor cases.
- **Non-infringement of lawfully granted privileges:** Tax privileges (such as incentives and exemptions) granted by law should not be arbitrarily revoked.
- **Valorisation:** Tax obligations expressed in nominal terms should be periodically adjusted for inflation.
- **Protecting the interest of the treasury:** Safeguarding taxpayer rights should not compromise the treasury's solvency or impede necessary public spending.

2 **Legal Principles**

- **Legalism:** Taxes must be established by law, not imposed or altered through administrative discretion.
- **Non-discretionary nature:** Tax obligations should be clearly defined in legislation, minimising officials' interpretative power.
- **Trust:** Taxpayers should be well-informed about tax laws, have participation rights, and be treated fairly in administrative proceedings.
- **Non-retroactivity:** New taxes should not apply to actions or events that occurred before they were introduced.

The above principles reflect what their authors considered right or wrong (fair or unfair) regarding public tributes; more broadly, they mirror prevailing intuitions or conceptions of justice. Some of these principles may be in conflict. For example, legalism does not fully align with pragmatism, and balancing the interests of both the taxpayer and the state invariably requires compromise. By juxtaposing these principles, one can attempt to reconstruct the underlying principles of justice and potentially connect them to established theories in social philosophy.

For instance, the ability-to-pay theory and the principle of vertical equality, which allows for differentiating taxpayer situations and assigning varied fiscal burdens, align with the principle of protecting the state's financial interests as well as principles of efficiency and pragmatism. Together, these principles support the maximisation of social utility, echoing the utilitarianism of Bentham and Mill.

The majority of socio-political principles – including the theory of taxes as reciprocal benefits, the principle of horizontal justice, the protection of taxation sources and taxpayer property, and the non-confiscatory nature of taxation – point towards safeguarding the natural rights of citizen-taxpayers, aligning with justice in libertarian terms. Additionally, many technical rules, such as those governing the creation of tax law and the conduct of tax proceedings, are derived from libertarian principles, prioritising the protection of taxpayer rights and freedoms.

Contemporary reasons for tax compliance

Today, the most straightforward reason people pay taxes is fear of possible sanctions, including criminal liability. Intuitively, the so-called deterrence theory seems plausible: as taxes are generally seen as an unpleasant duty, people would likely avoid paying them if not for the threat of penalties. Thus, the decision to evade taxes becomes a calculated gamble, with the evader weighing the costs and benefits of taking the risk. However, deterrence theory does not fully explain tax compliance, which is surprisingly widespread.

While the state and its officials may sometimes seem almost omniscient, they are not. A rational cost-benefit analysis of tax evasion would have to consider the probability of detection and audit. Although governments are increasingly inventing new tax surveillance methods, the likelihood of detection and audit remains relatively low. A reasonable gambler might have plenty of incentive not to pay taxes. This does not mean that deterrence and the threat of enforcement or penalties are irrelevant; a shift towards a softer tax policy does not increase compliance, as a perceived lower risk of punishment actually results in more cheating (Sheffrin, 2013, p. 166). But deterrence alone does not tell the whole story.

It appears that a substantial number of people pay taxes because they believe it is morally right to do so; they possess high "tax morale". What is tax morale? It is the intrinsic motivation of a specific population of taxpayers to pay taxes, independent of potential enforcement or penalties (Alm & Torgler, 2006; Pasternak-Malicka, 2013). Tax morale is crucial for tax system efficiency. High tax morale among taxpayers helps lower collection costs without reducing revenue, as individuals voluntarily pay taxes and avoid fraud and evasion. According to empirical research, a reduction of tax morale by one unit could lead to a 20% increase in the grey economy (Torgler, 2007, p. 191).

Folk justice as a determinant of tax morale

What factors contribute to this tax morale or the willingness to pay taxes voluntarily? As discussed in Chapter 4 human beings are moral agents, and their decision-making often incorporates intuitive judgements of fairness. Most individuals do not use complex ethical theories but rely on "folk justice" – a set of intuitive and culturally influenced ideas about fairness.

If we aim to increase taxpayers' tax morale, we must first identify those sensitive folk values. Fortunately, extensive research can help us in this regard (Torgler et al., 2008). Among the findings, Sheffrin highlights the importance of "deservingness" (Sheffrin, 2013, p. 43). People generally accept certain tax incentives and privileges as long as they perceive them as "deserved" – for example, benefits for the disabled, incentives for investors who contribute to economic development, or support for caregivers. Conversely, they tend to reject subsidies viewed as undeserved, such as direct cash handouts for the homeless, regardless of the reasons for homelessness, or universal basic income. People are also more inclined to tax undeserved income than income perceived as deserved.

Saez and Stancheva have empirically examined, weighted, and modelled the impact of certain independent or deontological values among taxpayers, such as libertarian freedoms like ownership protection (Saez & Stantcheva, 2016). Sheffrin also draws attention to "voice" and "respectful treatment" (Sheffrin, 2013, p. 4), both of which are aspects of procedural justice. Folk justice appears sensitive to how taxpayers are treated during tax procedures, irrespective of the final tax outcome. "Voice", or the opportunity to participate in the process and meaningfully influence the outcome, applies to both drafting and implementing new tax laws, as well as ensuring respectful treatment in specific tax procedures.

Additionally, social influence plays a strong role, as our tax morale is easily affected by the behaviour of others. Higher perceived tax evasion erodes the intrinsic motivation to pay taxes (Torgler, 2007), while higher perceived compliance boosts tax morale (Alm et al., 1992). As strong reciprocators, people are more willing to pay taxes when they feel their contributions lead to benefits they can enjoy. This sentiment contradicts the utilitarian "ability to pay" principle, which asserts that taxes are not intended as compensation for specific government-provided goods or services. Economists and political thinkers generally dismiss the equivalence principle. However, people often base their willingness to pay taxes on the concept of "fiscal exchange" (Leder et al., 2010). Similarly, beliefs about government efficiency also matter: the more convinced we are that the government is misusing our money, the less willing we are to contribute (Aguirre & Rocha, 2010).

The tension between folk justice and tax efficiency

Despite broad principles guiding tax policy, a persistent tension exists between the utilitarian goals of policy-makers, who prioritise efficiency, and the folk justice values held by many taxpayers. This tension is especially evident in the trade-off between efficient tax collection and perceptions of fairness. Governments often favour policies that maximise revenue with minimal administrative cost, while taxpayers assess fairness through concepts like equality, reciprocity, deservingness, and transparency – values that do not always align with utilitarian goals.

One clear example of this tension is the Value-Added Tax (VAT) or other forms of indirect taxation on goods and services. From a utilitarian perspective, VAT is efficient: it generates significant revenue with low enforcement costs and is difficult to evade. However, VAT is regressive in terms of distributional impact, violating principles of horizontal equality. Lower-income households, who spend most or all of their income on consumption, end up shouldering a proportionally heavier tax burden than wealthier households, who save or reinvest a larger share of their income. For instance, consider two families: one with an annual income of €30,000, spending 90% of it on consumption, and another with an income of €500,000, saving 50%. With a VAT rate of 20%, the tax burden relative to income for the first family is 18%, while for the second family, it is just 10%.

Furthermore, VAT raises procedural justice issues. The tax burden is largely invisible to consumers, as VAT is embedded in the price of goods and services. This "invisibility" can lead to cognitive biases, where taxpayers underestimate how much they actually pay in VAT, thereby reducing transparency and potentially eroding trust in the tax system. Most respondents in Poland are unaware of their VAT contributions. It illustrates how the tax exploits isolation biases to achieve high efficiency – VAT constitutes about 18% of treasury inflows in EU countries.

Another example is wealth and inheritance taxes. From a utilitarian perspective, these taxes are both fair and efficient: wealth, especially in forms like real estate, is easy to monitor, and transfers through inheritance are straightforward to track. But from a folk justice viewpoint, wealth and inheritance taxes are deeply contentious. Many people see them as a form of "double taxation" on assets that were already purchased with taxed income. This perception contradicts the libertarian values of property rights and the desire to pass wealth to descendants, creating strong public opposition – even among people who are unlikely to be affected.

Consider two more hypothetical families. The first family possesses substantial inherited wealth, with assets valued at €50 million, primarily in land, residential properties, and financial instruments. These assets yield an annual passive income of about €2.5 million before tax. Of this, €1.5 million comes from rental income, taxed at a flat rate of up to 12.5%, and €1 million from dividends and capital gains, taxed at 19%. In Poland, real estate taxes are negligible, and passive income is not subject to mandatory social security or healthcare contributions, resulting in a total levy of around 15% on the family's passive income.

The second family, by contrast, consists of two high-earning professionals with a combined annual income of €150,000. In Poland, this income level is taxed progressively, with rates up to 32%. Additionally, they must pay social security contributions, which amount to roughly 40% when split between employer and employee, plus a mandatory healthcare levy of 9% on net income. In total, their tax and social security burden is about 48% of their gross income.

This contrast highlights the perceived unfairness in the tax system. While the first family enjoys relatively low taxes on passive income, the second family faces a high tax burden on earned income. Even when high-value wealth and inheritance taxes are proposed to address inequality, they encounter strong resistance based on folk justice principles, such as the belief that assets should not be taxed repeatedly. Cognitive biases like "overconfidence", where people are overly optimistic about their future wealth, also contribute to public resistance, as many believe they or their descendants may someday be affected.

Capability approach: An imperfect but applicable theory of justice?

Nobel Prize-winning economist Amartya Sen has proposed a "non-ideal" theory of justice that combines broad consequentialism with respect for individual rights (Sen, 2009). At the core of Sen's approach is a vision of the human being encompassing two key elements: the recognition that people are diverse in many ways, which no theory of wealth distribution can ignore, and the assertion that people possess inalienable rights and freedoms. This second element aligns Sen closer to libertarians than to utilitarians. However, unlike most libertarians, Sen holds that individual rights cannot be divorced from the consequences of actions (viewed broadly). In this respect, he employs what is known as consequentialist reasoning. Unlike traditional utilitarianism, which measures social welfare solely in terms of aggregate outcomes, Sen's approach considers individuals' capabilities – their real opportunities to pursue the lives they have reason to value (Robeyns & Byskov, 2023; Sen, 1985).

Following Sen's approach, we can identify two groups of capabilities relevant to tax justice: those related to agents' monetary utilities (such as income opportunity, wealth-building potential, access to free or low-cost public services, and public infrastructure that enhances the quality of life). These are crucial in determining whether changes in the tax system are worthwhile, but they do not dictate the specific nature of those changes. Additionally, there are capabilities tied to "folk values" relevant to tax justice, such as the opportunity to participate in public consultations regarding tax changes or the ability to receive financial assistance when poverty arises from factors beyond one's control. At least three sources identify these folk values and provide intersubjective reasons to value them: regular social research, "the voice" of public consultation on tax changes, and legal precedents. Some findings from social research have been referenced above.

The non-ideal aspect of Sen's approach lies in its lack of a requirement for an optimal solution. Instead, it advocates for selecting the best available alternative, one that is at least "not worse" than the others under consideration. In other words, while we may not always be able to determine which configuration of capabilities is best, we can reject unacceptably unfair options.

Let us revisit the case studies discussed above through the lens of the capability approach. The case study shows that VAT contradicts horizontal tax justice and folk fairness intuitions. Nevertheless, it remains highly efficient, primarily due to its "hidden" nature and the shifting of collection costs onto entrepreneurs, who themselves do not bear its financial burden. The government, therefore, has little incentive to alter this situation by educating people about the tax, its mechanics, and its inherent unfairness. However, the implications of a non-ideal theory of justice offer an alternative perspective.

Firstly, unfairness may be tolerated if it is alleviated or compensated in other ways. Tax rates can be adjusted so that they are higher for goods and services mainly consumed by more affluent taxpayers and lower for those consumed by less affluent ones. Additionally, indirect subsidies can protect the least affluent from price increases. Perhaps most crucially, a "fiscal exchange" could be fostered by educating the public on tax efficiency and demonstrating how tax revenues are used for the benefit of the least advantaged, potentially through dedicated, special-purpose funds.

Secondly, low public awareness of the VAT mechanism, its significance, and its consequences have drawbacks. VAT is especially susceptible to fraud, leading governments to spend significantly on deterrence. VAT morale is low; small entrepreneurs often fail to report taxable sales, and consumers generally tolerate this, showing little concern if a VAT receipt is issued. This behaviour crowds out honest taxpayers, who find themselves outcompeted by those who evade taxes, further compounding the tax's unfairness. The capability approach advocates for transparency, education, and a "no-worse" solution.

Wealth and inheritance taxes face strong opposition from taxpayers, as they conflict with fundamental libertarian values: protection of ownership, unrestricted freedom to pass on inheritance, and no "double taxation" on the same income (since assets were ostensibly purchased with already taxed income). The capability approach does not favour reforms that go against prevailing folk intuitions. However, in the "comprehensive outcome", conflicting fairness intuitions about undeserved wealth and under-taxed income are also relevant. Thus, the capability approach could advocate for tax reforms targeting such undeserved wealth and income. Given the sensitivity of this issue, where competing values are at play, any potentially threatened libertarian freedoms should be counterbalanced by reinforcing other values, such as taxpayer "voice" and procedural guarantees.

The "voice" could be strengthened by extended public consultations (with outcomes genuinely considered), potential referendums, and a substantial *vacatio legis* (the period between a law's enactment and its implementation). Procedural guarantees should also be reinforced, particularly regarding taxable asset valuation, with measures like a publicly accessible default asset valuation list and independent expert valuations.

Do we need a theory of tax justice at all?

If we accept the government's role in collecting taxes and allocating them for various purposes, we must establish rules for collection and distribution. These rules could remain vague, intuitive, and applied instrumentally, as they often were in the past. However, history shows that rules perceived as unfair often lead to violence, riots, and revolutions, which are ultimately harmful to people's well-being. Examples include the French Revolution and the American War for Independence. Conversely, the "great betterment", discussed in Chapter 1, coincided with an increasing share of public levies in GDP. Despite debates over specific allocations and military spending, this general increase in public levies contributed to improving people's welfare.

Given that taxation directly affects our sense of distributional justice and that our willingness to pay taxes depends on the perceived alignment between our fairness intuitions and the justice underpinning the tax system, the answer to this subchapter's question is affirmative. Yes, we need a comprehensive theory of tax justice – one that aligns with various intuitions and goals while serving as guidance for policy-makers and law enforcers. It does not necessarily need to be Sen's theory, but it should meet these criteria. Otherwise, tensions will rise, and tax collection efficiency will decline.

Note

1 https://www.servat.unibe.ch/dfr/bv093121.html/ (Accessed: December 2024)

References

Aguirre, B., & Rocha, F. (2010). *Trust and tax morale in Latin American & Caribbean countries.* [Online] Available at: https://extranet.sioe.org/uploads/isnie2010/basilia_fabiana.pdf [Accessed 25 October 2024].

Alm, J., Jackson, B., & Mckee, M. (1992, February). Estimating the determinants of taxpayer compliance with experimental data. *National Tax Journal*, *45*(1). https://doi.org/10.1086/NTJ41788949

Alm, J., & Torgler, B. (2006, April). Culture differences and tax morale in the United States and in Europe. *Journal of Economic Psychology*, *27*(2), 224–246. https://doi.org/10.1016/j.joep.2005.09.002

Brzeziński, B. (2017). *Prawo podatkowe. Zagadnienia teorii i praktyki*. Towarzystwo Naukowe Organizacji i Kierownictwa.

Keen, M., & Slemrod, J. (2021). *Rebellion, rascals and revenue. Tax follies and wisdom through the ages*. Princeton University Press.

Leder, S., Manetti, L., Hölzl, E., & Kirchler, E. (2010, April). Regulatory fit effects on perceived fiscal exchange and tax compliance. *The Journal of Socio-Economics*, *39*(2), 271–277. https://doi.org/10.1016/j.socec.2009.12.003

Mill, J. S. (2013). Utilitarianism. In *Complete works* (Kindle ed., pp. loc. 46246–47461). s.l.: Minerva Classics.

Musgrave, R. A. (1959). *The theory of public finance. A study in public economy.* McGrow-Hill.

Pasternak-Malicka, M. (2013, January-March). Mentalność i moralność podatkowa a reakcje gospodarstw domowych na obowiązek podatkowy. *Modern Management Review*, *XVIII*(20), 87–98. https://doi.org/10.7862/rz.2013.mmr.8

Rawls, J. (2005). *The theory of justice* (reissue edition ed.). Belknap Press. Harvard University Press.

Robeyns, I., & Byskov, M. F. (2023). The capability approach. In E. N. Zalta & U. Nodelman (Eds.), *The Stanford encyclopedia of philosophy* (Fall 2023 Edition). Metaphysics Research Lab, Stanford University. https://plato.stanford.edu/archives/fall2023/entries/capability-approach/

Saez, E., & Stantcheva, S. (2016). Generalized social marginal welfare weights for optimal tax theory. *American Economic Review*, 1(106). https://doi.org/10.1257/aer.20141362

Sen, A. (1985). *Commodities and capabilities.*

Sen, A. (2009). *The idea of justice*. Harvard University Press.

Sheffrin, S. M. (2013). *Tax fairness and folk justice*. Cambridge University Press.

Smith, A. (1776). *An inquiry into the nature and causes of the wealth of nations* (Cannan ed., Vol. 1). Methuen. https://oll.libertyfund.org/titles/smith-an-inquiry-into-the-nature-and-causes-of-the-wealth-of-nations-cannan-ed-vol-1

Stiglitz, J. E., & Rosengard, J. K. (2015). *Economics of the public sector*. W.W. Norton.

Strayer, P. J. (1958). *Fiscal policy and politics*. Harper.

Torgler, B. (2007). *Tax compliance and tax morale: A theoretical and empirical analysis*. Edward Elgar Publishing.

Torgler, B., Ihsan, C. D., Macintyre, A., & Schaffner, M. (2008). Causes and consequences of tax morale: An empirical investigation. *Economic Analysis and Policy*, *38*(2), 313–339. https://doi.org/10.1016/S0313-5926(08)50023-3

von Justi, J. H. G. (1762). Ausführliche Abhandlung von denen Steuern und Abgaben nach ächten, *aus dem Endzweck der bürgerlichen Gesellschaften abfließenden Grundsätzen, und zur Wohlfarth der Völker dienlichen Maaßregeln abgefasset*. Woltersdorff.

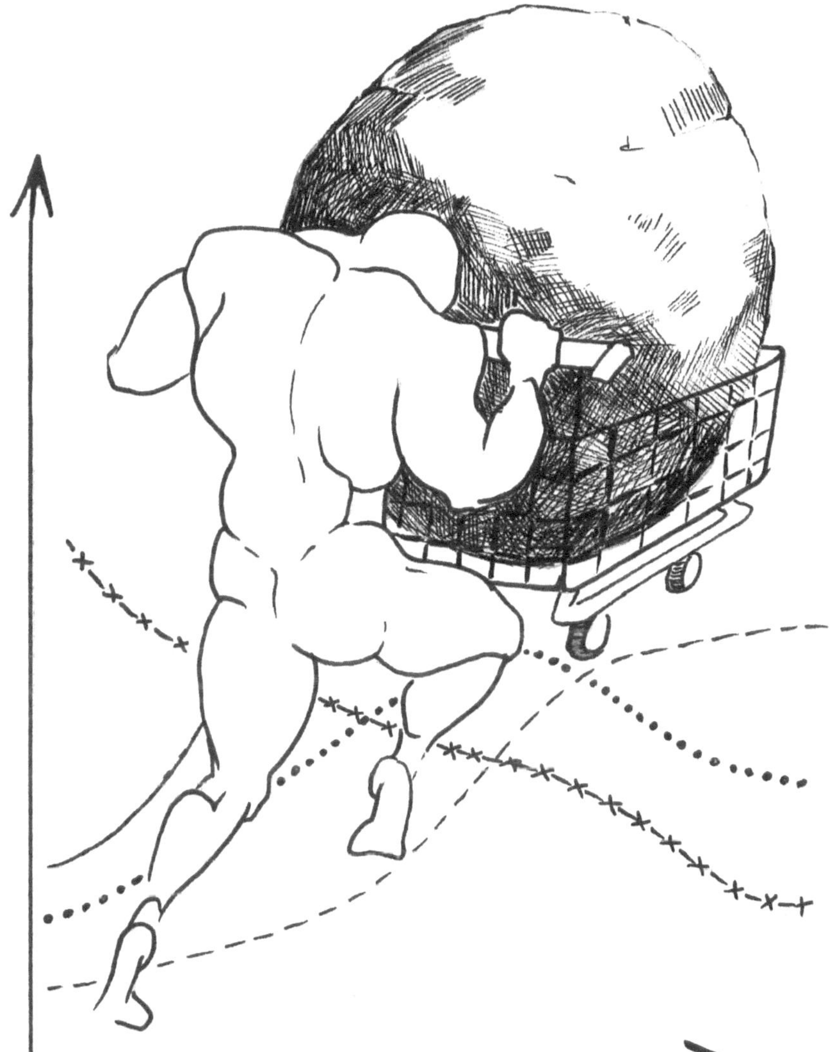

7

DOES WEALTH MAKE US HAPPIER?

In late 2011, Dan Price, CEO of Gravity Payment – a company specialising in credit card payment processing – noticed that one of his employees seemed unusually withdrawn and irritable. Jason Haley, an employee with a high school education earning around $32,000 annually, had been exhibiting signs of frustration for some time. Being curious about Haley's behaviour, Price approached him during a cigarette break and asked, "Seems like something's bothering you. What's on your mind?"

Haley's response was unexpectedly blunt: "You're ripping me off".

Price, caught off guard, defended his pay policy: "Your pay is based on market rates. If you have different data, please let me know. I have no intention of ripping you off".

Haley, however, refused to accept this explanation. "Data doesn't matter", he countered. "I know your intentions are bad. You brag about how financially disciplined you are, but that just translates into me not making enough money to lead a decent life".[1]

This exchange unsettled Price. He had long prided himself not merely on his financial discipline but on how well he treated his employees in the company he co-founded with his brother. Why, then, was Haley questioning his integrity? Could there be some truth to Haley's accusation? These questions weighed heavily on Price's mind.

The incident prompted Price to seek reassurance from family and friends, who generally support his policies. They reminded him that his pay practices adhered to industry standards and that as a CEO, his focus on financial discipline had been crucial to protecting Gravity Payments from the devastating effects of the 2008 financial crisis – a crisis that had nearly led to the company's liquidation. Despite this reassurance, Price found himself increasingly troubled. The more he reflected

DOI: 10.4324/9781003469384-10

on Haley's words, the more he began to question his own motives. Perhaps, deep down, his policies have been driven less by concern for his employees and more by his desire to safeguard the company's fanatical stability. The thought was unsettling: could Haley have been right all along?

This period of self-reflection marked a turning point in Price's career. Within three years of his conversation with Haley, Price implemented significant changes at Gravity Payments. He began by raising salaries across the company by 20% and, in April 2015, announced a groundbreaking initiative: the establishment of a company-wide minimum wage of $70,000 per year, more than double Haley's initial salary. To fund this increase, Price reduced his own compensation from over $1.1 million annually to $70,000 – a move that drew national attention.

The response to Price's decision was swift and polarised. Many celebrated him as a visionary leader taking a stand against wage inequality, with some hailing him as "the best boss in America". Others, however, dismissed him as a reckless idealist, warning that his actions could jeopardise the company's financial viability. Even Price's brother, who owned a third of Gravity Payments, opposed the decision so strongly that he filed a lawsuit against him. Nonetheless, the announcement captured widespread public attention, gathering over 500 million social media interactions and extensive media coverage across print and television.[2]

Amidst the public debate, a central question emerged: why had Price undertaken such a radical shift in his pay policies? What had driven him to take such a bold and controversial step to raise his employees' salaries to the specific amount of $70,000 a year?

The story of Dan Price provides a compelling entry point into a broader, universal question: does an increase in income lead to greater happiness? It is tempting to believe that it does. After all, who among us would not wish to earn more, eliminate the financial worries, or afford the holidays and experiences we dream of? The allure of financial security is undeniable, and the idea that "more money equals more happiness" seems intuitive. But is it truly the case?

Easterlin's paradox

Following the work of Arthur Cecil Pigou (1932), the British economist and founder of welfare economics, economists have traditionally assumed that changes in economic well-being – defined by measures such as income and wealth – serve as indicators of changes in social well-being, encompassing happiness and life satisfaction. This assumption aligns with the intuition shared by many: financial security is often viewed as a fundamental condition for a peaceful and fulfilling life. Even if one questions the extent of this relationship, it is difficult to deny that a lack of material security, i.e. poverty, is a direct path to unhappiness.

However, this seemingly inseparable link between economic well-being and happiness was challenged by the seminal study of American economist and demographer Richard Easterlin (1974). Drawing on survey data extending back to the 19th century, Easterlin examined the relationship between individuals' income levels and their reported sense of happiness. His findings supported the intuitive idea that, within a single country at a given time, individuals with higher incomes generally reported higher levels of happiness than their less affluent counterparts. This observation aligns with the case of Jason Haley and Dan Price: Haley, barely making ends meet, represents the dissatisfied lower-income individual, while Price, a millionaire CEO, exemplifies the self-satisfied high-earner.

Nevertheless, Easterlin's other conclusions were far less intuitive. When examining the relationship between income and happiness across countries, he observed that the correlation weakened significantly. Countries with vast disparities in wealth, such as Nigeria – where, in 1960, the real gross national product (GNP) *per capita* was only $134 – and West Germany – where the GNP *per capita* during the same period was $1860, reported surprisingly similar average happiness scores. Measured on a 0-to-10 scale, the difference in average happiness between these two countries was just 0.5 points. Furthermore, regardless of their wealth, most countries reported an average happiness score within a narrow range of 4.5 and 5.5 points. Poland, for example, with a GNP *per capita* of $702 at the time, reported an average happiness level of 4.4 points, placing it near the lower boundary of this range but still comparable to wealthier nations (Easterlin, 1974, p. 105, 106). These findings suggest that the relationship between wealth and happiness is not as straightforward as commonly believed.

The most intriguing dimension of Easterlin's research emerged when he examined the relationship between changes in income and changes in happiness over time. Analysing data from the United States between 1946 and 1970, Easterlin noted that despite significant economic growth – marked by a 65% increase in gross domestic product (GDP) *per capita* – people's average reported happiness remained almost unchanged. This striking disconnect between rising wealth and stagnant happiness levels became known as Easterlin's paradox.

The relevance of this paradox continues to be debated in contemporary studies. Data from the annual *World Happiness Report*, based on surveys conducted by the Gallup Institute, provide a nuanced perspective. The report suggests that, in general, people in wealthier countries tend to report higher level of happiness. For example, a doubling of GDP *per capita* is correlated with a modest 0.7-point increase in happiness. However, when examining changes over time, the relationship between GDP *per capita* and happiness is far less clear-cut. Among the 125 countries analysed in the report, 43 demonstrated a pattern where an increase in wealth was accompanied by a decrease in happiness – a finding consistent with Easterlin's original observations. These countries include, among others, the United States, Japan, the Netherlands, Sweden, Canada, Egypt, and India.

In contrast, the remaining 82 countries showed a positive correlation between wealth and happiness or, in some cases, a simultaneous decline in both indicators. For instance, in nations such as China, Nigeria, Russia, Turkey, Germany, and

Poland, rising wealth was accompanied by increases in reported happiness. Conversely, in countries like Ukraine, Venezuela, Jordan, and Italy, decreases in wealth were associated with declining happiness levels (The Economist, 2019).

Does this mean that only in certain contexts do people become both richer and happier? Why does Easterlin's paradox occur at all?

Treadmill of happiness

The first explanation of the noted paradox was proposed by Easterlin himself. According to him, a person's sense of happiness does not increase as their income increases because, simultaneously, their standard for assessing their income level also changes. People simply adapt to their living situation. For example, studies have shown that individuals who win a significant sum of money in the lottery are not happier in the long term compared to other members of society. Even more surprisingly, individuals who experienced traffic accidents and became disabled do not report lower long-term happiness than others. These findings suggest that each person has a built-in personal "happiness thermostat" that maintains their sense of happiness at a relatively consistent level, even when circumstances change drastically (Brickman et al., 1978). This adaptation phenomenon highlights that a person's sense of happiness is predominantly determined by personality and temperament, while external circumstances have relatively little impact. Consequently, even significant life events, whether positive or negative, tend to affect happiness only temporarily before individuals return to their baseline level.

This adaptation mechanism also plays a role in the relationship between income and happiness (Layard & De Neve, 2023, p. 214). While an increase in income provides new opportunities, it simultaneously raises individuals' aspirations. Entering a higher level of wealth often results in the consumption of more expensive goods and services. For instance, someone earning a higher income may feel inclined to allocate more money to their wardrobe, purchasing very expensive shirts instead of those at the more modest prices they previously paid. However, this shift in behaviour offers only a temporary boost to happiness. Over time, the new expenditure becomes normalised, and the sense of happiness reverts to its prior level.

Thus, it appears that we are locked in what might be described as a "treadmill of happiness", and, like hamsters, we run in it constantly. Much like hamsters running on the wheel, we expand effort and resources in the pursuit of happiness, only to find ourselves back at the same baseline. This dynamic is not merely an individual phenomenon but has a broader social dimension. Researchers have identified a connection between this cycle and the human tendency to compare oneself with others. For example, studies have calculated that a 1% increase in a neighbour's income has a comparable effect on an individual's life satisfaction as a reduction in their own income by the same amount (Anand, 2016). Such rivalry directly influences behaviour. For instance, research has found that when a woman's husband earns less than her sister's spouse, the woman becomes more likely to take employment in order to maintain a standard of living comparable to her sister's (Layard, 2005, p. 150).

Social comparisons are a powerful determinant of happiness. Each of us tends to evaluate our life success and overall satisfaction by comparing ourselves with others. Therefore, my sense of happiness is influenced less by the fact that I now earn twice as much as I did five years ago and more by the fact that my earnings, both then and now, remain close to the national average. In other words, what matters is relative income – how one's earnings compare to a social standard of wealth – rather than absolute income. As Easterlin explained, this phenomenon is similar to perceptions of height. When asked whether they consider themselves tall or short, individuals respond based on how their height compares to others in their community.

This tendency to compare ourselves with others also influences our consumption patterns. As income rises, people often begin to purchase goods that are not essential but serve to emphasise their social status. For example, they may spend money on luxury cars, extravagant weddings, or high-end suits. Early in the 20th century, the economist and sociologist Thorstein Veblen referred to this behaviour as "conspicuous consumption". Later in the 1970s, Fred Hirsch identified a specific category of these products, termed "positional goods". According to Robert Frank (2005, pp. 82–84), this type of consumption motivated by social comparison can have detrimental effects akin to an arms race.

For instance, if a lawyer chooses not to wear expensive suits like their peers, they may reduce their chances of attracting wealthy clients. Similarly, driving a smaller car than most people may increase the risk of fatal injuries in an accident. In fact, according to *The Economist*, the heaviest 1% of SUVs or trucks in the United States save lives for their occupants but cause more than a dozen deaths in smaller cars (The Economist, 2024). Thus, the "treadmill of happiness" is not solely an individual struggle but a social phenomenon. We find ourselves participating in this cycle because others do as well, and failing to do so may place us at a disadvantage. This raises a fundamental question: Is it truly in our interest to pursue happiness in this way?

Critics of the consumer culture argue that over-consumption leads to the wasteful use of resources, as well as the inefficient allocation of workers' time and skills. Rather than producing goods that improve the quality of life, society invests resources in creating items that many people could forgo if only others would do the same. Furthermore, the relentless pursuit of material possessions detracts from the time and energy we could devote to more meaningful pursuits, such as nurturing family relationships. The paradox of happiness thus highlights two crucial issues: first, the question of what constitutes well for individuals and society, and second, a challenge to the economic concept of rationality. If individuals consistently choose behaviours that do not enhance their well-being, can such behaviour truly be considered rational? (Bruni & Porta, 2005, pp. 15–17). While we begin this part of the book by examining various conceptions of well-being, we will address the issue of rationality in Chapter 17.

The "treadmill of happiness" also raises important questions for wage policy, such as those proposed by Dan Price. If individuals continually adapt to new conditions such that their overall sense of happiness remains unchanged, then introducing a minimum wage in a company might not achieve the intended goal of increasing employees' happiness. Instead, such a policy might only change the social standard regarding acceptable income levels. Nevertheless, alternative explanations of the happiness paradox may provide further insights into this complex relationship.

Social problems and citizens' happiness

Easterlin's paradox may arise not only because individuals adapt to new social standards as their income increases. Another dimension of this paradox emerges when economic growth is accompanied by an increase in social problems, such as alcohol and drug addiction, rising social inequality, and obesity. According to Jeffrey Sachs, one of the co-authors of the *World Happiness Report*, growing social problems are a significant factor in the diminishing sense of happiness that often accompanies economic development. Examining the situation in the United States, Sachs identifies what he describes as a state of social crisis. This crisis is evidenced by various troubling trends, including an increase in drug addiction, rising suicide rates, growing income inequality – where the wealthiest 1% of households in the United States earn as much as the poorest 70% – and a decline in social trust. Additionally, the United States mortality rate, or the number of deaths per population, is increasing, in contrast to trends observed in European countries and Canada (Sachs, 2017).

Sachs emphasises three social phenomena that have reached epidemic proportions and are particularly influential in reducing citizens' happiness: obesity, substance abuse, and depression (Sachs, 2018). Thus, while economic well-being may improve on one level, this improvement is often accompanied by social phenomena that offset the gain in happiness. If this explanation of Easterlin's paradox holds, then the argument made by Haley for a wage increase to ensure a dignified standard of living becomes even more compelling. Since social inequality is one of the issues that diminishes happiness, addressing wage disparities could contribute to alleviating this problem. Furthermore, if economic development exacerbates social issues like obesity, alcoholism, or drug addiction, one potential solution is to provide individuals with the resources they need to cope. For example, an increase in wages could enable individuals like Haley to access professional psychological support.

However, if these social problems are systemic in nature, they also require systemic solutions. Measures aimed solely at rising individual incomes may be insufficient to address the underlying causes. Increasingly, governments – whose quality of conduct clearly correlates with citizens' reported happiness (Layard & De Neve, 2023, p. 255) – are recognising this complexity. When formulating policy decisions, many are now looking beyond traditional economic indicators such as GDP and considering the broader impact of their policies on citizens' subjective well-being, as measured by their happiness or life satisfaction. A notable example is New Zealand, which implemented the world's first *Well-Being Budget*, in 2019.[3] This budget highlights four key priority areas intended to enhance social well-being: mental health, child well-being, supporting the aspirations of indigenous people, and increasing productivity while transitioning to a more sustainable economy.

By integrating subjective well-being into fiscal policy, the New Zealand government has committed to defining well-being objectives alongside traditional economic goals. For instance, the budget allocates $40 million towards suicide prevention, includes a $370 million package to combat domestic and sexual violence, and sets aside $229 million to encourage sustainable land use. These targeted measures illustrate a broader policy shift that explicitly prioritises citizens' happiness and well-being.

Nevertheless, the extent to which governments should intervene in promoting happiness remains a contentious issue. While some argue that state-led efforts to improve well-being are justified, others question whether such measures, if excessively applied, infringe on personal autonomy. This debate will be explored further in Chapter 9. For now, however, it is worth considering an additional challenge to Easterlin's paradox: the possibility that this paradox arises primarily from the way economic well-being (wealth) and social well-being (happiness) are measured.

Easterlin's paradox not so paradoxical

Economic well-being is commonly measured by GDP *per capita*. In simple terms, this is the total value of goods and services produced by the citizens of a country in a given calendar year, divided by the number of those citizens. Social well-being, on the other hand, is measured through surveys. For instance, the *World Values Survey*, the largest global survey of attitudes and values, includes questions on both feelings of happiness and life satisfaction. Respondents evaluate their happiness qualitatively, choosing among options such as "very happy", "rather happy", "not very happy", or "not at all happy". Life satisfaction, in contrast, is measured on a ten-point scale, using an approach introduced by psychologist Hadley Cantril. In this approach, individuals are asked to imagine a ladder with ten rungs, where the top rung represents the best possible life they can envision. Respondents then decide which rung they feel they are on at a given time. The higher the rung, the greater the satisfaction with life.

The methods used to measure these quantities – GDP for economic well-being and surveys for social well-being – may themselves influence the occurrence of the happiness paradox. While GDP *per capita*, as an economic measure, can grow indefinitely, subjective well-being measures such as happiness or life satisfaction face inherent limitations. For example, happiness scales are capped by design: an individual can only report being "very happy" or select the maximum value of 10 on Cantril's ladder. This upper limit in measurement creates a situation where subjective well-being cannot increase beyond a certain point, regardless of further economic growth.

This limitation in measurement is not unique to happiness. A comparable example can be seen when comparing GDP to human life expectancy. Over time, GDP and life expectancy are well correlated; however, life expectancy cannot grow indefinitely because it is constrained by biological limits. In contrast to the objective determinants of human biology that cap life expectancy, the ceiling for subjective well-being is determined by the conventions of the measurement scale itself (Coyle, 2014, p. 111). Thus, the appearance of a plateau in happiness levels despite rising GDP may not entirely reflect a genuine stagnation in subjective well-being, but rather a limitation in how we define and quantify it. This issue of measurement conventions is discussed further in Part III of this book, in Chapter 13.

If the way happiness is measured influences the interpretation of Easterlin's paradox, a related question arises: at what level of wealth do individuals stop reporting greater happiness or life satisfaction? Identifying the income "saturation point" for happiness has become a significant focus of research in recent years. Studies suggest that this threshold varies depending on how subjective well-being is defined. For example, annual income levels above which well-being ceases to increase are $95,000 for well-being, defined as life satisfaction, and between $60,000 and $75,000 for well-being, interpreted in terms of emotional experience (positive or negative feelings). These values also vary regionally. In eastern European countries and the Balkans, the corresponding thresholds are approximately $45,000 for life satisfaction and $35,000 for emotional well-being (Jebb et al., 2018).

This research provides a clear context for the decision made by Dan Price to offer his employees a minimum salary of $70,000 per year. Price's decision reflects his awareness of studies on happiness saturation points, particularly the work of Nobel Prize-winning economists Daniel Kahneman and Angus Deaton. Their research established that, for residents of the United States, the happiness ceiling occurs at an annual income of $70,000 (Kahneman & Deaton, 2010).

Ultimately, this leads us to a moderately positive conclusion regarding the title question of this chapter. The evidence suggests that income growth has a clear positive effect on happiness – at least up to a certain point. Beyond this threshold, additional income has diminishing returns, and other factors, such as social inequality and systemic challenges, become more influential in determining overall well-being.

Notes

1 https://www.inc.com/magazine/201511/paul-keegan/does-more-pay-mean-more-growth.html (Accessed: February 2020).
2 https://www.theguardian.com/society/2015/nov/29/future-of-work-dan-price-gravity-ceo-cut-own-pay-to-give-staff-increased-minum-wage (Accessed: February 2020).
3 https://treasury.govt.nz/sites/default/files/2019-06/b19-wellbeing-budget.pdf (Accessed: November 2024).

References

Anand, P. (2016). *Happiness explained: What human flourishing is and how we can promote it*. Oxford University Press.

Brickman, P., Coates, D., & Janoff-Bulman, R. (1978). Lottery winners and accident victims: Is happiness relative? *Journal of Personality and Social Psychology*, *36*(8), 917–927. https://doi.org/10.1037/0022-3514.36.8.917

Bruni, L., & Porta, P. L. (Eds.). (2005). *Economics and happiness. Framing the analysis*. Oxford University Press.

Coyle, D. (2014). *GDP: A brief but affectionate history*. Princeton University Press.

Easterlin, R. A. (1974). Does economic growth improve the human lot? Some empirical evidence. In P. A. David & M. W. Reder (Eds.), *Nations and households in economic growth: Essays in honor of Moses Abramovitz* (pp. 89–125). Academic Press.

Frank, R. H. (2005). Does absolute income matter? In L. Bruni & P. L. Porta (Eds.), *Economics and happiness: Framing the analysis* (pp. 65–90). Oxford University Press.

Jebb, A. T., Tay, L., Diener, E., & Oishi, S. (2018). Happiness, income satiation, and turning points around the world. *Nature Human Behaviour*, *2*(1), 33–38. https://doi.org/10.1038/s41562-017-0277-0

Kahneman, D., & Deaton, A. (2010). High income improves evaluation of life but not emotional well-being. *Proceedings of the National Academy of Sciences*, *107*(38), 16489–16493. https://doi.org/10.1073/pnas.1011492107

Layard, R. (2005). Rethinking public economics: The implications of rivalry and habit. In L. Bruni & P. L. Porta (Eds.), *Economics and happiness: Framing the analysis* (pp. 147–169). Oxford University Press.

Layard, R., & De Neve, J.-E. (2023). *Wellbeing: Science and policy*. Cambridge University Press.

Pigou, A. C. (1932). *The economics of welfare* (4th ed.). Macmillan.

Sachs, J. D. (2017). Restoring American happiness. In J. F. Helliwell, R. Layard, & J. D. Sachs (Eds.), *World happiness report 2017* (pp. 178–187). Sustainable Development Solutions Network.

Sachs, J. D. (2018). America's health crisis and the Easterlin paradox. In J. F. Helliwell, R. Layard, & J. D. Sachs (Eds.), *World Happiness Report 2018* (pp. 146–159). New York: Sustainable Development Solutions Network. https://s3.amazonaws.com/happiness-report/2018/CH7-WHR-lr.pdf

The Economist, 2019. Economic growth does not guarantee rising happiness. *The Economist*, 21 March. https://www.economist.com/graphic-detail/2019/03/21/economic-growth-does-not-guarantee-rising-happiness

The Economist, 2024. What to do about America's killer cars. *The Economist*, 5 September. https://www.economist.com/leaders/2024/09/05/what-to-do-about-americas-killer-cars

8

SHOULD WE OPEN BORDERS FOR ECONOMIC IMMIGRANTS?

Fear of strangers

In 2015, Europe experienced one of the most serious immigration crises, mainly related to the war in Syria and the unstable political situation in many African and Asian countries. Hundreds of thousands of migrants tried to enter the old continent, mainly by sea, reaching Italy and Greece in particular. This episode, almost negligible in the scale of the entire phenomenon of global migration, caused widespread political controversy within and between EU member states. According to many, it contributed to the Brexit referendum and the strengthening of the position of populist-conservative groups. Similar sentiments also began to prevail in the country that was built by migrants, the United States, and anti-immigrant rhetoric brought President Donald Trump to office.

Immigrants are strangers who inspire fear. Opponents raise a number of accusations against them (or rather against their settlement in developed countries). They point to the increase in crime rates, mainly in its most dangerous form, terrorism. They highlight the destruction of the local labour market, with the lowest paid and least skilled local workers being victims and losing their jobs or having to accept lower wages in competition with immigrants. They point to the budgetary costs, the drain on the welfare system. Immigrants from developing countries relocate, relying mainly on the usually generous welfare systems of rich countries. And finally, there is a dominant fear of preserving the cultural achievements of the Western world, of destroying the foundations of our prosperity by importing patterns of behaviour that are precisely responsible for making poor countries poor, of undermining our cultural identity, of disappearing our languages, our literature, but also the institutions of the liberal-democratic order. Fear of the destruction of those elements of civil society that make us trust and cooperate with each other.

DOI: 10.4324/9781003469384-11

Is there anything to fear? Firstly, let us present some figures to make us aware of the scale of the phenomenon we are talking about or may discuss in the future.

At the peak of the immigration crisis in Europe, there were around 2.3 million irregular border crossings in 2015–2016 and 1.3 million asylum applications in the European Economic Area (EEA) countries in 2016.[1] With Europe's current population of over 0.5 billion, this adds up to around 2.5 per mille. In comparison, Australia receives three times as many immigrants per year, relative to its population, and the most likely estimate is that around 1.1 million workers from Ukraine were employed in Poland in 2018 (Growiec et al., 2019). This is evidenced by the fact that, following the outbreak of full-scale armed conflict in Ukraine, an estimated 8 million refugees swept through Europe. According to UNHCR data, as of 14 March 2024, nearly 6 million refugees from Ukraine were registered in Europe,[2] of which approximately 4.2 million were benefiting from temporary protection.[3] And in terms of the alleged migration crisis, almost nothing worrying happened. Thus, if it had not been for the media attention and the clustering effect in two countries (Italy and Greece), which were unprepared for such a situation, the number of refugees in 2015–2016 would have gone unnoticed. However, the number of those willing to change their place of residence will not decrease. In 2019 there were about 270 million people born outside their country of residence in various countries around the world, representing about 3% of the world's population. Most in Australia (about 28%), Canada (about 22%), Germany, and the United States (about 14–15%), and least in China (close to 0%), among others. According to the Gallup Institute, there are about 750 million people worldwide willing to do so, representing about 40% of the adult population in developing countries (Clemens, 2011; The Economist, 2019d). This huge number represents about 10% of the world's population. And the climate change will likely strengthen this trend. What could happen if this massive number of people moved across borders? Our fearful intuitions are completely at odds with what economists say (and count). It would be much, much better. For everyone or almost everyone.

Economists see it differently

Regardless of which stream the economists studying the various aspects of labour migration come from, they generally agree that the basic measure of well-being is global gross domestic product (it is a different matter whether it is a valid and accurate measure, but we write about that in the next section, in Chapter 13) will generally increase with the relaxation of migration policies of developed countries. Michael A. Clemens, one of the main proponents of such a policy, estimates that the elimination of emigration barriers would lead to an increase in global GDP of between 67 and 147%. Averaging out, there is an opportunity ahead to double the wealth of the entire world and thereby lift millions of people out of poverty. He perversely titles his article on these estimates, "Trillion-Dollar Bills on the Sidewalk" (Clemens, 2011). By comparison, the complete removal of trade barriers could lead to a mere 4.1% growth. English economists (Barrell et al., 2010) have calculated that post-accession immigration to the United Kingdom from central and eastern European countries contributed 1.7% to GDP growth in 2004–2007. According to estimates by Polish economists, the inflow of Ukrainian workers to Poland in 2013–2018 contributed 11% to Polish GDP growth (Growiec et al., 2019).

However, the biggest beneficiaries of a world without borders would be the immigrants themselves and their families. Widening income inequalities in different parts of the world lead to wage gaps that are hard to imagine. Low-skilled workers in Haiti, Nigeria, or Egypt earn ten times less than similarly skilled workers in the United States (Clemens, 2011). The difference in earnings between Poland and Ukraine in different groups of workers is estimated to be three to five times![4] Even if we assume they will not earn as much as local workers once they arrive in the destination country, the financial benefits are still enormous.[5] In turn, the money earned is most often sent to families in the country of origin, further contributing to the fight against local poverty and making a significant contribution to that country's GDP. It is estimated that the total value of such transfers in 2022 was USD 630 billion.[6] For many countries, they represent more than 1/3 of their annual GDP (Tonga, Haiti, or Tajikistan). For Ukraine, this amount (coming largely from Poland) amounted in 2021 to USD 14 billion, which is about 7% of the country's GDP and was expected to rise by 22% after the Russian invasion in 2022.[7] This is a key compensation that seems to outweigh the very negative effect of migration, which is the intellectual drain of the sending country. This is because, in the first phase of migration, the young and well-educated citizens usually decide to migrate and are also the most productive. This can also be seen in the statistics of Ukrainians arriving in Poland, more than half of whom have higher education (Growiec et al., 2019). However, economists also argue that this effect has a paradoxically positive outcome. This is because workers staying in the country earn slightly more and are more motivated to educate themselves (The Economist, 2011). In turn, emigrating workers often return with capital, stimulating entrepreneurship in their country of origin. This effect has probably contributed to the explosive growth of the IT business in India (The Economist, 2019e).

In addition to the increase in GDP, consumers in the host country also benefit directly, mainly due to a slight decrease in the prices of many products and services and an increase in the range of products on offer. Immigrants produce goods and provide services that benefit host-country residents. Immigrant settlement is usually accompanied by an increase in property prices, benefiting property owners and local property developers.

The benefits listed above are mainly of a so-called static nature. Still, economists emphasise that the most important are the dynamic benefits arising from the complex relationship between incoming migrants and the local community and between sending and receiving countries. A commonly observed effect is an increase in entrepreneurship. Immigrants or their children are the founders of 45% of Fortune 500 companies. They are also three times more likely to be the authors of patent applications (The Economist, 2019e). Economists also analyse so-called *political externalities*, which can be both positive and negative. The positive ones include "voting with one's feet" – one of the most important and effective ways of influencing policy change in the country being left. And it is not just totalitarian regimes from which persecuted social groups are fleeing but also flawed democratic countries in which, however, the policies pursued contribute to deepening poverty. An oft-cited example is Venezuela, from which some 4.6 million citizens (1/7 of the population) have left since 2014, thus voting against the presidency of Nicolas Maduro. The diaspora contributed significantly to the fall of Apartheid in South Africa and today contributes to criticism of regimes in China and North Korea (The Economist, 2019b).

But perhaps the economists are wrong?

Economics is not a science that allows for foolproof reasoning. We wrote about this in Chapter 3. It may, therefore, be worth looking a little more carefully at the concerns expressed about economic migration and assessing them reliably in the context of the available knowledge.

Let's start with crime and terrorism. The most frequently cited example in Europe is Sweden, where during the aforementioned emigration crisis in 2015 some 162,000 asylum applications were made. This represented almost 2% of the country's population.[8] Sweden had for years been renowned for its liberal asylum policy, accepting around 40,000 asylum seekers each year. However, it was not prepared for this number, and the rules in place at the time included financial support for those awaiting an asylum decision and a ban on working. This inevitably had an impact on the social situation, including an increase in crime. However, most of the opinions expressed were so exaggerated that the Swedish embassy in Poland decided to make an official statement, citing a range of data on the alleged crime rates in immigrant communities.[9] In fact, since 2010, there have been only two recorded acts of terrorism in which five people were killed. This corresponds with figures from other countries. Bryan Caplan reports that in the United States, the risk of dying from a terrorist attack is three times lower than from a lightning strike and 350 times lower than the risk of dying in a car accident (Caplan & Weinersmith, 2019). For the past 25 years, despite liberal immigration policies, crime in Sweden has been declining. In 2015, however, it registered an increase, temporarily returning to 2005 levels. In Sweden, too, it is the foreign-born who are more often suspected of committing crimes (2.5 times) than the native-born. With such statistics, however, Sweden appears to be the exception rather than the rule. In the United States, the crime rate for foreign-born people is one-third lower than for Americans. Naturalised immigrants are model citizens five times less likely to conflict with the law (Caplan & Weinersmith, 2019). A comprehensive study conducted by the National Academy of Sciences (National Academies of Sciences, Engineering, and Medicine, 2015, p. 327) on the integration of immigrants into American society surprises with the conclusion that "studies demonstrate that immigrants and immigration are associated inversely with crime. Immigrants are less likely than the native-born to commit crimes, and neighborhoods with greater concentrations of immigrants have much lower rates of crime and violence than comparable non-immigrant neighborhoods".

Another revealed concern is the destruction of the local labour market. Are local workers really losing their jobs and earning less? Generally no. Almost all studies did not confirm a decrease in average wages in the host country. Some, however, indicated that such a decrease could be observed among the lowest-paid and least-skilled workers, in some cases by as much as about 5% (Borjas & Katz, 2007). The same research also indicates an increase in the salary of educated local workers. This is justified by their natural progression to higher positions. This is because local workers will always have an advantage over immigrants in terms of fluency in the language and local institutional settings, making them natural managers (The Economist, 2019c). However, such a decline in wages has not been recorded in cases of particularly massive migration, such as the liberation of the labour market for Black South Africans after the fall of Apartheid or the accession of central and eastern European countries to the EU in 2004. The more than one million workers from Ukraine who came to Poland in 2014–2018 and roughly another million who came after the Russian invasion in February 2022 also did not cause a decline in wages in the lower-income decile, which on the contrary increased by around 30% in 2014–2018[10] and wage growth continued between 2022 and 2024 but was more modest in real terms due to inflation.

Immigrant workers also tend to be net contributors when it comes to the tax system, i.e. they contribute more to it than they receive from it. This is understandable, given that most of them come to work and earn. In this respect, however, the figures vary from country to country. As a rule, countries such as the United States, Australia, and especially the United Arab Emirates fare better in this respect, i.e. the net balance is clearly in favour of the budget. The situation is worse in Europe and especially in the Scandinavian countries, where the welfare system is particularly generous. However, it must be borne in mind that social systems, which also include pensions, mainly support the elderly (and economic migrants are usually not part of this group), which is a problem in itself since they are usually not the poorest group in society today.

A particular set of concerns relates to the assimilation of immigrants and the "importation" into richer countries of cultural patterns that either directly conflict with local culture or law (e.g., attitudes towards women) or not directly violate the delicate fabric of social trust and solidarity, leading to the destruction of institutions that contribute to the wealth of developed countries. These types of concerns are the most difficult to analyse. It is unclear how to study these aspects, especially since, as we wrote in Chapter 1, the factors that have led to "great improvement" over the last two centuries are at least partly disputed. Assimilation is most simply measured by the fluency level in the host country's language.

Here, the data are more optimistic than one might expect. Even in the United States, known for the creation of specific enclaves of nationality, by the second generation, 88% of immigrants are fluent in English (Caplan, 2012, p. 11). Attempts to measure the level of assimilation through knowledge of local culture and history are problematic, as a significant proportion of the local population presents this knowledge at a very low level.[11] Almost as quickly as linguistic assimilation, there is also adaptation to the established liberal democratic institutions. Its importance, however, is lessened by the fact that even naturalised immigrants show a moderate interest in politics and participation in democratic elections (Caplan, 2012, p. 9). They are least likely to abandon their religion, which, in the case of Islam, a religion commonly associated with a particular organisation of state power and terrorism, raises peculiar emotions. However, the way in which religious practices are carried out and their impact on daily life is being significantly modified.[12] Concerns about quantitative dominance due to the elevated fertility rate, characteristic of some African cultures, are also misplaced. It decreases with a change of residence. The average Somali woman who has six children in Somalia has only two children after moving to Norway (The Economist, 2019a).

On the other hand, the fact is that in more racially and culturally diversified communities, levels of social solidarity, as measured by the share of public redistribution in GDP, decline (Alesina et al., 2001). One of the more interesting analyses of the importation of adverse cultural patterns was presented by two American economists, M.A. Clemens and L. Pritchett in the form of the so-called epidemiological model (Clemens & Pritchett, 2019). Based on various research results and making very conservative assumptions, they developed an economic model to calculate the maximum level of migration at which negative "epidemiological" effects, mainly expressed in terms of productivity losses, do not occur. In this model, the key variables are the level of low productivity transmission from the sending country to the receiving country, the rate of assimilation resulting in productivity equalisation, and the level of migration density that can negatively affect transmission and assimilation. In other words, they assumed that the higher the ratio of migrants to residents, the higher the level of low productivity transmission to the host country and the slower their assimilation may be. According to their calculations, an annual influx of migrants of about 4% of the local population does not cause this "epidemiological effect". If this model turned out to be correct, we could receive about 18 million people in Europe a year without any fear that they would "infect" us with low productivity. It is worth mentioning that one of the most serious problems in Europe is a greying society, a growing number of pensioners and a shrinking workforce. According to the latest Eurostat projections, by 2100 Europe will be about 27 million people short and the population will be significantly older. People aged 65 and over will account for 32% of the population, up from 21% in 2022. The current pace of migration will not compensate for this effect.[13]

Is it our moral duty to open our borders?

Suppose the cited data on the mutual benefits of economic migration leads us to conclude that borders should be opened. In that case, this means that we are more or less consciously forming judgements about what is good (and what we should strive for, and thus what is our moral duty) and what is bad (and what we should avoid). Moreover, these judgements are formed on the basis of a certain ethical standard that is characteristic of many economists. According to the conviction expressed by David Hume, there is no logical transition from what "is" to what "ought" to be. In other words, the justification of our moral duties must be based on at least one normative premise. Those inclined to recognise an obligation to open borders on the basis that it leads to a doubling of global wealth and the lifting of millions of people out of poverty form their judgements on the basis of the hypothetical effects to which the action leads. If these effects turn out to be beneficial for the majority of people (both the inhabitants of the host country and the emigrants), then the action that leads to them becomes a moral obligation.

However, the caveat can always be raised that the benefits and costs of relaxing migration policy are not equally distributed. Indeed, as the studies already cited prove, most people would benefit considerably (e.g., property development businesses, landlords, immigrants, and their families). Still, the situation of others may deteriorate (e.g., the lowest-paid and least-skilled workers may lose their jobs). In view of this, opening borders would lead to injustice. The economic answer to the charge of unfair distribution of costs and benefits is to apply a compensation standard. Those for whom the opening of borders turns out to be particularly beneficial can simply compensate the people who are disadvantaged because of it. One could imagine, for example, an additional tax on immigrant labour or an entry fee levied on every immigrant entering the local labour market. The funds obtained in this way would then be transferred to people for whom the new situation would prove disadvantageous.

Why is there still no free movement of people and no possibility of working anywhere in the world if it is in everyone's interest? Perhaps one reason is that, for many people, prosperity, especially economic prosperity as measured by material wealth, is not the most important thing. Multiplying wealth on a global scale may be important, but something far more important from a moral point of view is respect for people's rights and freedoms and concern for the well-being of fellow citizens first and foremost. Do people for whom respect for the rights and freedoms of individuals is the basic standard for judging actions have any reason to be in favour of opening up borders to immigration? Let us try to answer this question by analysing a thought experiment formulated by the American philosopher Michael Huemer (Huemer, 2010). Let us imagine Huemer proposing a man named Marvin, who is in desperate need of food. He is in danger of starvation. Perhaps someone has stolen his food supply, or some natural disaster has destroyed his crops. However, Marvin has a plan to get out of his predicament. He intends to go to the local market, get a job with a local entrepreneur, earn money, and then buy something to eat. He knows he will find people willing to employ him and sell him food. Now imagine that someone, e.g., Sam, actively tries to prevent Marvin from getting to the market and carrying out his rescue plan. As a consequence, Marvin starves to death. Note that not only does Sam not help Marvin in an extremely difficult situation he does not allow Marvin to help himself by making voluntary exchanges with people who are willing to do so.

The thought experiment referred to is intended to make us realise that immigration restrictions violate the rights of individuals to move freely and to enter into voluntary relationships with other people, which in extreme cases leads to the violation of a fundamental human right, namely the right to life. The conclusion of Huemer's argument is the belief that people, in principle, have the right to settle and live where they want, i.e. they have the right to migrate unless there are some special cases in which the enforcement of this right leads to adverse consequences. Such consequences could be, for example, those analysed by economists: the negative impact of immigration on the local labour market, the significant burden on the host country's social system caused by the influx of immigrants, the threat posed by immigrants to the local culture. However, if the economists are right, as we have already written about, none of these cases occurs.

One more reason that may lead people to question the right to immigration is the belief that we should take special care of our loved ones, members of the family, the village, the region, and the country. Intuitively, it seems apt to believe that while we are obliged to respect the fundamental rights of all people, we have special moral duties towards those with whom we have close relationships. In other words, we value the well-being of those close to us more than that of potential immigrants living in distant countries. The question is whether the demand for open borders requires the adoption of an extremely cosmopolitan attitude, i.e. the recognition that my homeland is the whole world and that all people form one great community in which every person has the same moral value, and therefore that their well-being is as morally significant as that of our fellow citizens. Such an attitude would be incompatible with a position of special duties towards loved ones. But does the opening of borders require such a radical cosmopolitan attitude? The American economist Dani Rodrik made an attempt to answer this question. He formulated an economic model in which he assumes, among other things, that 60 million people want to emigrate from poor countries to highly developed countries to work there. He then compared the hypothetical loss to the inhabitants of the host countries associated with a decline in wages of the least skilled workers, calculated according to a conservative model but still acceptable in a given society, with the benefits received by immigrants taking up work there. He noted that the benefits of immigrants are more than four times the acceptable losses of local residents. Let us assume that each immigrant counts as one and that the sum of the benefits obtained by all immigrants represents the welfare of that community. Assume further that the sum of the losses of local residents represents the welfare loss of that community. What weight should be given to the welfare of local residents if their loss in community welfare is to offset the increase in welfare gained by immigrants? The answer to this question is simple: the welfare of an individual resident of the host country must count for more than four times the welfare of an individual immigrant. So, it turns out that relaxing migration policy does not require adopting a position of radical cosmopolitanism. We can value the well-being of members of our community much more and still advocate a substantial opening of borders for labour immigration (Rodrik, 2017).

Thus, no matter what standard of moral evaluation one advocates, whether it is the sum of beneficial social effects, respect for human rights and freedoms, or duties towards those with whom one has close relationships, there are reasons to argue that opening borders to economic migration constitutes a moral duty. However, the persuasive power of these arguments depends largely on the quality of the research carried out by economists. If their work is reliable, we gain a basis for making informed moral judgements about labour immigration.

Why is it so difficult to persuade local voters?

Despite all these economic and moral arguments, attitudes to labour immigration remain quite reluctant. A significant proportion of voters in the developed world are convinced that the influx of "aliens" is too high. This is the view of 59% of voters in the United Kingdom, 37% in the United States, and 17% in Canada, traditionally with a very liberal immigration policy (Clemens, 2011, p. 67). These results translate into relevant policy choices. An interesting aside remains that once we come to co-exist with other cultures, our attitude towards them becomes friendlier. These are, among others, the results of a study on the attitudes of Poles towards workers from Ukraine (Personal Services, 2019). Pro-immigration political choices in localities characterised by multiculturalism are also a characteristic recurring pattern. The referendum to ban the construction of minarets in Switzerland lost in localities with a Muslim minority population, while it won where there was no minority at all (Göle, 2016). Apparently, this co-existence triggers a set of human characteristics responsible for extensive cooperation between alien community members. This extensive cooperation among humans is a unique trait among mammals and is most likely the source of *Homo sapiens'* evolutionary success as measured by the scale of numerical and territorial expansion. However, it has long been a mystery to evolutionists and anthropologists how it evolved. Today's most plausible hypothesis involves cultural evolution linked to collective or multilevel selection. In the most general terms, competition in nature involves not only individuals but also whole communities and the cultural patterns they develop, some of which prove more and others less adaptive. However, for some homogenisation of cultural patterns to take place in the area of a given community, a specific mechanism is required at the level of an individual, which in this case is our unusual tendency to imitate other members of the community, also known as conformist transmission (Stoelhorst &

Richerson, 2013; Tomasello, 1999). This imitation, mimicking patterns of behaviour that are most common in a given group, is highly adaptive; however, it leads to the development of symbolic markers such as language or dress that distinguish members of a community and make them hostile to other groups. Strangers in such a model pose a double threat. They can become carriers of less adaptive patterns, but above all, they can "parasitise" on the cooperative qualities of group members. However, the history of the cultural evolution of the human species, at least since the time of Neolithic settlement and the emergence of large communities, is a story of constant struggle with these contradictory tendencies. On the one hand, we reveal the tendency for widespread cooperation enforced somewhat economically; on the other, we struggle against inter-group hostility and in-group parasitism. N. Steward has rightly summarised it in the 2011 Berkeley Wealth Report: "The brain is mainly set up for wandering around on the savannah picking up berries. We're stuck with that sort of Stone Age brain, trying to do modern financial decisions making with it" (Berclays Wealth, 2011).

Notes

1 https://www.europarl.europa.eu/topics/en/article/20170629STO78630/asylum-and-migration-in-the-eu-facts-and-figures (Accessed: December 2024).
2 https://data.unhcr.org/en/situations/ukraine (Accessed: December 2024).
3 https://www.consilium.europa.eu/en/infographics/ukraine-refugees-eu/ (Accessed: December 2024).
4 https://www.pulshr.pl/wynagrodzenia/place-w-polsce-i-na-ukrainie-roznice-nawet-pieciokrotne,55666.html (Accessed: December 2024).
5 The wage gap between Ukrainian and Polish workers, which cannot be explained by other factors related to their skills and productivity, is around 10%. In doing so, they are often employed in positions below their professional qualifications (Growiec et al., 2019).
6 https://www.worldbank.org/en/news/press-release/2022/05/11/remittances-to-reach-630-billion-in-2022-with-record-flows-into-ukraine (Accessed: December 2024).
7 https://finance.ec.europa.eu/system/files/2022-09/220927-joint-statement-remittance-ukraine_en.pdf (Accessed: December 2024).
8 https://www.migrationpolicy.org/article/sweden-turns-welcoming-and-restrictive-its-immigration-policy (Accessed: December 2024).
9 https://www.swedenabroad.se/pl/embassies/polska-warszawa/faq—cz%C4%99sto-zadawane-pytania/jakie-s%C4%85-fakty-na-temat-migracji-i-przest%C4%99pczo%C5%9Bci-w-szwecji/ (Accessed: December 2019).
10 https://stat.gov.pl/obszary-tematyczne/rynek-pracy/pracujacy-zatrudnieni-wynagrodzenia-koszty-pracy/struktura-wynagrodzen-wedlug-zawodow-w-pazdzierniku-2018-roku,5,6.html (Accessed: December 2024).
11 In the United States, most Americans cannot name the decade of the 19th century in which the Civil War took place. And according to a 2014 study by TNS Global, most Poles fail a simple test covering the most important events in Polish history (http://www.tnsglobal.pl/archiwumraportow/files/2014/04/K.026_Polacy-wobec-historii_O02a-14.pdf).
12 Particularly interesting research in this regard is presented in the monograph "Muzułmanie w Europie" (Göle, 2016).
13 https://www.euronews.com/next/2023/04/04/china-sees-first-population-decline-in-six-decades-where-does-the-eu-stand (Accessed: December 2024).

References

Alesina, A., Glaeser, E., & Sacerdote, B. (2001). Why doesn't the United States have a European-style welfare state? *Brookings Papers on Economic Activity*, *2*, pp. 187–254. https://doi.org/10.1353/eca.2001.0014

Barrell, R., Fitzgerald, J., & Riley, R. (2010, March). EU enlargement and migration: Assessing the macroeconomic impacts. *Journal of Common Market Studies*, *48*(2), 373–395. https://doi.org/10.1111/j.1468-5965.2009.02056.x

Berclays Wealth. (2011). yumpu.com. Retrieved June 12, 2021, from https://www.yumpu.com/en/document/read/12809801/risk-and-rules-the-role-of-barclays-wealth

Borjas, G. J., & Katz, L. F. (2007). The evolution of the Mexican-born workforce in the United States. In G. J. Borjas (Ed.), *Mexican immigration to the United States* (pp. 13–56). The National Bureau of Economic Research. https://doi.org/10.7208/chicago/9780226066684.003.0002

Caplan, B. (2012). Why should we restrict immigration? *Cato Journal*, *32*(1), 5–24.

Caplan, B., & Weinersmith, Z. (2019). *Open borders. The science and ethics of immigration*. First Second.

Clemens, M. A. (2011). Economics and emigration: Trillion-dollar bills on the sidewalk. *Journal of Economic Perspectives*, *25*(3), 83–106. https://doi.org/10.1257/jep.25.3.83

Clemens, M. A., & Pritchett, L., 2019. The new economic case for migration restrictions: An assessment. *Journal of Development Economics*, *138*, pp. 152–164. https://doi.org/10.1016/j.jdeveco.2018.12.003

Göle, N. (2016). *Muzułmanie w Europie. Dzisiajsze kontrowersje wokół islamu*. Wydawnictwo Karakter.

Growiec, J., Wyszyński, R., & Strzelecki, P., 2019. *The contribution of immigration from Ukraine to economic growth in Poland*. [Online] Available at: https://www.nbp.pl/badania/seminaria/31x2019.pdf [Accessed 09 01 2020].

Huemer, M. (2010). Is there a right to immigrate? *Social Theory and Practice*, *36*(3), 429–461. https://doi.org/10.5840/soctheorpract201036323

National Academies of Sciences, Engineering, and Medicine (2015). *The integration of immigrants into American society*. The National Academies Press.

Personal Services. (2019). *Barometr imigracji zarobkowej. II półrocze 2019. Ukraiński pracownik w Polsce*. Wrocław: Personal Services. Retrieved 01 14, 2020, from http://personnelservice.pl/pl/biuro-prasowe/raporty

Rodrik, D. (2017). *Is global equality the enemy of national equality?* (HKS Working Paper No. RWP17-003). Harvard University, John F. Kennedy School of Government. https://doi.org/10.2139/ssrn.2910603

Stoelhorst, J. W., & Richerson, P. J. (2013, June). A naturalistic theory of economic organization. *Journal of Economic Behavior & Organization*, pp. 45–56. https://doi.org/10.1016/j.jebo.2012.12.012

The Economist (2011). Drain or gain?. *The Economist*, 26 May.

The Economist (2019a). The backlash. Fear of the unknown. *The Economist*, 16 November.

The Economist (2019b). Voting with your feet. The greatest liberty. *The Economist*, 16 November.

The Economist (2019c). Low-skilled migrants. Labourers and loved ones. *The Economist*, 16 November.

The Economist (2019d). Migration. A world of walls. *The Economist*, 16 November.

The Economist (2019e). Skilled migrants. Lightbulb in their luggage. *The Economist*, 16 November.

Tomasello, M. (1999). *The cultural origins of human cognition*. Harvard University Press.

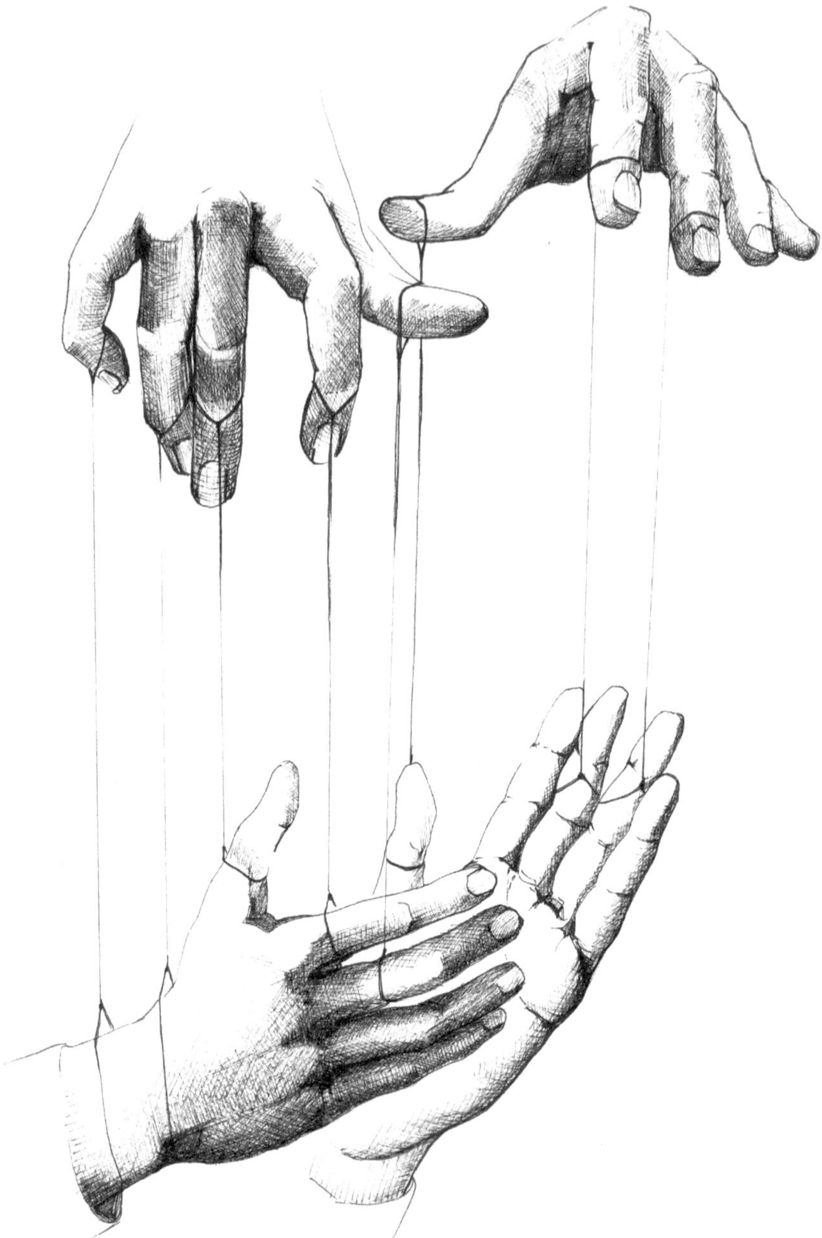

9

IS A STATE ENTITLED TO "NUDGE" CITIZENS?

An economist proudly claims that he has been attending the gym regularly since his university days. Like most of us, he occasionally feels unmotivated, faces competing priorities, or simply lacks the energy to exercise. However, remarkably, he has never missed a single workout. How has he achieved this? His secret lies in his choice of gym, an extraordinarily expensive luxury facility. As a student, he even allocated 8% of his income to cover this cost. When teased by colleagues for spending so much on something they accessed at a fraction of the price, he would respond, "It makes more sense to spend 8% of your income on something you actually use than to pay $50 a semester for something you never go to". For him, the high cost of the subscription ensured that the guilt of wasting money outweighed any temporary lack of motivation.[1]

In contrast, most people do not approach gym subscriptions so strategically. Many of us, when purchasing memberships, end up paying not to go. Research conducted in the United States found that individuals who purchase monthly, auto-renewing subscriptions often fail to visit the gym frequently enough to justify the cost. On average, they use the gym less than twice per week, which is the threshold at which the subscription would become financially worthwhile. This systemic overestimation of workout frequency leads to higher-than-expected costs per visit, often exceeding what they would have paid with a pay-per-visit model. Additionally, many subscribers procrastinate when it comes to cancelling their memberships, allowing costly contracts to continue into subsequent billing cycles (DellaVigna & Malmendier, 2006). This lack of rationality among customers is skilfully exploited by businesses, which leverage consumer overconfidence and inertia to maximise profits by promoting auto-renewing subscriptions.

The challenges of rational decision-making extend far beyond gym memberships. For instance, people often struggle to make optimal choices when it comes to

DOI: 10.4324/9781003469384-12

their health. Many overindulge in alcohol, smoke cigarettes, take drugs, consume unhealthy foods, or drink excessive amounts of sugary beverages. These behaviours increase the risk of obesity, cardiovascular disease, respiratory cancer, and depression. Although adults undeniably have the right to make decisions about their own lives, there are instances where small external interventions, called "nudges", could encourage healthier and more beneficial choices. A common example of such a nudge is the inclusion of graphic warnings on cigarette packaging. By mandating tobacco companies to display images of diseased organs along with warnings about the harms of smoking, governments aim to dissuade individuals from engaging in harmful behaviour, ultimately for their own good.

Recognising our own cognitive and motivational limitations, we can take deliberate steps to "hack" our behaviour, as illustrated by the economist's decision to use the financial burden of an expensive gym subscription as a motivator. However, while individuals may attempt to counteract their own weaknesses, businesses often exploit these same vulnerabilities for profit, as seen in the marketing of auto-renewing subscriptions. Meanwhile, governments intervene in an attempt to influence personal choices, ostensibly for the benefit of public health. This raises a critical question: How is it possible for individuals, businesses, and governments to exert such influence over decisions that seem, at first glance, entirely personal? And, more importantly, is the state justified in using nudges to guide citizens' choices?

Thinking traps

The development of experimental economics, particularly behavioural economics – a topic discussed in greater detail in Chapter 14, has called into question the traditional vision of the economic man, or *homo oeconomicus*. This idealised figure is assumed to be perfectly rational, possessing complete knowledge, calculating flawlessly to maximise profit, and always acting in their best interest. However, it has become evident that ordinary individuals often deviate significantly from this ideal.

The divergence becomes especially pronounced in situations requiring difficult decisions. These are decisions that require self-control, involve complex or infrequent choices, provide limited feedback, or occur in areas where we lack well-informed preferences. In such cases, we are prone to errors and oversimplifications. For example, maintaining regular exercise routines or moderating the use of stimulants requires considerable self-control, which may explain why so many unmet New Year's resolutions revolve around these behaviours.

Similarly, infrequent and high-stakes decisions – such as choosing a course of study, selecting a life partner, or buying a house – often leave us little opportunity to learn from experience, especially mistakes. A person who consumes a high-fat diet over many years may not receive immediate feedback about its negative health effects until she suffers a heart attack.

Decisions about a major medical procedure further complicate matters, as they involve trade-offs that are difficult to conceptualise. For instance, how does one decide whether to undergo a surgery that might extend life by three years but carries a 30% risk of impotence or incontinence? As Thaler and Sunstein (2008) point out, it is difficult to imagine the lived experience of losing control over one's bodily functions. This makes it nearly impossible to weigh such outcomes rationally and translate the available options into a clear sense of what the future experience would entail.

In this type of situation, instead of systematically gathering and analysing the necessary information, we often resort to simplifying decision-making shortcuts (rules of thumb), known as heuristics. While heuristics help us navigate a complex world, they also lead to systematic cognitive biases that can distort our judgement.

One such heuristic is the anchoring heuristic, where we rely heavily on the first piece of information we encounter, which subsequently shapes our perception of the situation. For example, when students were asked, "Are you happy?" followed by "How often do you date?", researchers found a weak correlation between their responses (0.11). However, when the order of the questions was reversed, the correlation increased significantly (0.62). The thought of dating frequency acted as an anchor, influencing the evaluation of happiness. A student might think, "I can't remember the last time I dated, therefore, I must be unhappy" (Thaler & Sunstein, 2008).

Another common heuristic is the availability heuristic, which leads us to estimate the likelihood of events based on how easily examples come to mind. For example, many people erroneously believe that homicides are more frequent causes of death than suicides. This misjudgement arises because homicides are widely publicised in the media, while suicides are less likely to be reported. Consequently, vivid or memorable examples skew our perception of probabilities. Psychologists describe this as a tendency to believe that what is more mentally accessible occurs more frequently.

A pervasive cognitive bias related to decision-making is loss aversion. Thaler and Sunstein, in their bestselling book "Nudge: Improving Decisions about Health, wealth, and Happiness", highlight that the pain of losing something is roughly twice as intense as the pleasure of gaining the same thing. This bias is closely tied to the endowment effect, where we overvalue what we already own and resist trading it, even if such an exchange would benefit us. For instance, I may cling to an old, unfashionable pair of jeans so that I don't wear them anymore because I find it emotionally easier to buy new ones than to part with the old ones. This reluctance to let go of possessions often results in unnecessary clutter, but the implications of the endowment effect extend beyond personal belongings. It can make people resistant to change of any kind, even when maintaining the status quo is suboptimal. This reluctance explains why cancelling subscription services such as Netflix, Spotify, or an auto-renewing gym membership often feels disproportionally difficult.

Another critical factor influencing our decisions is the way information is presented, a phenomenon known as the framing effect. Our choices often depend not on the facts themselves ("bare facts") but on how they are framed or interpreted. For instance, individuals are more likely to consent to a surgical procedure if told that 90 out of every 100 patients are alive five years later, compared to being informed that 10 out of every 100 patients died within five years of the operation. Although both statements convey the same statistical reality, the positive framing of survival rates appears to be more persuasive than the negative framing of mortality rates (Thaler & Sunstein, 2008).

While heuristics are not inherently detrimental because they help to simplify sometimes overwhelmingly complex world, they can, in many cases, lead to decisions that are not in our best interest. For example, subscribing to a gym membership with an auto-renewal feature might feel like a commitment to a healthier lifestyle. However, when the initial enthusiasm to exercise wanes, the cognitive bias towards maintaining the status quo often leads us to keep paying for the membership, even when we stop using it. Rather than quitting immediately, we procrastinate, resulting in unnecessary expenses.

Behavioural economists have turned these biases into an opportunity. They argue that the very cognitive biases that lead us astray can also be leveraged to benefit us. By carefully redesigning the context in which our decisions are made, whether through slight changes in how options are described, altering default settings, or modifying the framing of choices, it is possible to guide people towards better outcomes. Thaler and Sunstein (2008) refer to these subtle interventions as "nudges", illustrating the concept with the example of a school cafeteria.

Choice architecture

Imagine, as Thaler and Sunstein suggest, that we have the opportunity to arrange the goods in the school cafeteria however we like. For example, we could place their favourite candy bars, sugary drinks, and crisps on the shelves at the pupils' eye level. These are products that the children themselves would be inclined to choose. However, if we prioritise their health, we might instead place fruit and fresh juices in the most prominent and accessible areas. While these healthier options may not be the children's preferred choices, they are certainly better for them. Alternatively, we could organise the goods based on our financial interests, displaying the items that yield the highest profit. Regardless of the approach, one thing is certain: the arrangement of merchandise on the shelves will inevitably influence the choices made by consumers.

In this scenario, the school cafeteria owner becomes responsible for shaping the context in which purchasing decisions are made. Whether consciously or unconsciously, the owner acts as a kind of "architect of choice". This choice architect has the power to significantly impact behaviour, which can be used to positive effect. The responsible cafeteria owner understands that, while healthy food is best for children, they may struggle to exercise self-control when faced with the temptation of crisps or sugary drinks placed directly in their line of sight. By intentionally arranging the cafeteria's offerings, the owner can design the decision-making environment to encourage better, in this case, healthier choices. Thaler and Sunstein argue that children may naturally choose healthy foods if they possess the same knowledge and self-discipline as adults, but since they lack these traits, nudges can guide them towards better decisions.

State institutions sometimes act in a manner similar to the cafeteria owner by shaping the decision-making context of citizens. For example, the law passed by the Polish parliament obliged companies to establish Employee Capital Plans (PPKs) to help people accumulate additional savings for retirement. Contributions to PPKs are made jointly by employers and employees, with the state adding an annual quota bonus. Under the law, employees aged 18–54 are automatically enrolled in PPKs by their employers, who enter into agreements with selected financial institutions on behalf of their employees. Since PPK is a voluntary saving programme, employees can opt out at any time by submitting a written declaration. However, if they take no action, they remain enrolled in the plan, and contributions continue to be deducted from their salaries.

The legislator's decision to make automatic enrolment the default option was a deliberate attempt to increase participation rates. It is reasonable to assume that more people will save for retirement when they are automatically enrolled with the option to opt out, compared to the scenario where they have to actively express their desire to join. Making participation a default option is an example of a "nudge" implemented by the state for the benefit of its citizens. Experts widely agree that inadequate additional savings will result in future pensioners relying solely on compulsory pension insurance, leading to very low income levels in retirement. In simple terms, individuals have to save voluntarily for their old age or risk facing poverty. However, experts also recognise that individuals often fail to act rationally when planning for the future. Most people prioritise present consumption over future needs and therefore save less than they should. Thankfully, another behavioural tendency – the preference for status quo – can be leveraged to benefit individuals. It is the aforementioned desire to leave things as they are, to preserve the status quo. If the default option is participation in PPKs, few people will choose to opt out. Many will likely think, "Since I'm already enrolled, I might as well stay", or "I'll withdraw next week", and then forget to take future action.

Just as the cafeteria owner influences children's choices by strategically arranging merchandise, legislators influence citizens' decisions by setting the default option for voluntarily saving plans, like PPKs. In both cases, the respective choice architecture is designed to push people towards decisions that are in their best interest, even if they are not fully aware of the benefits. However, the analogy diverges when we consider the different audiences involved. While the cafeteria owner is nudging schoolchildren, who may lack the knowledge or self-discipline to make healthy choices, state institutions are nudging adult citizens, who are fully entitled to make autonomous decisions about their lives. This raises an important ethical question: Should we accept that the state, through policy decisions, assumes the role of the school cafeteria owner and shapes the context of choice so that citizens, like children, are guided towards what is deemed to be good for them? Thaler and Sunstein's answer lies in their concept of so-called libertarian paternalism (Thaler & Sunstein, 2003).

Libertarian paternalism

Derived from the Latin word "pater", meaning "father", paternalism reflects the "paternal" attitude of state institutions towards their citizens. Much like a father who insists on forcing his children to eat vegetables instead of sweets for the sake of their health, the state, in certain circumstances, compels citizens to act in their own best interest or to refrain from actions that may harm them. For example, the law mandates wearing seatbelts while driving, using child safety seats for young children, and prohibiting the use of telephones while driving. As citizens, we are expected to abide by these regulations, even if we believe we should have the autonomy to decide what risks we are willing to take with our own lives.

Economists have traditionally opposed the paternalistic tendencies of the state. Many adhere to a principle articulated by John Stuart Mill, one of the founding figures of classical liberalism. Mill claimed that "… the only purpose for which power can be rightfully exercised over any member of a civilised community, against his will, is to prevent harm to others. His own good, either physical or moral, is not a sufficient warrant. He cannot rightfully be compelled to do or forbear because it will be better for him to do so, because it will make him happier, because, in the opinions of others, to do so would be wise, or even right" (Mill, 1859). In other words, individual freedom should only be limited to preventing harm to others; beyond that, everyone knows what is best for themselves. Mill was convinced that any attempt by institutions to decide what is good for an individual would likely produce worse results than if the person were left to make decisions independently.

Thaler and Sunstein, however, challenge the assumption that people always know what is best for them. They argue that economists' aversion to paternalism rests on several misconceptions: firstly, that individuals reliably act in their own interest; secondly, that sensible alternatives to paternalism exist; and thirdly, that paternalism necessarily entails coercion. Experimental studies reveal that people, guided by cognitive biases and heuristics, frequently make decisions that are detrimental to their well-being. For instance, people often fail to save adequately for retirement or pay for gym membership without actually attending. When tested empirically, the assumption that individuals are the best judges of their own interests often proves false (Thaler & Sunstein, 2003, p. 175).

Are there sensible alternatives to paternalistic interventions? Frequently, the answer is no. Individual choices do not occur in a vacuum; the conditions in which decisions are made are always shaped by "choice architects". Consider the example of the school cafeteria. Displaying fruit and fresh juices prominently to encourage children to eat healthy could be viewed as paternalistic. This is true. But would it be preferable to arrange the cafeteria to maximise sales of sweets and snacks, which children naturally crave, or to prioritise profits for the cafeteria owner? Since the cafeteria owner has to structure the space of choice in some way, they might as well prioritise promoting the health of the children. Importantly, this approach does not eliminate the option to purchase crisps or sweets; these items remain available in the cafeteria. Rather, the choice architect gives a slight "nudge" towards healthier options, such as fresh juices and fruit, which are in the children's long-term best interest.

This form of paternalism does not rely on coercion, as in the case of mandatory seatbelt laws, but instead seems to preserve individual freedom while subtly guiding people towards better choices. Thaler and Sunstein (2008) describe this approach as libertarian paternalism. The term reflects its dual nature: "libertarian" because it preserves freedom of choice and "paternalism" because it seeks to influence people to lead longer, healthier, and better lives.

A "rational" pearl in an irrational "shell"

The attraction of libertarian paternalism lies in its challenge to the assumption that people know best what is best for themselves. However, if we reject this belief, what alternative do we accept? Must we concede that the institutions of the state should decide what is better for citizens? Proponents of libertarian paternalism firmly reject this option. In their view, a "nudge" from the state should guide citizens towards choices they themselves would make if they possessed perfect knowledge and were free from cognitive errors and weakness of will. The goal is to ensure that people's "true" desires, such as healthy eating, are realised, rather than fleeting impulses, such as consuming crisps instead of a nutritious lunch. Human beings, they argue, are akin to rational pearls encased within a shell of irrational desires and cognitive errors (Infante et al., 2016). The role of the choice architect, then, is to design decision-making environments that illuminate this rational core of human nature.

The dualistic vision of humanity – as composed of a rational pearl and an irrational shell – does not, however, resolve a fundamental problem inherent in libertarian paternalism. Specifically, how do state officials determine what is genuinely good for people? Behavioural economists, working in their laboratories, are only able to test the irrationality of the shell, but what the pearl itself looks like remains a matter of pure speculation. We can only hypothesise how a person with perfect knowledge, free from cognitive biases and weakness of will, might behave. For instance, it seems reasonable to assume that a rational individual would want to be healthy and live a long life. Yet, the details of such behaviour are far from straightforward. Is every instance of alcohol consumption or indulgence in sweets an irrational act? Is every decision to prioritise spending in the present over saving for the future inherently flawed? Certainly not. Determining whether a perfectly rational person would, in a particular context, choose to consume more alcohol or save more money requires us to engage in speculative guesswork.

Even if it were somehow possible to ascertain what decision a rational actor might make, another challenge arises: by what means should the state encourage people to act in alignment with their rational nature? The essence of nudges lies in leveraging individuals' irrational tendencies (such as the tendency to preserve the *status quo*) to guide them towards decisions they might make if they were perfectly rational. This approach does not aim to help people overcome the limitations of their irrational shell; rather, it seeks to exploit those very limitations for their own benefit. Consequently, the practice carries an inherent element of manipulation. The central question becomes whether the state has the right to "nudge" citizens, essentially, whether it has the right to manipulate people under the guise of acting in their best interest.

Scepticism towards state interventions leads us to doubt the validity of answering this question in the affirmative. While it may be difficult to completely avoid forms of state paternalism, a well-governed state should not rely on manipulation. Instead, it should enhance the cognitive capacity of its citizens, equipping them to make informed decisions independently. Just as a diligent economist hones their skills through consistent practice, people aware of their cognitive limitations and weaknesses of will can, in many cases, learn to make better decisions on their own.

Note

1 https://qz.com/754344/the-case-for-joining-an-expensive-gym (Accessed: November 2024).

References

DellaVigna, S., & Malmendier, U. (2006). Paying not to go to the gym. *American Economic Review*, *96*(3), 694–719. https://doi.org/10.1257/aer.96.3.694

Infante, G., Lecouteux, G., & Sugden, R. (2016). Preference purification and the inner rational agent: A critique of the conventional wisdom of behavioural welfare economics. *Journal of Economic Methodology*, *23*(1), 1–25. https://doi.org/10.1080/1350178X.2015.1070527

Mill, J. S. (1859). *On liberty*. J. W. Parker & Son. Retrieved from https://www.econlib.org/library/Mill/mlLbty.html

Thaler, R. H., & Sunstein, C. R. (2003). Libertarian paternalism. *American Economic Review*, *93*(2), 175–179. https://doi.org/10.1257/000282803321947001

Thaler, R. H., & Sunstein, C. R. (2008). *Nudge: Improving decisions about health, wealth, and happiness*. Yale University Press.

PART III

Methodology and Economics

2%
Y = 3/√53
-6

10

HOW DO ECONOMISTS REASON?

Hume's fork

David Hume, the father of empiricism and modern reflection on science and human cognition, is the author of a typology that today goes by the name of "Hume's fork". Analysing the foundations of our knowledge of the world, he concluded that they are quite weak and based on beliefs that are more expressions of our faith and aesthetic judgements than the "hard" evidence we would expect from science. In this chaos of beliefs, however, two areas stand out. Wherever "magnitude and number" appear, where we carry out deductive reasoning on the basis of assumed axioms and rules, these will reliably lead us to unambiguous results. Within the accepted rules of geometry, the square of the hypotenuse of a right-angled triangle will always be equal to the sum of the squares of the two legs (Pythagoras' theorem). Within the sentential calculus, the falsity of the conjunction of two sentences will always mean that either both sentences are false or one of the two. The second area is reasoning based on facts deduced from sensory experience. This experience can be unreliable. Nevertheless, if we accept that a fact has occurred, we can derive other facts from it on the basis of a known relation between facts (e.g., causality). All the rest is just a matter of "style and feeling, not reason", including moral beauty. The rest, Hume suggests, "Commit it then to the flames: for it can contain nothing but sophistry and illusion" (Hume, 2007, p. 120). Such thinking, later reinforced by Kant's systematics of the sciences and the philosophy of science of the Vienna Circle, still shapes our conception of science today, to which we will include biology and mathematics but leave normative ethics instead to philosophers.[1] Hume's fork also defines the method used as follows: precise, deductive analysis and reasoning in the formal sciences, observation, experiment, and generalisation in the empirical sciences. What method does economics use?

DOI: 10.4324/9781003469384-14

From arbitrary assumptions to irrelevant conclusions

Methodology is the science of research methods used in specific fields of knowledge. It usually has a dual dimension: a descriptive one, showing what methods are actually used by representatives of a given science, and a normative one, indicating what methods should be used and how they should be applied correctly. Economics is one of the social sciences, so it should not be surprising that its research methods are also appropriate to other social sciences, such as history, sociology, and psychology. However, its strong, theoretical character sets this science apart and has shaped how it has been practised for many years. Economists think in theoretical models. We write about this in more detail in the next chapter. At Hume's fork, economics seems to be pointed at the same end as geometry and logic. This was expressed by the Nobel laureate in economics, Wassily Leontief (1905–1999), in summarising in 1982 the nature of the economic articles published in the American Economic Review. Indeed, it turned out that 54% of the texts dealt with mathematical models and a further 11.6% of the texts involved non-mathematical, theoretical analyses, both without any empirical data.

> Page after page of professional economic journals are filled with mathematical formulas, leading the reader from sets of more or less plausible but entirely arbitrary assumptions to precisely stated but irrelevant theoretical conclusions.
> *(Leontief, 1982, p. 104)*

However, this paradigm has changed significantly over the last 30–40 years. This is acknowledged, among others, by one of the leading philosophers of economics, Daniel Hausman, in one of his interviews (Hausman et al., 2017). We have written about these developments when discussing the possibility of making accurate predictions on the basis of economic theory, the relationship between wealth and happiness, and the permissibility of government "nudging" citizens.[2] We will also write about them in the following chapters: Chapters 11 and 14. Finally, we will also mention methodological paradigm shifts in economics in the chapters in the last part of the book that deal with the relationship of economics with sociology, demography, cognitive psychology, and evolutionary theory. In other words, everywhere we look, we see the constantly evolving method of economics. However, the fact that it is changing in a more empirical direction does not mean that theoretical models have left academic textbooks and scientific journals. Despite the development of empirical methods, they are still the hallmark of this science, at least in relation to its most mainstream version, neoclassical economics. How did such a paradigm have dominated this science for centuries?

Historical development of economic methods

Although economics is traditionally derived from the Scottish philosopher Adam Smith (1723–1790) and his major work, *An Inquiry into the Nature and Causes of the Wealth of Nations (1776)*, so the methodological culmination of the classical period in economics was the analyses of John S. Mill (1806–1873) and the so-called marginal revolution by Leon Walras (1834–1910), William S. Jevons (1835–1882), and Carl Menger (1840–1921). Mill is probably associated by many with utilitarianism in ethics and empiricism in science. However, his proposed characterisation and method of economics had relatively little in common with empiricism. Mill treated economics as an a priori science, in the likeness of geometry. For, in his view, this science made certain simplified assumptions about the motivations and behaviour of individuals in the market, abstracting from all other aspects of their psychology other than the desire to make a profit, which it then extended to a given population, deductively deriving certain necessary laws from them. These simplistic assumptions were somewhat later dressed up in the label *homo oeconomicus,* with a strongly pejorative (especially in the literature) meaning. With this perception of economics, the analogy with geometry seems apt, for no one expects perfect points, straight lines or equilateral figures to exist in physical reality. Nevertheless, this idealisation serves us to deductively establish a number of necessary relationships, which primarily help us to understand the reality around us and may also have their own non-ideal applications. Suppose economics also establishes certain necessary relations on the basis of these simplified assumptions. In that case, no one should expect that these assumptions accurately depict reality nor that these necessary relations relate to observable and repeatable regularities in social and market reality. For their primary function is to *explain* and *understand,* not to *predict*. In a way, Mill's philosophy was an attempt to salvage the previous achievements of classical economics from the misguided predictions of Ricardo and Malthus, which we wrote about in Chapter 3. In the next chapter, we will present one such theoretical model of Ricardo – the so-called comparative advantage model. Not long after Mill, following his paradigm, the marginalists proposed a theoretical model of price formation in the market that moved away from its reliance on the value of the labour put into producing a particular product, instead proposing the concept of so-called diminishing marginal utility. In the case of Walras and Jevons, this was also combined with the extensive use of mathematical analysis tools to illustrate the demand and supply functions and the states of a hypothetical market equilibrium, first partial and then general. Today, almost every microeconomics textbook discusses these issues in a highly theorised and mathematised way. Until the 1970s, economics was dominated by market equilibrium models. Based on Walrasian assumptions, they attempted to take into account all price drivers across the economy and thus became immeasurably more complex. A partial end to these models was only brought about by the so-called Lucas critique, which introduced an element of so-called reflexivity into economic discourse.[3] Their modern successors, widely used mainly in central banks, are stochastic-dynamic general equilibrium models. A third marginalist, Carl Menger, simultaneously initiated the so-called Austrian School in economics, which went in a slightly different direction, although equally theoretical. The successors of the Austrian School are somewhat outside the mainstream of modern economics, but their relevance to science was and still is important. Austrians rejected the mathematisation of economics, recognising that mathematical analysis tools are useless for economic analysis. Their unsuitability is rooted in radical market uncertainty associated with a consistently applied methodological individualism (von Mises, 1996). Advocates of this position maintain that the underlying factors in any market analysis are individuals' motivations, plans, and actions which are conditioned by the actions of other individuals observed in the market (Hayek, 1937). Although Austrians, like the classics, make a priori assumptions about the introspectively knowable motivations of individuals and attribute rationality and a focus on the realisation of individual benefits, these dynamically adjusted plans create situations of mathematically irreducible complexity. Any attempt to determine states of presumed equilibrium in the market is doomed to failure. This does not change the fact that the basic research method of the Austrian School is theoretical analysis, deduction based on a priori assumptions and thought experiments. On the other hand, historical-inductive methods (observation of repeated phenomena in the economy and generalisation of conclusions into fixed causal relationships) and the consistent use of statistics in economics are programmatically rejected.

At the other end of Hume's fork lie the historical-inductive method and methods derived from the falsificationism of Karl R. Popper (1902–1994). There are many different types of induction, but the one that seems of interest from the point of view of economics consists, in simple terms, of the experimental search for recurring regularities in market reality and their generalisation into economic laws. Many economic laws came about not through a theoretical-deductive analysis of the assumptions made but precisely through observing these regularities. This is how, among others, Nicolaus Copernicus drafted the law on the displacement of a stronger coin from the market by a weaker one, later called Copernicus-Grescham's law (Kopernik, 1526). In modern times, the use of this method has been inspired by the historical sciences, particularly in Germany, and by the emerging sociology. In both fields, the basis for editing any more general conclusions is, first of all, the accumulation of a sufficient amount of data that can be analysed inductively. In the social sciences, and in economics in particular, the data collected are themselves subject to construction and interpretation.[4] In order to calculate the average per capita income in a given market and during a given period, which we can then use in a historical-inductive analysis, we must, for example, first determine which elements shaping this income are to be taken into account and which are not, and who is to be included in the population taken into account.[5] The foundations for such processing and data collection were laid, on the one hand, by sociologists and, on the other, by American economists from the institutional school, who in 1920 founded the *National Bureau of Economic Research*, which is still in operation today. Examples of such research that are particularly well-known in economics include Max Weber's (1864–1920) analyses of the impact of religion on the economic development of specific regions in Germany (Weber, 2002).[6] More contemporary is the historical-inductive research on the relationship between inflation and unemployment, conducted by Alban W. Phillips (1914–1975). The relationship he established was later called the Phillips curve (Phillips, 1958). Although the institutionalists were criticised by mainstream economists and Austrians for their approach, which, according to the latter, only added confusion to economic theory, their research provided many arguments supporting or challenging mainstream theories.

Falsifying the predictions of economic theories has become another milestone in the development of economic methods. The theoretical basis for this approach was laid by the Austrian philosopher Karl R. Popper (Popper, 2002). In simple terms, he considered that the essence of a scientific theory is not the inductive generalisation of observations but formulating of such a theory, whose integral parts are the resulting empirical predictions that are suitable for confrontation with observable reality. Only a theory that incorporates these falsifiable predictions is scientific. Popper's thought initiated the development of the philosophy of science in a direction that increasingly took into account the knowledge of how scientists actually work, create, correct, and refute their concepts. In economics, falsificationism had its direct reception in the thought of the British economist Terence Hutchison (1912–2007) (Hutchison, 1938), who made a strong critique of the a priori-deductive methods of the classical school and in particular against assumptions derived from psychological introspection. He considered that most of the so-called pure economic theory claims were tautological and, therefore, unscientific. A more contemporary position was represented by Mark Blaug (1927–2011) (Blaug, 1992) and Milton Friedman (1912–2006). The latter, in particular, stirred up much controversy with his radicalism. Friedman, a Nobel laureate in economics mainly associated with the neoliberal policies of the United States under President Ronald Reagan, is also the author of a widely commented methodological essay (Friedman, 2008). When, in the wake of successive economic crises that eluded the analysis of neoclassical economics, economists began to move towards more extensive verification of their claims by empirical methods, the main effort of this verification was focused on the theory's assumptions. This was because it was recognised that their "unrealisticness", their inadequacy to experience, was primarily responsible for the inaccurate predictions of these theories. Friedman attacked such a thesis and reversed the problem from an extreme instrumentalist position. It is not the realism of the assumptions that should be of concern but the predictions themselves. Only the accuracy of the predictions of a given theory can tell us whether it is good or bad, or, in other words, whether it is useful from the point of view of a particular state policy. The assumptions themselves may be false or even arbitrary and unfalsifiable.

However, falsificationism in economics faces a significant problem. If these Popperian criteria were to be applied consistently, recognising as scientific only those theories that have falsifiable predictions as part of them, it could also turn out that very little of the entire science of economics would remain. For most of these predictions are not only falsifiable but also falsified. The Phillips curve has been revised at least twice but still does not illustrate the current relationship between unemployment and inflation. Prices do not respond flexibly to changes in demand, and the monetary mechanism, which underpins the activities of central banks, has essentially ceased to function in recent times.

However, the above disputes have led to a gradual increase in interest in empirical research in economics based on in-depth analysis of aggregated data. This has also given rise to a science treated as ancillary to economics, namely econometrics, which is mainly concerned with developing mathematical and statistical tools for analysing relationships between economic variables. Undoubtedly, in addition to the methodological shift in this direction, the growing stock of data collected mainly by public administrations (although more recently also, or perhaps even primarily, by private enterprises, often with a global reach) and the possibilities of processing this data ever more rapidly thanks to IT systems have also contributed to this. In this last element, some philosophers of science see a breakthrough in the methodology of the social sciences (Kinkaid & Ross, 2009; Rosenberg, 2009). It would be related to the recently fashionable *big data* research, for which the Internet is becoming an invaluable source of data, and artificial intelligence techniques are becoming a tool for processing data, allowing, for example, semantic analysis of information available on the Internet.[7]

Also linked to falsificationism are experimental methods in economics, which, together with *big data* analyses, represent the latest, most recent stage in the methodological development of this science.

Contemporary economic research methods

When, in 1982, the aforementioned Leontief complained about the over-theorisation of economics by analysing the methods used in scientific publications, he found, among other things, that among the studies that could be classified as empirical, it was primarily the analysis of published or generated elsewhere data that dominated (22.7% of all studies and 66% of empirical ones). Experiments and artificial simulations, on the other hand, increased progressively from 0.5 to 1.9% between 1972 and 1981 (Leontief, 1982, p. 104). According to cross-sectional data based on a review of scientific publications, experiments in economics already account for 6% of all research, as does purely theoretical research based on textual analysis. In contrast, analyses of published and generated elsewhere data (45%) and (perhaps somewhat surprisingly) surveys (39%) dominate (Sagan, 2016, p. 112). Thus, if one were to rank contemporary empirical or quasi-empirical research methods in economics according to their popularity, they could be divided into three main categories:

1 Analyses of published or generated elsewhere data,
2 Questionnaires and surveys, and
3 Observations and experiments.

The latter will be deliberately omitted, as we devoted a separate chapter to them (Chapter 14).

Analysis of published or generated elsewhere data

With a broad understanding of the "data" being analysed, it should come as no particular surprise that this method has been, and continues to be, dominant in economics from the very beginning of the science. Smith, in his flagship work, conducts many such analyses. Among other things, he reviews interest rates in England, France, and the Netherlands, changes in the wages of labourers, in the prices of gold, silver, and wheat over four centuries. Thomas Malthus does the same, whose essay is derived from data on the size of the population in the poorest social strata, the demand for labour, and the amount of wages paid (Malthus, 2011). Even economists consistently applying Mill's a priori method were keen to refer to examples from the market to illustrate their theses. The ongoing contemporary dispute between monetarists and neo-Keynesians[8] has also been resolved by using specific examples of national economies applying policies similar to one or the other school of economics and referring to macroeconomic data alleged to represent the effect of these policies. However, the fundamental problem with such an application of this method lies in the selective choice of relevant data. Many effects, which are also responsible for the predictive difficulties of economics, result in the same or very similar policies, leading to quite different results. Therefore, such qualitative comparisons are very unreliable and are more often used for rhetoric and argumentation than for establishing causal relationships in the economy. On the methodological side, however, it can be said that at the two opposite ends of the analysis of the found data lie two types of research that can serve to establish these causal relations from the scientific perspective of the frog and the eagle. These are case studies, often linked to so-called counterfactual analysis and econometric analyses of a range of economic variables.

Case studies are empirical qualitative studies of a specific economic phenomenon conducted in its natural environment, taking into account the context in which the phenomenon occurred. These studies involve the analysis of a quantitatively limited number of occurrences of a phenomenon or even a single occurrence. Their purpose is usually to establish the cause of specific observed effects considered to be of interest from an economic point of view, regardless of whether these effects are positive or negative. Thus, case studies can be carried out to determine the causes of the deep crisis of public finances in Greece and the associated economic recession and high unemployment, as well as to determine the causes of the long-term double-digit GDP growth in China. This method is also very popular in management science. It was widely used by one of the most prominent economists in organisation and management theory, Peter F. Drucker (1909–2005). In one of his flagship works, he describes the cases of companies such as Sears, Ford, and IBM (Drucker, 2006).

Particularly valuable within the framework of this method, from the point of view of establishing causal relationships, are analyses of similar cases where a similar intervention led to different results. This is because it is possible, through comparison, to isolate the variables that determine the different paths of events. An example of such an analysis can be found in Roger Backhouse (Backhouse, 2010), where he compares the effects of Leszek Balcerowicz's reforms in Poland and Yegor Gaidar's in Russia. Both "shock" economic therapies had similar assumptions and implementation methods. However, while the return to economic growth in Poland was relatively quick, Russia was still struggling with recession for many years.

Big data analysis is nowadays especially fashionable (because there is much talk about it). In fact, it is a buzzword that refers to any method involving processing large amounts of data to establish or falsify hypothetical regularities. Their peculiarity is the need to use computer or artificial intelligence techniques. Beyond these techniques, the processing of these data is computationally inaccessible. At the root of these methods are classical econometric techniques, which involve creating an econometric model on the basis of existing data, presenting the relationship between the response variable and explanatory variables in the form of an equation or system of equations. Computer techniques are not essential with a limited number of explanatory variables, although they greatly facilitate calculations. However, as the number of variables increases, the model's complexity level increases at a rate that does not allow it to be constructed without a computer. An additional problem is hypothesising which variables can act as explanatory variables and which are irrelevant. This is usually the role of the economist. However, the number of potential variables is infinite. A computer algorithm can help to hypothesise what variables should be tested.

Scenario analyses are another commonly used method, which involves less existing data and more expected data, already aimed directly at predicting the development of the studied events in a defined future. In textbook terms, these are studies aimed at establishing causal relationships between the analysed system and an unstable environment (Sagan, 2016, p. 144). They have been encountered by anyone with a model business plan in hand. This is because usually, in addition to the so-called transactional environment (e.g., factors directly shaping the financial performance of the company), it also distinguishes the contextual environment (e.g., assumptions regarding the economic developments in a given market, or the exchange rate, inflation rate, cost of credit, etc.), and depending on one and the other factors, three to four scenarios are constructed as follows: pessimistic, realistic, and optimistic (sometimes also surprise). This method is very characteristic of economics, as it allows the sensitivity of a given model to a changing contextual environment to be analysed and optimal measures to be selected depending on the likelihood of a given scenario occurrence and the consequences that follow. A contemporary, advanced development of the scenario method are all simulation models, including agent-based simulation models. The latter are another example of the application of modern computational techniques to economics. In addition to the transactional and contextual environment, an agent (or rather multiple agents) with a defined function of its behaviour is introduced into these models. By running a simulation, the researcher observes the development of different scenarios by manipulating variables in the transactional and contextual environments as well as variables describing the agents' behaviour. Such models are used to analyse public transport and the behaviour of employees in a company or investors in the financial market.

The last method based on existing data analysis to be discussed is cost-benefit analysis. In principle, it is one of the primary methods used both in micro- and macroeconomics, which can aim both at the evaluation of the effects of current actions within the framework of a given intervention or public policy, as well as at a prospective evaluation covering the future, expected effects of the outlays made. Such an analysis may be reduced to financial analysis only. Only direct financial outlays and benefits are taken into account. It is usually used in companies where the essential parameter is to obtain a certain rate of return on investment. However, it can also be an extended economic analysis, where indirect costs, such as *opportunity costs*, are also taken into account. The results of such analyses are sometimes not evident. An example of this is the discussion around so-called *sin taxes*, a tax on the consumption of harmful substances such as alcohol, nicotine, or high-sugar drinks. The British *Institute of Economic Affairs* has produced a series of reports calculating the net cost to the UK budget of the consumption of certain stimulants. Taking into account tax revenue, healthcare costs, crime, or premature death, it was found that alcohol and nicotine consumption has a positive budgetary effect, mainly resulting from relatively early deaths (at or shortly after the end of working age), which leads to significant savings in the pension system. On the other hand, a strongly negative budgetary effect is caused by overweight, caused, among other things, by excessive consumption of sugars (The Economist, 2018).

Questionnaires and surveys

The frequency with which economists turn to questionnaires and surveys may come as a surprise, given that this method is traditionally associated with sociology or psychology. However, the surprise should be significantly lessened when we recall that in neoclassical economics, the fundamental element is a rational individual making utility-maximising decisions. What an individual does or intends to do (in the light of rational expectations theory) is, therefore, central to economic analysis. For these analyses to take place, we need to gather the relevant knowledge. An important part of the research involving published or elsewhere generated data mentioned above is based on data collected precisely by survey methods. It is worth giving a few examples.

- *The Labour Force Survey* (LFS) has been conducted by many countries since the 1940s and 1950s. EU member states are now expected to submit LFS results for every quarter to Eurostat. The survey is carried out in accordance with the methodology of the International Labour Organisation, which, by surveying a sample of households, aims to determine the economic activity (employed, unemployed, economically inactive) of people aged 15–74.
- *The Household Budgets Survey* (HBS), a national survey focusing mainly on household expenditure on goods and services. They are conducted in all EU countries. They were launched in most EU member states at the beginning of the 1960s. Eurostat has been collecting and publishing these data every five years since 1988.
- *The Purchasing Managers' Index* (PMI) is an indicator describing the prevailing trends in the economy in manufacturing and services, which was developed by the *Institute for Supply Management* and is calculated on the basis of surveys of business managers that include questions on data such as new orders, inventories, current production, subcontractor deliveries, and employment.

One specific panel method worth mentioning at the end relates to philosophical constructivism in economics, the so-called Delphi method.[9] Given the fact that economic experts can differ significantly in their assessments of the market situation, even though they have the same data, constructivists have developed a method based on the assumption that the collection of these divergent opinions and their qualitative analysis can allow for better prediction as to the economic variables of interest to the researcher. The method, therefore, involves first selecting experts who can be members of a research panel and then bringing about an interaction between the panel members to discuss and exchange views. The interaction is moderated and observed, and the level of agreement and disagreement is measured. Finally, these results are aggregated and analysed quantitatively and qualitatively, and final conclusions are drawn (Sagan, 2016, p. 142).

Fork or spoon?

The juxtaposition of the above methods together with those we have described so far or will still be writing about in the following chapters makes Hume's classic two-pronged fork lose its sharpness and the spaces between its prongs fill with hybrid analyses. It thus resembles a spoon with holes in places, drawing from a social soup to strain out the interesting contents. On the one hand, we have mathematical models with precise results, criticised for the unrealistic nature of their assumptions and their inability to make reliable predictions; on the other, we have observations made using various techniques whose conclusions are so general that they cannot be falsified or are falsified as soon as they are formulated. In the chapter on the difficulties of predicting economic crises, we wrote about this predictive impotence of economics, drawing attention to specific features of social reality, such as the complexity, reflexivity, and adaptive nature of human behaviour. Hume did not analyse these features. However, he was convinced that the three areas of human knowledge that he distinguished, namely a priori (deductive-analytic), a posteriori (derived from experience), and aesthetic-moral, were qualitatively different and that some coherent typology of science could be constructed on their basis. However, this need not be the case, and economics can exemplify that this is not the case. Leaving aside the issue of the philosophical-mathematical dispute over the sources of our mathematical concepts,[10] the fundamental problem lies in facts and values. There is no such thing as pure facts or sense experiences detached from a moral context. Since Popper, philosophers of science have boldly spoken of "theorised" observation. Our observation is selective. We find some facts interesting and ignore others. We observe selected facts according to attributes imposed by a previously accepted, even temporarily and very primitive theory. The existing data, which we use in empirical economic research, are not only preselected and processed according to some theory (not necessarily economic), but they are also "value-laden". We wrote about this extensively in Chapter 4 and we will also touch on this topic in Chapter 13. Classical and neoclassical economists were very keen to present their theories in a way that indicated their complete independence from the economist's professed value system. According to Hume's postulate, economics as an "almost exact" science was to remain free of value judgements and describe only objective facts and the relations between them. This was to be the domain of positive economics, while value judgements were to be the domain of normative economics, which was to respond to essentially ethical problems, i.e. the goals of economic or social policy, as revealed in the light of positive economic theory. From the outset, such a division was questionable. The most strident critics came from the Marxist school. For them, all scientific activity, and in particular that of the social sciences, is subordinated to the ideology of a particular social class. However, there was also criticism among other economists, who noted how many value-laden elements were to be found in apparently objective economic theories. Others, in turn, pointed out that certain normative postulates (realised overarching goals, values) are in fact, formed in the course of economic activity rather than being pre-determined or resolved (Blaug, 1992, p. 130). Today, probably no reasonable person would argue that there is no problem here. However, at least three positions can be distinguished:

1 Optimistic, assuming that freedom from value judgements is more challenging to achieve in the social sciences but possible nevertheless;
2 Pessimistic, assuming that such freedom is not possible and that we should deal with the normative burden in other ways;
3 "Metanormative", recognising that such freedom is not only impossible, but actually ethically undesirable.

Most research economists seem to lean towards the optimistic version. Most economic philosophers, on the other hand, tend towards the pessimistic one. The metanormative position is related to the fact that many economic theories, treated instrumentally, lead to postulates contradicting our moral intuitions. In Chapter 4 we give, among others, the example of Summers' shocking memorandum. The problem is that these ethical involvements of economic theories can be seen clearly where the consequences mentioned appear shocking to us and are not seen where, at least at first sight, they remain within the scope of a shared ethical belief system. Their apparent invisibility, however, does not mean that these ethical assumptions are not there or should not be there. On the contrary, they should be identified and discussed. For "A social science that sought to efface the moral dimension from its descriptions and explanations would simply serve the interests of some other moral conception" (Rosenberg, 2016, p. 288).

Notes

1 Positive ethics, or ethology, on the other hand, which involves the study of the actual moral beliefs of individuals and communities, would be classified as a science.
2 Chapters 3, 7 and 9.
3 We wrote about it in Chapter 3, pointing out that this phenomenon is one of the limitations of the social sciences, determining their poor predictive ability.
4 Which, in effect, leads to the creation of such, constructional measure-models in economics, which we write about in Chapter 13.
5 Let us try to give some non-obvious examples: the products of a home farm, free Internet access, alimony payments, income resulting from the increase in value of the dwelling owned and used, income from foreign transfers from relatives, income of illegal immigrants residing in the area or students, income received by people temporarily working outside the area under study, etc.
6 We write about these in more detail in the last section of the book in Chapter 16.
7 An example of such research is presented in the next chapter (Chapter 11), where, in the specific messages, the relationship between the frequency of occurrence of words with an optimistic or pessimistic emotional charge and macroeconomic indicators is analysed (Nyman et al., 2018).
8 In simple terms, it can be said that this dispute concerned the loosening or tightening of state fiscal policy and its impact on economic growth. Monetarists are rather in favour of state financial discipline and very cautious handling of public debt and financial

impulses, whose stimulating effect on the economy would follow from Keynesian macroeconomic models. Cf. (Rzońca, 2007).

9 We wrote more about constructivism in Chapter 3, but it is also discussed in the next chapter on models.

10 In a certain simplification, one can say that only mathematical Platonism assumes objective and independent existence of mathematical entities (G.Frege). Alongside it, however, an equally strong position is mathematical constructivism, which recognises that mathematical concepts are derived from our perception of the world shaped by evolution (H.Poincaré) as well as mathematical empiricism, which assumes that sensory experience is at the root, while mathematical abstraction is a secondary activity of our mind (J.S. Mill).

References

Backhouse, R. E. (2010). *The puzzle of modern economics. Science or ideology?*: Cambridge University Press.

Blaug, M. (1992). *The methodology of economics or how economists explain*. Cambridge University Press.

Drucker, P. F. (2006). *The practice of management*. Harper Business.

Friedman, M. (2008). The methodology of positive economics. In D. M. Hausman (Ed.), *The philosophy of economics. An anthology* (pp. 145–178). Cambridge University Press.

Hausman, D. M., Gorazda, M., & Kwarciński, T. (2017). O przydatności ekonomii, celach polityki publicznej i znaczeniu filozofii ekonomii. *Zarządzanie Publiczne*, *42*(4), 102–109. https://doi.org/10.15678/ZP.2017.42.4.08

Hayek, F. A. (1937). Economics and knowledge. *Economica*, *IV*(February), 33–54.

Hume, D. (2007). *An enquiry concerning human understanding*. Oxford University Press.

Hutchison, T. W. (1938). *The significance and basic postulates of economic theory*. MacMillan and Co.

Kinkaid, H., & Ross, D. (2009). The new philosophy of economics. In H. Kinkaid & D. Ross (Eds.), *The Oxford handbook of philosophy of economics* (pp. 3–34). Oxford University Press.

Kopernik, M. (1526). *Monetae cudendae ratio*. [Online] Available at: http://la.wikisource.org/wiki/Monetae_cudendae_ratio [Accessed 08.08.2013].

Leontief, W. (1982). Academic economics. *Science*, *217*(4555), 104–107. https://doi.org/10.1126/science.217.4555.104

Malthus, T. R. (2011). *An essay on the principle of population*. Retrieved 02.18.2011, from Library of Economics and Liberty: http://www.econlib.org/library/Malthus/malPop3.html#VII.20

Nyman, R., Kapadia, S., Tuckett, D., Gregory, D., Ormerod, P., & Smith, R. (2018, January). *News and narratives in financial systems: Exploiting big data for systemic risk assessment*. Retrieved 12.15.2018, from Bank of England. Working paper No 704: https://www.bankofengland.co.uk/working-paper/2018/news-and-narratives-in-financial-systems

Phillips, A. W. (1958, November). The relationships between unemployment and the rate of change of money wages in the United Kingdom 1861–1957. *Economica*, *25*(100), 283–299. https://doi.org/10.1111/j.1468-0335.1958.tb00003.x

Popper, K. R. (2002). *The logic of scientific discovery*. Routledge.

Rosenberg, A. (2009). If economics is a science, what kind of science is it. In H. Kinkaid & D. Ross (Eds.), *The Oxford handbook of philosophy of economics* (pp. 55–67). Oxford University Press.

Rosenberg, A. (2016). *Philosophy of social science*. Westview Press.

Rzońca, A. (2007). *Czy Keynes się pomylił? Skutki redukcji deficytu w Europie Środkowej*. Warszawa: Wydawnictwo Naukowe Scholar.

Sagan, A. (2016). *Metodologia badań ekonomicznych.* Wydawnictwo Uniwersytetu Ekonomicznego w Krakowie.

Smith, A. (1776). *An inquiry into the nature and causes of the wealth of nations* (Cannan ed., Vol. 1). Methuen. https://oll.libertyfund.org/titles/smith-an-inquiry-into-the-nature-and-causes-of-the-wealth-of-nations-cannan-ed-vol-1

The Economist (2018). The price of vice. "Sin" taxes-eg, on tobacco-are less efficient than they look. *The Economist*, 28 July.

von Mises, L. (1996). *Human action: A treatise on economics*. Foundation for Economic Education.

Weber, M. (2002). *The protestant ethic And the spirit of capitalism: And other writings*. Penguin.

11

WHAT MODELS DO ECONOMISTS USE?

Models instead of scientific laws

Economists love models. Few sciences are as fond of creating models as economics. Dani Rodrik, a well-known American economist of Turkish origin, even took the liberty of saying that economics as a discipline thrives precisely by growing its library of models (Rodrik, 2015). Physics and chemistry, which are somewhat treated as model sciences, use the notion of scientific laws, principles, and theories. This is not to say that these sciences have no models, but they are not the quintessential models. They enter the area of the practical application of specific laws and theories, where engineers dominate, or the exact opposite area, that of theoretical physics and cosmology, where the empirical possibility of testing specific theories is strongly limited. The analogy is not coincidental. In economics, drafting universally applicable laws is difficult, and some say impossible.[1] Others also argue that because scientific laws, by definition, demand a certain universality, i.e., that they apply always and everywhere, economics does not formulate such generalisations. Even if individual economists did use the term, what lay beneath it was quite distant from the classical understanding of the laws of science (Hardt, 2017). Economists, on the other hand, have been constructing models since the very beginning of this science. These are both "engineering" ones, which are supposed to represent some simplified version of the solution to be implemented, and highly theoretical ones, which, based on more or less arbitrary assumptions, are supposed to give us a picture of some economic universe, as well as many others.

DOI: 10.4324/9781003469384-15

In order to neatly tell what models are in economics but also what models are in general, it is best to use a few, not too complicated, examples at the outset:

1 In his flagship work, which for many years became a de facto textbook on economics, David Ricardo, in the chapter on foreign trade, edited the model of so-called comparative advantage (Ricardo, 1821). In this model, he presented two countries, England and Portugal, that produce wine and cloth. In England, producing a unit of cloth requires the work of 100 people for a year, while producing a unit of wine requires 120 people for a year. In Portugal, the same cloth unit requires the labour of 90 people and wine 80. Portugal is, therefore, more efficient in producing both wine and cloth. Intuitively, therefore, it seems that it should not be interested in any purchases from England, as they will probably be more expensive due to the higher production costs. On closer inspection, however, this intuition proves unreliable. If Portugal commits all its human resources to wine production and England to cloth production, the global volume of wine and cloth in both economies will increase. If, on the other hand, we treat the above units of labour directly as the total cost of producing the corresponding unit of wine or cloth, it can be seen that however much lower the price of a unit of wine in England is than 120, it will be attractive. In contrast, if Portugal earns 40 (120–80) on wine exports, it is even profitable for it to "top up" on cloth imports. In such a model, both countries gain from specialisation resulting from relative comparative advantage. This model (somewhat more complex in the original) was and is still used today as an argument for free international trade.
2 In 1494, in Venice, a Franciscan friar, Luca Pacioli, published a synthetic treatise describing the rules of double-entry bookkeeping, which in principle are still used today and which is considered the basis of modern bookkeeping (*Summa de arithmetica, geometria, proportioni et proportionalità*). The double-entry rule means that every economic operation in the company is entered in two accounts, *debit* and *credit,* reflecting the principle that the value of all the company's assets equals the value of their financing sources (debt or owners' capital). These abstract rules nowadays allow us to treat every balance sheet and profit and loss account as a kind of company model. It does not tell us what a company does or how many people it employs, but it does tell us the value of its assets, what categories these assets are made up of and how they are financed. It also tells us what revenues the company generated in the reporting period, what costs it generated by type and whether it made a profit or a loss.
3 In 1949, New Zealand economist Alban W.H. Phillips (then a student at the *London School of Economics*) constructed a hydraulic machine. This analogue computer simulated the workings of the British economy, mainly through the lens of financial flows, depicted by coloured fluid circulating in plastic transparent tubes, controlled (or calibrated) by valves placed there. MONIAC (*Monetary National Income Analogue Computer)* was intended to represent how the

flow and accumulation of the fluid changes in individual tanks, representing the various components of the economy, government, businesses, imports and exports, and households, depending on manipulable variables, interest rates, taxes, or exchange rates. The machine, which was primarily intended for educational purposes, was also used to make economic predictions (Ng & Wright, 2007).

4 In 2018, a group of economists from the Bank of England conducted a study involving a complex analysis of the relationship between two types of data: commonly used indices denoting economic sentiment (e.g., PMI – *Purchasing Manager's Index*) and an indicator constructed for the study (RSS – *Relative Sentiment Shift*) describing changes in the mood of the narrative used in various types of reports and commentaries on the stock market or economic situation. The second indicator was based on the predominant use of phrases or words denoting excitement or anxiety. Based on this analysis, which can be described as *big data*, they constructed a predictive model to predict how economic indicators would behave depending on the change in mood of the preceding narrative in stock market reports. In simple terms, the model illustrates a hypothesis that goes somewhat against the grain of mainstream economics, according to which it is not economic changes that affect sentiment indicators but the dominant way they are presented in professional reports (Nyman et al., 2018).

The above examples were chosen to avoid using complex mathematical equations for simplicity. However, most economic models described in textbooks or scientific articles are a set of more or less abstract equations describing relationships between economic variables. The above examples also have underlying specific functions or mathematical equations. The comparative advantage associated with production costs and relative prices in the market is calculable when the actual data are substituted. A specific equation can express the principle of double entry in accounting or rather a set of equations where the sums of the entries on the credit and debit sides are always equal. If they are not, it usually means that a mistake has been made somewhere in the entries or someone has robbed us, and we have not yet discovered this. At the core of MONIAC, on the other hand, is a set of equations describing the functioning of the economy based on a mathematical interpretation of Keynes' general theory. Analyses in big data are usually complex, computer-based calculations on Gigabytes of data.

What is a model?

Considering the examples above, the issue seems simple: a model is a simplified picture of some reality. However, if we go deeper, things are a bit more complicated. This simplification can have a very different nature and purpose. The scaled-down replica of Christopher Columbus' flagship, the *Santa Maria*, standing on a shelf, is a model that performs mainly aesthetic (it looks nice) and informative functions (it allows us to imagine such a ship in reality). However, it omits many irrelevant details, and an attempt to place it on the water would inevitably fail. Such a model is sometimes called iconic. Another example of such a model is a map of a territory. The map does not "work". There are no variables to manipulate or test the terrain under their influence. It is just a coded image that allows one to move around in a marked space. The map can, however, be used as an "insert" for a mathematical model, which, e.g., like the *Google Maps* application, calculates how long it will take us to get from Krakow to Berlin by car, given the traffic density. The map then becomes the provider of a number of relevant variables. In economics, examples of iconic models are various types of economic measures or their specific settings, such as the balance sheet and profit and loss account of a company.

The same *Santa Maria*, equipped with adjustable sails and balanced in a way that corresponds to a real caravel, placed in a wind tunnel, will allow us to observe how such sailing ships behaved in different wind directions. Such a model, usually mechanical, will be called a simulation model (Grobler, 2006) and it will be extremely useful to engineers but unlikely to be used in economics (although this function could be assigned to some market and behavioural experiments[2]). MONIAC, which looks like such a model, is a mathematical model where flows of coloured liquid in tubes have been used to illustrate the various interdependencies. The precise definition of such a model, sometimes also called a semantic model, is quite complex. Let us imagine that, as a budding economist, I would like to describe the operation of some selected part of the economy, e.g., a company. Indeed, in this description, I will use some language (e.g., English) and formulate some sentences that I consider to be true. These sentences can be of various types: they can be statements of fact, according to accepted principles (e.g., *this company has 300 employees).* They can also represent inferences I have made (e.g., *because any company with more than 250 employees is large, and the company described here has 300 employees, therefore it is large*). I may also describe the relationship between the various attributes of that company (the variables describing it), e.g., *large, medium, small, profit, revenue, market valuation*, and the like. I can, for example, state that *a company with higher profits achieves a higher market valuation.* Suppose I now transform my sentences into another language (e.g., the language of mathematical symbols). In that case, this transformation will be a mathematical model if the equivalents of these transformed sentences are equally true. Let us take the last sentence describing the relationship between a company's profit and its market valuation and label any two companies with indices 1 and 2 and price and profit with the symbols C and z, respectively. I can write the above sentence as a formula:

$$\forall p_1, p_2 : z_1 > z_2 \rightarrow C_1 > C_2$$

I read it as follows: for every p_1 and p_2 it follows that if z_1 is greater than z_2 then also C_1 is greater than C_2. If my statement is true, then transforming it into a formula like the one above should keep it true. Such a simplified model allows me to carry out "experiments" similar to the simulation model, but using only different values substituted for the variables and the mathematical transformations allowed in the given language. In this way, by making certain assumptions about existing economic relationships (e.g., a company's profit determines its market valuation) and accepting them as true, I can observe how other variables will behave in my mathematical model and compare the results obtained with those observed in reality. Ricardo's comparative advantage model is such a mathematical model. Despite its simplified description, it is accompanied by a number of assumptions, such as that each country has an interest in the global increase in the quantity of goods and services it purchases, and the more its citizens purchase them, the more fully their preferences are satisfied and the richer they are. MONIAC is also a mathematical model. However, the set of relations expressed in equations therein, controlling the flows of a coloured liquid simulating cash, is much more complex.

When economists talk about models, they are actually, according to the above classification, referring exclusively to mathematical models. Dani Rodrik, mentioned above, defines them as simplifications, presenting the functioning of a specific mechanism in isolation from other disturbing factors. The model is supposed to depict the causal interactions and how they produce specific effects. However, Rodrik also presents economic models using the metaphor of a fairy tale or parable. These traditional literary forms actually share a specific set of characteristics with economic models. They use model objects, humans or anthropomorphised animals, with particular, invariant virtues or vices guided by simplified motives of action (jealousy, greed) and placed in a clear, isolated context. The fairy tale does not care about the realism of the characters and setting. However, the moral of the tale is key: honesty pays off, he who laughs last laughs, don't kick the man who is lying, etc. Similarly, in the economic models, the objects placed there are simplified: they have a clear motivation boiling down, for example, to the desire to get rich, the surrounding world is most often limited to similar objects and to different representations of this wealth, as well as random economic shocks deliberately introduced there, which induce the subject to act according to his motivation. In turn, the story unfolds according to the logic of causal and conditional relations (what if …). In the end, the moral is the most important, and it takes the form of indications for economic policy: free international trade promotes the wealth of countries, or an increased money supply in the market increases the demand for goods and services. The most exciting analogy, however, is the incalculable number of fairy tales, which often present contradictory morals with only slightly changed circumstances. The same is true of economic models. Many of them lead to contradictory conclusions as a result of modifications of key assumptions.

Do economic models represent any economic reality?

The iconic model of a company in the form of a balance sheet and profit and loss account seems to represent such a reality. Experienced accountants will smile at this point, recalling the old anecdote in which the chief accountant, when asked about the company's financial results, replies, "And how much the management board would like it to be?". Even, it would seem, strict accounting rules leave a considerable margin of interpretation for so-called creative accounting. What is, however, the subject of the most tremendous disagreement between economists and economic philosophers is the nature of mathematical models. Note, that Ricardo did not analyse the actual production costs or wine and cloth prices in Portugal and England. His model detaches itself from this reality, only showing certain relationships that occur under certain conditions. MONIAC was of a similar nature. Here, however, some attempt was made to calibrate it, i.e. introduce into the equations such values and coefficients that would correspond to those observed (or constructed[3]) in the economy. Transitorily, there was even success in the form of an approximate correspondence between the readings and the data from the economy. However, the model itself is also rich in prior assumptions, the validity of which seems to determine the results obtained. These assumptions take the form of so-called idealisations and *ceteris paribus* conditions. Idealisations are conditions assumed in the model for some objects or variables that we know are not present in the real economy. Such an idealisation is the assumption that the only factor relevant to human action in the market is the desire to get rich. Thus, a number of emotions we know from introspection, such as love or fear, are deprived of market relevance. It is idealistic to assume in the perfect competition model that the actors involved in market transactions are perfectly informed about all relevant factors affecting the transaction terms, i.e. they have perfect market knowledge. The *ceteris paribus* condition means that all other factors not included in the model remain constant. Suppose we assume that the price of a specific good (e.g., a residential apartment) depends on the demand for it (the number of people willing to buy it) and its supply (i.e. the number of flats available on the market). In that case, we ignore the possibility of a demand shock on the market connected with an epidemic of a new influenza strain, which causes potential buyers to rather refrain from buying, saving their money for the future.[4]

As it is not difficult to see from the example of the models described above, they contain a whole set of idealisations and *ceteris paribus* conditions that make them appear to be a somewhat distant picture of the modelled reality. In spite of this, scientific realists will argue that economic models, with all the simplifications (or *isolations*, as some say) described above, still represent an essential feature of the modelled reality, its essence or at least certain tendencies that may or may not always reveal themselves in the economy. Their manifestation, however, is not crucial. It is a matter of understanding the dominant causal mechanisms that the modelled reality conceals and accurately explaining them. A model that properly represents these mechanisms is an explanatory model. A model that does not have them, or does not have them to a sufficient degree, is inferior, even if it has the potential to generate more accurate predictions. Hence, much excitement is being aroused by the increasingly widespread predictive models constructed using the achievements of modern computer science in processing large data sets, such as artificial intelligence, neural networks, and machine learning. Although their ability to predict specific economic quantities is often better, this dominant causal mechanism is implicit. The model is, therefore, not an aid to understanding the economic reality being modelled. In a way, the narrative model of economists from the Bank of England is such a model. True, it reveals relationships between the analysed variables and even hypotheses about the direction of causal interactions, but it cannot explain the mechanism of these interactions.

Assessing whether a model representation is more or less accurate or plausible must also take into account two additional factors: the purpose for which the model is built and the audience to which it is directed (Hardt, 2016). A model of a company will look different if its addressee is an investor facing a decision on whether to take a stake in the company, different if it is a manager considering becoming CEO, and different if it is a legislator deciding to support that company during an economic crisis to avoid mass layoffs. In each of these cases, appropriate comments on the model revealing, among other things, the idealisation assumptions and the *ceteris paribus* conditions should resolve the scope of the model applicability and the elements that constitute its similarity to the modelled object.

However, given these two additional elements of model objectives and addressees, instrumentalists would say that this hypothetical veracity of models is irrelevant. After all, the purpose of an economic model is to solve a concrete problem, which can be reduced to whether or not to invest in a given enterprise or whether or not to remove barriers to international trade. The model is, therefore, not any representation of an alleged reality but is only an instrument for achieving the goal set by the creator or user of the model. This is why this position is called instrumentalism.

The Gospel truth, true enough and not a shred of truth

Such a classification of truth was formulated by the Polish philosopher Józef Tischner. He wrote a history of philosophy using a specific Polish highlanders' dialect, where he also prized their commonsensical approach to complicated philosophical problems (Tischner, 2018). This well-known Polish Christian philosopher had very little to do with the philosophy of science and even less with the philosophy of economics. Nevertheless, his conception of truth had this realist strand, the conviction of the existence of an external reality independent of us, cognisable mainly through the analysis of the language with which we describe this reality. The method was typical for phenomenologists; philosophers considered themselves Edmund Husserl students. The chase for truth and search for the most appropriate method of its cognition is typical for philosophical realists. We wrote about the dispute between realists and constructivists in the chapter "Why can't economists predict future crises?". However, this dispute emerges in a special way precisely in the discussion about models. Thus, on the occasion of the dispute about the "veracity" of models, it is worth taking a slightly closer look at constructivism itself. It has a fundamental problem: constructivism is at odds with our everyday experience or conviction. Each of us is essentially a naïve realist. We believe that the world really is as we see it. Even if we have taken a basic course in biology and know that a two-dimensional image is projected onto our retina, which then has to be interpreted by our brain as three-dimensional, and that colours are only a representation of a specific wavelength of light, we will still, in our everyday experience, confidently claim that grass is green. It is what it is, or it is not. Actually, we don't know. Millions of years of biological evolution have shaped our cognitive apparatus precisely so that we can survive and spread our genotype. Alternatively, put another way, those whose perception of the world was better suited to these ends, whether it was more or less "true", survived and reproduced. Donald Hoffman, one of the contemporary cognitive philosophers, even puts forward a very radical thesis and proves it mathematically: this "veridical perception" of the world is not conducive to the survival and spread of the genotype. "Fitness beats truth" (Hoffman, 2019). The model of the world we apply is dominated by other purposes than its resemblance to the "real" world. Worse still, the more complex this model is, the more variables it contains, the further away it is from the supposed truth. Because of these biological-evolutionary conditions, we have no access to it. Scientific constructivists have taken reasoning based on these assumptions much further. If our mental model of the world is a construct subordinated to gene propagation, so much more can scientific models of the world be. Not only do they arise on the basis of this mental model but we also use its secondary constructs, such as the spoken language, for their construction. This, in turn, is culturally conditioned. The structure of language and the concepts created within it strongly shape our ideas about the world. The world in which we use money as an instrument for the exchange of goods and services is a completely different world from the world of barter. It is a world in which we begin to attribute monetary value, to the dismay of humanists, to every possible manifestation of social life. This is just one of the economic concepts we use in our models.[5] We cannot break out of the world shaped by concepts. There is no extra-conceptual cognition. So-called facts are nothing more than relations between concepts. This is how constructivists put it. Why do we need models, then? More or less, for the same reasons that our mind creates certain models of perceived reality, it gives it a three-dimensional character, colours, smells, and shapes. Each of these elements fulfils some sub-goal. They enable us to move about, to distinguish ridges from abysses, poisonous substances from edible ones, and to find promising partners for possible future offspring. According to constructivists, scientific models also pursue some partial goals. They should only be judged by the extent to which they achieve these goals and not from the point of view of their supposed veracity, which is inaccessible to us. Models are "empirically empty". Only when they are filled with an appropriate narrative as part of the realisation of the goal set before them can one assess to what extent the goal is actually realised. Here, however, two divergent strands can be identified. For instrumentalists, the objectives set before the models can be varied, but most often, they involve some kind of prediction of the future economic situation or a presentation in a way that is clear to the audience regarding the consequences of the assumptions made. In such a view, neither the assumptions' veracity nor the mechanism's veracity some relevant relationship revealed in the model is important (Friedman, 2008). For postmodernists, on the other hand, like the American economist Deirdre McCloskey, for example, the exclusive function of models will be their argumentative power (McCloskey, 1983). Any search for truth in models, accurate predictions or a presentation of the consequences of assumed complexities, which can instruct certain economic decisions, are manifestations of the "commandments of modernism in economics" (McCloskey, 1998, p. 143). They do not have any significant meaning. Models are "metaphors without ornaments". They must be analysed with the tools appropriate to literary criticism. They are the stories of economists who, using an acknowledged modernist paradigm, try to convince other economists or policymakers of their worldview and make decisions that suit it. Like Rodrik, McCloskey could, therefore, readily use the metaphor of the model as a fairy tale, except that its only function would be to persuade the addressee to follow the moral. On the other hand, the fairy tale characters and the circumstances in which the fairy tale writer has placed them are only meant to give the impression of resemblance to real characters and worlds.

Plurality of models

In the next chapter, "Why are handsome men not smart?", we will point out that the many different conceptions of causality have led some philosophers of science to believe that arguing about which conception is accurate makes no sense. It may simply be that we use many different categories of causality depending on the purpose for which we apply the concept. It may be somewhat similar to models. Although we create a specific conceptual category, we lump very different objects into it, which are also characterised by different purposes and levels of abstraction from our observations captured in everyday language. Rodrik, who seems firmly grounded in a realist interpretation of economic models, points out that they serve at least three different functions. Firstly, they clarify the nature of the hypotheses made, drawing attention to what their logical consequences might be, and on what they depend. In this way, like Ricardo's model of comparative advantage, they can open our eyes to non-intuitive possibilities. Secondly, they are a manifestation of the accumulation of our knowledge, at least in the sense that they expand the set of possible plausible explanations of certain economic phenomena. Thirdly, they provide a basis for designing studies to test specific hypotheses empirically or for economic policy interventions. In the latter case, the model can also serve an argumentative function. Ricardo's model of comparative advantage is essentially "empirically empty". It serves only to illustrate the consequences of the assumptions made about foreign trade. Its historical context, on the other hand, was *strictly* argumentative. This illustration of consequences served to convince decision-makers in favour of unrestricted, duty-free trade. The actual consequences were irrelevant. The enterprise model of the balance sheet and profit and loss account, or more broadly, the accounting principles, is also empirically empty as long as we do not fill it with actual data. Then, from the point of view of the specific objective of recognising the company's assets and financial situation, it becomes a decent and operationally usable approximation of such a situation. The data contained in the model, or more precisely, their specific combination, can be used to make predictions about the current and future value of the company and thus convince potential investors of the profitability of their investment. These predictions, in turn, can play a key role in a macroeconomic model of the economy based on Keynes' mathematical theory. They make it possible to predict the size of the unemployment or inflation rates. In turn, because of these predictions, they also allow difficult decisions to be made on "quantitative easing", designed to introduce a large amount of cheap money into the market to stimulate economic activity. The last model of shaping economic sentiment indicators through narratives, on the other hand, is almost purely predictive. This is because it allows, based on a prior analysis of the content of stock market reports, to determine the expected value of these indicators in advance, thus anticipating the onset of an economic slowdown.

Notes

1 We write about this, among other things, in the chapter "Why can't economists predict future crises?"
2 We write more about economic experiments in the chapter "Is economics an experimental science?"
3 The caveat about constructed rather than observed quantities stems from the fact that in economics most variables are themselves models and are to some extent constructed rather than observed. We write about this in more detail in the chapter "Why do we rely on GDP in modern economics?". At this point, it is sufficient to note that if the variable is the profit of a company, it is the result of using an iconic model such as the profit and loss account to calculate it.
4 Indeed, the distinction between idealisations and *ceteris paribus* conditions is not so obvious in the social sciences. In particular, with regard to the latter, we can both assume that certain factors do not act at all (*ceteris absentibus*), or that they take on certain constant values (*ceteris constantibus*), or that admittedly they do act but within a certain range of values that we consider normal (*ceteris normalibus*).
5 We draw attention to this in chapter "Why do we rely on GDP in modern economics?", where we write more extensively about economic concepts and measures and their operationalisation.

References

Friedman, M. (2008). The methodology of positive economics. In D. M. Hausman (Ed.), *The philosophy of economics: An anthology* (pp. 145–178). Cambridge University Press.
Grobler, A. (2006). *Metodologia nauk*. Aureus.
Hardt, Ł (2016). Modele w ekonomii. In M. Gorazda, Ł. Hardt, & T. Kwarciński (Eds.), *Metaekonomia. Zagdnienia z filozofii ekonomii*. Copernicus Center Press.

Hardt, Ł (2017). *Economics without laws: Towards a new philosophy of economics*. Palgrave Macmillan.
Hoffman, D. (2019). *The case against reality: Why evolution hid the truth from our eyes*. W.W. Norton & Company.
McCloskey, D. N. (1983). The rhetoric of economics. *Journal of Economic Literature, XXI* (June 1983), 481–517.
McCloskey, D. N. (1998). *The rhetoric of economics*. The University of Wisconsin Press.
Ng, T., & Wright, M. (2007, December). Introducing the MONIAC: An early and innovative economic model. *Reserve Bank of New Zealand: Bulletin*, *70*(4), 46–52.
Nyman, R., et al., 2018. *News and narratives in financial systems: Exploiting big data for systemic risk assessment* [Online]. Available at: https://www.bankofengland.co.uk/working-paper/2018/news-and-narratives-in-financial-systems [Accessed 15 December 2018].
Ricardo, D., 1821. *On the principles of political economy and taxation* [Online]. Available at: http://www.econlib.org/library/Ricardo/ricP1.html [Accessed 03 June 2013].
Rodrik, D. (2015). *Economics rules: The rights and wrongs of the dismal science*. W.W Norton & Company.
Tischner, J. (2018). *Historia filozofii po góralsku*. Wydawnictwo ZNAK.

12

WHY ARE HANDSOME MEN NOT SMART?

Why write about causality at all?

After all, everything is clear. If regular polls were carried out, it would quickly become apparent that the majority of those questioned would have no problem in correctly identifying cause-and-effect relationships in the reality around us, whether these are relationships in the material or social world. A pedestrian, the writer Berlioz, slipped on the sunflower oil spilt in the street by Annushka and fell so awkwardly under the tram that his head was cut off.[1] The cause of Berlioz's severed head is, therefore, the oil spilt by Annushka. The rising wages mean that people have more money, so they buy more, and prices rise. The cause of inflation is, therefore, the increased income of the population. Simple economics. Why complicate it? And yet, in practice, establishing causal relationships is not so simple at all.[2] At the same time, it is important, especially for economists who, on the basis of their supposed knowledge of these relationships, recommend governments to introduce certain economic programmes.

The examples indicated reveal two essential features of our human and scientific thinking about reality. Firstly, it is all-embracing causal – in almost every observed sequence of events, we look for causes and effects. In fact (as numerous studies in cognitive psychology indicate), we are unable to think about the world in any other way than causally. We also perceive connections between events where there are none (or where it is impossible to identify them with tools slightly better than our intuition). Imagine for a moment that you are an independent person and, in order to spice up your social life, you regularly go on dates with friends you meet at social events or on social networks. After a while, you notice a strange pattern. Although the partners you meet have varying levels of attractiveness (for simplicity's sake, let's assume a handsome/unhandsome dichotomy), the handsome ones are more likely to appear dumber. Experience suggests that nature compensates for

DOI: 10.4324/9781003469384-16

a beauty deficit with greater intellectual ability. The fact that this is not the case, however, is described further on.

Secondly, we explain the world causally. The most common conception of scientific explanation in the philosophy of science (i.e. the conception of what scientific explanation is and when it is considered good) refers to causation. Pointing to spilt oil as the cause of a traffic accident and thus the death of the writer Berlioz, although singular in nature, is a scientific explanation. Since economics aspires to be a science, it demands similar explanations.

Regularity versus causality mechanism

Both of the above examples also reveal our basic, intuitive understanding of causality: whenever events occur regularly, immediately one after the other, and remain in spatial "contact" with each other, we can say that the earlier was the cause of the later. The first to define causality in this way was the Scottish philosopher David Hume (1711–1776) (Hume, 2000). This definition is the basic reference point and constitutes the so-called regularity theory of causality. However, it soon became apparent that it was not very accurate. Indeed, there are many cases in which regularly and immediately consecutive events are not causally related. A falling barometer reading regularly precedes a change in the weather, but the barometer does not cause this change. There is, therefore, a need to distinguish causal processes from the mere co-occurrence of phenomena. An idea for this might be, for example, to examine the actual "tangency" or the requirement for some "marker" to be carried between causally related events. The example of the oil spill seems to illustrate this well. Each sequence of events appears to be in physical connectivity with the previous one and the next one (although as we descend to the quantum level, this is no longer so obvious). The second example (causes of inflation), referring directly to causal interactions in economics, is already more problematic from this point of view. For this reason, such a concept (Salmon, 1998) finds moderate application in economics, ceding the fields to the so-called mechanistic concept. The latter, in the most general terms, boils down to the assumption that there are certain pathways of causal links that are linear in nature, and we will speak of a mechanism when we identify all the causes mediating between the initial and final events and how they interact with each other. However, we are not looking for physical "tangency" or "markers" transferred between events. In the example of rising prices, such a path is identified. We also have a description of how the mediating variables interact (e.g., people have more money than they spend more), which is in the nature of common generalisations. What is lacking in this example is putting them into a mathematical relationship (e.g., as much more money will be spent in the market as people earn more). However, it has to meet several conditions for the mechanism to work. In the social sciences, and economics in particular, the most problematic are the conditions of invariability under intervention and the condition of modularity. The former states only that if, instead of a 10% pay rise, a 25% pay rise were executed, the underlying generalisation (the more money, the more purchases) would not change. The latter states that if one of these generalisations would nevertheless change for some reason (e.g., despite increased purchases, prices do not rise), this is without affecting the other generalisations (e.g., the fact that as people earn more, they spend more) (Woodward, 2002). The modularity condition is difficult to capture in the above example with inflation, as the generalisations indicated there are on the same "causal path". This means we are presented with a single sequence of related causes and effects (A causes B, B causes C, and C causes D) with no side effects (e.g., A causes B, but B may also change due to side cause Z). Such an unambiguous pathway means that a change in the preceding generalisation (A causes B) must necessarily affect the subsequent ones (but not vice versa). However, let us imagine that we describe these generalisations by some linear relationships:

1 In a given period, consumers spend exactly as much as they earn.
2 Inflation over a given period increases by exactly the percentage by which consumers spent more money in the market.

In the event that the first generalisation changes and is expressed in a slightly different formula (e.g., it turns out that consumers spend only part of their income and save the rest), however much the amount of spending in a given period in the second generalisation changes, the modularity condition assumes that this will not affect the established relationship. The value of inflation will change, but the expenditure-inflation relationship will not. We will return to the problematic nature of these conditions at the end of the chapter.

Note, however, that in the example with oil, we are dealing with a sequence of events, where inferences as to their causal connections are made either on the basis of previously observable regularities, which we thus treat as common and ordinary, or on the basis of the same regularities transformed into universally valid laws of physics. If one loses her balance when she slips, she usually falls over. According to the Newtonian law of universal gravitation, she falls over because the earth's attraction acts on her. A tram whose driver notices a pedestrian falling over on the tracks will not brake on the spot because the frictional force of the brake pads against the wheels will not balance the inertia of the tram, which is related to the principles of dynamics. An intuitive or scientific knowledge of these generalisations allows us to create a sequence of causal inferences. If the writer Berlioz had taken to the air due to an oil spill, where he would have collided with Boeing 474, there would have been a gap in our causal reasoning that would have been difficult to explain. Economists trying to fill these gaps find themselves in a similar situation. Newton, however, had it simpler. Between the mass of a moving body, the force of friction and uniform deceleration, there are repeatable linear relationships that are relatively easy to establish by appropriate measurement, arriving at the equation $a = F/m$. The same relationships in economics are never absolutely repeatable and rarely linear. To identify them, we must turn to probability calculus and statistics.

Co-variability of variables and causality in the Granger sense

Let us return to the example of rising salaries and prices. There, we have a number of variables occurring in the hypothetical causal sequence indicated, which can take different values. Such a variable would be both the money supply in a given period[3] (which in turn consists of wages and subsidies received) and the averaged[4] change in prices between the beginning and end dates of that period (i.e. inflation, if prices are rising). However, it is certainly not the case, as would follow from the exemplary generalisations described above, that an increase in the money supply by a certain unit X, will cause a direct increase in prices by some unit aX proportional to X. For consumers will spend the money obtained at different times and in different amounts on different things. It may also be that some will decide to increase their savings, while others will take out additional loans, hoping they will be easier to repay. In such a situation, we can only test whether there is any correlation between these different consumer behaviours and inflation. In other words, whether there is a relationship between the values taken by the variable *PP* (money supply) and the values taken by the variable ΔC (price change) over a given period. To establish this relationship, we examine what is the probability that a specific change in ΔC accompanies a change in PP. To establish this probability, we need to analyse the changes in *PP* and ΔC over a given period. Theoretically, we can do this by designing an appropriate experiment or analysing historical data. In practice, it will more often be by analysing historical data. We are interested in how large the change in ΔC was in those time segments that preceded the change in *PP* (1), and in those in which *PP* remained constant (2). If there is no difference between the two cases, it means that ΔC is independent of *PP*. However, if we find a difference, it indicates that *PP is the* cause of ΔC in the *Granger* sense.[5] Although it sounds somewhat complicated, including the change in *PP in* the model allows us to better predict the subsequent changes in ΔC over time than if we used only the historical changes in ΔC alone for this purpose (Granger, 1980). The co-variability of variables can be measured in various ways, but the most popular method is calculating the Pearson correlation coefficient. This coefficient takes values from -1 to 1. Values of 1 and -1 indicate perfect correlation or inverse correlation (the more the first variable increases, the more the second variable decreases). A value of 0 indicates no correlation at all, i.e. a completely random distribution of results. Correlation and temporal succession allow us to infer causal relationships imperfectly. Imperfectly, because statisticians, econometricians, and social science methodologists repeat it like a mantra: *correlation is not causation.* And rightly so. Indeed, there are compelling reasons for this (Reiss, 2013):

1 Correlations are symmetrical, while causality is not. Establishing correlations between variables X and Y does not tell us which occurs earlier and which occurs later. With the continuous evolution of variables over time, simply establishing temporal succession as an additional condition for causality can be problematic.

2 The correlation of two variables does not preclude that there is a third variable that is a common cause of the correlation. The change in the barometer reading and the change in the weather in the example above will undoubtedly be correlated but not causally related. Indeed, the common cause is a change in atmospheric pressure caused by the movement of air masses.
3 Many variables in economics are conceptually related, so they will be correlated by definition (e.g., gross domestic product and gross national product). We write about this in more detail in Chapter 13.
4 If different variables share a common trend (e.g., increasing), the test will show a correlation despite the lack of causation. Comparing the size of the Nigerian population and property prices in London over the last 20 years will probably show a correlation due to the increasing trend in both cases. However, it would be difficult to imagine any causal links here.

For the above reasons, it is also problematic in economics to use the so-called Reichenbach's principle, which holds that if we have two correlated variables, A and B, then either variable A is the cause of variable B, or B is the cause of A, or there is a third variable C, which is the common cause of A and B.

Over-representation of not-so-smart men among the handsome

Reichenbach's principle, often expressed with the slogan "*no correlation without causation*", will also not work if we, often unintentionally, preselect data for *correlation* analysis. Imagine a simple experiment. We toss 100 times two identical coins, which, by assumption, land completely randomly on a tail or on a head on the table. We record the results only if one of them (any of them) lands on a tail. Looking at the table we have made, which probably contains around 75 entries, we notice a surprising regularity: every time the first coin lands on a head, the second lands on a tail. The relationship is clear. Does this mean that the outcome of the first coin affected the outcome of the second? Of course not. The preselection we made and discarding all "head-head" results from the record introduced a so-called collider into the system. There is no relationship between the result of the first and second coin. Both results, however, affect the selective recording (collider), which thus shows an apparent relationship between the results (Figure 12.1).[6]

This preselection fallacy is prevalent in both scientific research and everyday life. Let's return to the example described at the beginning of the chapter, where, based on dating observations, one could conclude that handsome men seem intellectually weaker. However, this is not an accurate observation. The distribution of both attributes (handsome/unhandsome) may be entirely random. What is not random, however, is the selection of dating partners. One can take a chance with a handsome man about whose intellectual abilities one knows nothing. Or one can take a chance with an unhandsome one who has piqued our intellectual curiosity, but the unhandsome one, about whom we know nothing, will be eliminated in the

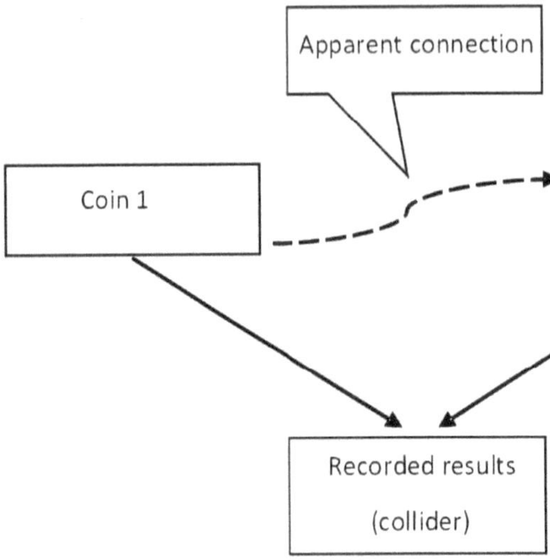

FIGURE 12.1 Collider

Source: Own compilation based on Pearl and Mackenzie (2018)

run-up. With such a preselection, we will have a clear over-representation of stupid and handsome ones. A similar problem occurs in scientific research. It was first observed in medicine when researchers attempted to establish the correlation (or implicitly the causes) of specific ailments by studying hospitalised people, forgetting that not everyone with a particular ailment ends up in the hospital. However, it is also common in economics. When we try to answer whether large corporations pay less income taxes (implicitly, whether they avoid paying them), we usually analyse the share of taxes in companies' revenue within the group of entities above a certain turnover threshold (i.e. large ones). Almost every such analysis leads to a positive conclusion. The big ones pay relatively less tax. It is only that the preselection according to turnover becomes a collider and introduces an overrepresentation in the studied group of, for example, financial institutions, which, by definition, have a very high revenue but low profitability (because they earn interest or commissions on transactions), and therefore pay lower taxes in relation to turnover than small and medium-sized enterprises.

Intervention and controlled and natural experiments

All is not lost, however. If science had been based on establishing causal relationships merely by examining the correlation of variables, it would have taken us much longer to arrive at today's knowledge and would have been burdened with a number of erroneous, difficult-to-verify hypotheses. The beginning of modern science (usually placed somewhere in the 16th–17th century with an indication of Galileo and Newton) coincided with the experimental method

(Galileo) and the mathematical-deductive method (Newton). In turn, the theoretical basis for experimentation was provided by the British empiricist John Locke (1632–1704) (Locke, 1841). We devote to experiments Chapter 14. This is because, although they are not very popularly used, they are quite commonly regarded as the "gold standard" for resolving theoretical doubts and have been particularly appreciated by the Nobel Committee recently. At this point, however, they should be mentioned as a postulated method for checking causal relationships in economics. If we observe two events that hypothetically form a cause-effect pair, the simplest method of testing this relationship is to intervene in the alleged cause (making some change by eliminating, reducing or amplifying it) and observe how this change will affect the alleged effect. The causal hypothesis was wrong if it did not affect it at all. If, on the other hand, it does affect, then theoretically, we not only confirm the causal relationship but, assuming reproducibility of the results, we can establish (calibrate) the mathematical relationship. However, something that seems extremely simple in physics becomes incredibly complicated in the social sciences. Here, we will point out just three problems:

1 The problem of hidden common cause: It was mentioned above using the example of the correlation between the barometer reading and a change in the weather. We also wrote that the presence of this common cause leads to a correlation that suggests a non-existent causal relationship. With a simple diagram (as in Figure 12.2), an experiment involving a change in the value of a variable that is a hypothetical cause will reveal the absence of a correlation. Thus, if we manually move the pointer of the barometer or place it in a barometric chamber to force a change in the readings, this will not

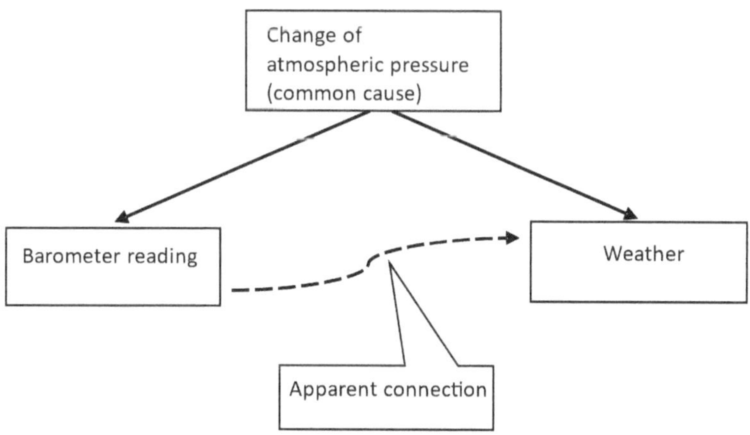

FIGURE 12.2 Common cause

Source: Own compilation

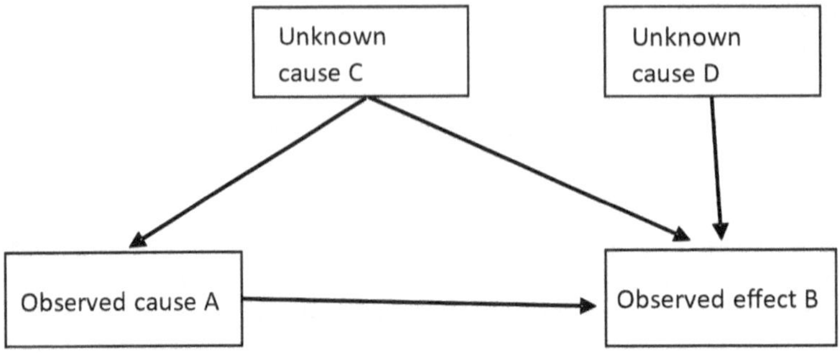

FIGURE 12.3 Unknown causes

Source: Own compilation

change the weather. However, if the correlation looks like in Figure 12.3, a simple intervention to change the value of variable A will show a change in the value of variable B and will confirm that A is the cause of B. Still, the relationship between A and B will be unstable due to unknown additional intervening causes (one common cause C and one side cause D). In turn, the intervention will not reveal the relationship at all if the unknown side cause D has a negative effect (i.e. counteracts the manifestation of effect B). The way out of this situation is to randomise (i.e. randomly select) the population of variables A on which the experiment is conducted. This randomisation is intended to make the effects of C and D also being randomly distributed, leading to the establishment of the actual relationship between A and B. An experiment based on such a scheme is called a *randomised controlled trial* (*RCT*).

2 The problem of transferability (transportability) of results: Running even a randomised experiment under laboratory conditions does not ensure that the results are applicable outside the laboratory. In economics, such experiments most often take the form of experiments on factors influencing individual economic decisions. This strand has led to the emergence of behavioural economics, experimental economics, as well as neuroeconomics, and thus to the exposure of a number of deviations from standard rationality, resulting either from the functioning of our cognitive apparatus or from the effects of specific psychoactive substances (e.g., oxytocin enhancing the tendency towards cooperative behaviour).[7] However, if we realise that the structure of causal interactions in the market almost always resembles that in Figure 12.3, these C and D disruptive factors in the laboratory, outside the laboratory multiply exponentially (E, F, G, H, … etc.) and are not necessarily determined by a randomly selected population, but result from the extra-laboratory environment in which this population has been placed.

3 The problem of experimentability: Experimentation in economics accounts for a small percentage of the research carried out. We write about this in more detail in Chapter 10. This is not only due to the general bias of economists towards experimentation but, above all, to the fact that much of economic theory is not amenable to experimentation in general. In particular, this applies to almost the entire field of macroeconomics. In many cases, the only chance to establish causal relationships is to rely on natural experiments, i.e. historically occurring situations in which an intervention in an economic variable has intentionally or accidentally occurred. Thus, there is research on the effect of the minimum wage on possible unemployment rates or the effect of the number of immigrants on resident wages, described in Chapter 8.

Multiple causality and perpetual experimentation

Among philosophers and economic methodologists, the view has recently begun to prevail that no single universal concept of causality or universal and reliable method of identifying it exists. We use different concepts and methods depending on the subject of our study and its purpose. Above, we have already identified four different concepts, starting with the oldest regularity theory, followed by statistical, mechanistic, and interventionist accounts. Each of these is accompanied by some set of distinctive methods for identifying causal relationships such as historical induction (i.e. observation of historical regularities), correlation and the statistical *Granger-causality* test, and experiments. Some, like the aforementioned Pearl, place these concepts on a "ladder of causality", recognising that in addition to differing in their purpose, they also differ in their level of cognitive (or mathematical) complexity. Regularity and statistical concepts are used to make predictions about what values economic variables will take in a certain future. The interventionist concept is used to create guidelines for specific policies at the micro level (e.g., specific rules for efficient business management) or at the macro level (i.e. rules for e.g., welfare growth). At the top of this ladder, another concept of so-called counterfactuals is placed. Historically, it also derives from Hume, who, in the same work, but in a different place, proposed a slightly different definition of causality, referring to a hypothetical but non-existent situation (if A had not occurred, then B would not have occurred either) (Hume, 2000). This conception requires the use of our human imagination to create a possible though non-existent world that differs from ours only in that cause A does not occur. Why do we need such a concept? Pearl rightly points out that it is used to assign responsibility for specific actions or omissions and to set limits to that responsibility. When company X accuses company Y for failing to perform a contract entered into between the companies and that company X has, as a result, lost a profit of Z euros, counterfactual reasoning is required to establish the connection between company X's actions or omissions.

All the indications are, therefore, that the social sciences and especially economics, reveal the peculiar nature of the concept of causation, which presents itself like a capacious bag, housing very different concepts and methods, whose contents are united only by our conceptual construction, the label given to it.

Many conceptions of causality, or causal pluralism, which do not reveal themselves with such intensity in the natural sciences, may also be the result of the peculiarities of the world of social relations. We write about this in more detail in Chapter 3. If the hypotheses formulated there are valid, this world is governed by a far greater level of complexity (however one measures it) and by the principle of uncertainty and reflexivity. The latter, in turn, leads to reflexive causal interactions. This means, in some simplification, that the arrows in Figures 12.1–12.3 could point in either direction directly or indirectly (creating circular interactions). There are many indications that, at least in some areas, this is the case. If so, the concept of mechanism, of which these graphs are a simplified expression, will have a very limited scope of application in economics. The mechanism requires the aforementioned invariability due to intervention and modularity. With multidirectional interactions, even some of which are feedbacks, both conditions will not be able to be met. Any intervention can therefore lead to a rearrangement that disrupts previously known generalisations and produces new ones. To translate this into more straightforward and practical language, perhaps one day, another public subsidy programme increasing people's income will cause its beneficiaries not to be interested in further earning and multiplying their consumption. They will start spending less, and prices will fall instead of rising. If this is the case, economists are condemned to a relentless pursuit of revealing new generalisations and causal relationships, an endless natural experiment.

Notes

1 We hope that readers will recognise in this story one of the earliest episodes from the novel "The Master and Margarita", by Mikhail Bulgakov.

2 The authors would be very reluctant to let this example, which is necessarily very simplified, become the basis for any economic knowledge of the readers. Although the relationship between money supply and inflation is often assumed in economic models, it is more complex and far more variables are involved.

3 The money supply is an economic term for the volume of money put into circulation and easily accessed demand deposits. In our very simplified model, it corresponds to the amount of money earned by consumers in a given period.

4 The question of how this averaging is or should be calculated is a separate issue, which is discussed in Chapter 13.

5 Clive Granger (1934–2009) was a British economist who won the Nobel Prize in economics in 2003 for the invention of statistical methods used to assess key properties of time series. Among other things, these methods are used to identify causal relationships between economic variables.

6 I quote both this and the following example from Pearl and Mackenzie (2018).

7 We write more extensively about this in the Chapter 17.

References

Granger, C. W. (1980). Testing for causality. A personal viewpoint. *Journal of Economic Dynamics and Control*, *2*, 329–352. https://doi.org/10.1016/0165-1889(80)90069-X
Hume, D. (2000). *A treatise of human nature*. Oxford University Press.
Locke, J. (1841). *An essay concerning human understanding*. Thomas Tegg.
Pearl, J., & Mackenzie, D. (2018). *The book of why: The new science of cause and effect*. Basic Books.
Reiss, J. (2013). *Philosophy of economics: A contemporary introduction*. Routledge.
Salmon, C. W. (1998). *Causality and explanation*. Oxford University Press.
Woodward, J. (2002, September). What is a mechanism? A counterfactual account. *Philosophy of Science*, *69*, 366–377. https://doi.org/10.1086/341859

13

WHY DO WE RELY ON GDP IN MODERN ECONOMICS?

Measurements in science and practice

On the surface, it seems that the issue of measures and measurement is extremely simple and intuitively understandable. Sometimes, mere observation is enough, which allows us to count the number of occurrences of a specific phenomenon (e.g., how many cars will pass through an intersection today). Sometimes, we need some kind of measuring device or standard for this. When Galileo Galilei dropped his objects from the Leaning Tower of Pisa, he used the height of the tower as a measure of distance. However, he also needed to measure or at least compare the time it took for two objects to fall, weigh them, and determine their volume. Each of these measurements is based on a number of assumptions. For example, such that the distance between the top of the tower and the base does not change between experiments. The stability of the measurement is also maintained by the scales and weights used, and the sand in the hourglass is always poured in the same unit of time. To determine volume, on the other hand, we need a specific theory or procedure (we can immerse an object in water and measure the amount of water displaced, or we can use the formula for counting the volume of a regular solid). However, the more we go into detail and the more our experiment depends on the accuracy of the measurement, the more problematic the measurement itself becomes. The experimenter's leaning in the tower window can change the distance covered by the object by up to several tens of centimetres, and no hourglass will measure time to the nearest second. Let's look at two other examples, more contemporary and familiar to us. A thermometer, as we know, is used to measure temperature. However, we have different types of thermometers based on a similar phenomenon: the thermal expansion of certain substances. This can be a metal (e.g., mercury) but also a spirit. Therefore, constructing a thermometer requires a

DOI: 10.4324/9781003469384-17

prior theory involving this thermal expansion, expressed mathematically, so that the relationship between temperature and the increase in volume by the substance in question can be established. It is also important to establish the scale. As we know, three different scales are commonly used and each was developed with a different application in mind. The Fahrenheit scale, where the reference point is the human body temperature, will be the best indication of how to dress. The Celsius scale, where the reference point is the freezing and boiling point of water, will find the best use in the kitchen, and the Kelvin scale, where the reference point is the state of energetic death or absolute zero, in scientific research. Quite similar is the case with distance measures, which seem to be the simplest. In the old days, they were generally anthropometric and varied depending on what was being measured and for what purpose. There were different measures for trade and others for agriculture. Hence fingerbreadths, feet, steps, ells, fathoms, or furlongs. The development of the sciences and the dependence of research on the accuracy and comparability of measurement forced a unification in the form of the SI system (*Système international d'unités* – the International System of Units), which, in terms of distance, is based on a standard of one metre. However, this standard is not used universally. For political reasons, it is not used in Anglo-Saxon countries, and for practical reasons, it is not used in maritime and aeronautical navigation. In the latter, the basis of distance measurement is the nautical mile, which corresponds to an angle of one minute on the globe, making it easier to convert distances and unit positions (latitude and longitude). However, since the earth is not a perfect sphere, one angular minute at different latitudes corresponds to different distances.

The old medieval measures, developed at a time of a burgeoning agricultural economy and trade in the old world, had their social specificity (Chwalczyk, 2019, p. 263):

1 They were meaningful, i.e. they reflected existing social relations. Measures used in agriculture were different from those used in trade. Measures of buying were different from those of selling. In turn, the differences ensured profit for privileged social groups.
2 They were strongly linked to their function. Ells were used to measure cloth, but feet measured distances in the field.
3 They were anthropometric, i.e. the primary standard was the person, their body parts, or performance.
4 They were also context-dependent, i.e. what was measured, where, and when.

With the development of science came the need to objectify and unify them. Gradually, therefore, modern measures lost their medieval specificity. However, two of their features still remain dominant. Firstly, modern measures are usually based on some kind of scientific theory, which enables their so-called operationalisation, i.e. the preparation of instructions on measuring and using them. This assumes that the theory is true, or at least plausible. Indeed, a change in theory would necessitate a change in measurement. Secondly, their use is still determined by their function, the purpose for which they were developed.

Measures in the social sciences

If measures describing the world of physical objects are far from being objective and accurate, and if even those scientifically standardised are dependent on a plausible theory and purpose for their use, what can be said of measures in the social sciences? In previous chapters, we have written about certain irremovable shortcomings of economics that make the creation of objective, circumstance-independent theories within it seem impossible. These include the complexity of the object of study, reflexivity (i.e. the interaction between a theory and its predictions) and the burden of value judgements. One would have to add to this a number of cognitive biases that distort our picture of reality, which we write about in the chapters on experimentation and rationality.[1] All this also translates into the way measures are constructed and used in economics. For let us consider what their basis is. We know a number of measures that economists use in their models, which are also commonly used in socio-economic popular journalism. The basic measure is price. However, one would be mistaken if one considered this measure objective and fixed, for we can observe it as an offer price (how much the seller is willing to sell for) or a transaction price (how much he actually sold for). We can also take many such offers and transactions in order to aggregate them (e.g., by averaging). However, there are much more complex measures. A business is usually described by its financial result, net assets, or a set of variables (measures) derived from financial statements. The economic situation of a country is determined by its gross domestic product (GDP – which we discuss in more detail below), the activity of citizens by the unemployment rate, and price changes by the inflation rate. Statistics are at the core of the aggregation of prices through all of the above indicators. Even the measurement of a company's financial result is partly based on statistical operations (e.g., the average consumption rate of fixed assets expressed by depreciation). One may venture the hypothesis that measurement in the social sciences, including economics, began with the development of the first statistical accounts by the Belgian mathematician Adolphe Quetelet (1796–1874) for the social physics of his time (Quetelet, 1835).[2] Statistics has terrible PR. It is said that there are lies, damned lies, and statistics, which is supposed to emphasise the falsification of the picture of reality made by statistical methods. There is something to it. Classical economists and economists from the Austrian School were highly sceptical of statistical methods and tried not to use them. Instead, they developed theoretical, mathematical models based on preconceived assumptions. Statistics were introduced into the salons of economics by the institutionalists, who, like the old mercantilists, were the first to use them to measure the economy. Today, we can do nothing without statistics. Even reluctant researchers make extensive use of statistically constructed economic variables. Statistics also perfectly captures what the act of measurement is all about. It is traditionally defined as the science that deals with data collection, organisation, analysis, interpretation, and presentation.[3]

Essentially, the emphasis should be on organisation and presentation. Human beings are not equipped to receive and analyse large amounts of data. In order to analyse them in any way, we need to organise and present them; in other words, simplify them. This, in turn, captures the essence of measurement itself. It allows us to transform the unobservable part of the world into the observable, resulting in "inscriptions" that allow us to "reduce" the world (Nowak, 2014). Such a definition applies to both physical measurements (temperature is an inscription indicating the unobservable energy of particles) and social measurements. In the case of the latter, this organisation and presentation of data is, by definition, done with all the stresses of our cognitive process. We organise data for a purpose. The purpose determines how they are organised. In organising them, we consider something to be right or wrong, good or bad. For this reason, we will consider some data and reject others. In one research, we will use the mean; in another, we will use the median or consider only the extreme values. Even the scale used will matter. It will make something seem much larger or almost equal. When we hear that, due to the COVID-19 epidemic, the German economy shrunk by 3.8% in 2020, we know it was not good. But more often than not, we do not think about what exactly this means or where the measure comes from.

Gross domestic product – A measure of the economy or welfare?

According to the definition used by the Eurostat, GDP is "a basic measure of the overall size of a country's economy" and equals to "the sum of the final uses of goods and services (all uses except intermediate consumption) measured in purchasers' prices, minus the value of imports of goods and services".[4] This final use is expressed in the currency of the country concerned and includes, in a simplified manner, the value of everything produced or provided as a paid service within the country in a given period. To determine this value, three approaches are possible:

1 It is possible to estimate what value has been added at each stage of service provision or production. This approach allows imported and exported goods and services to be captured appropriately. The former adds to GDP only to the extent that the activity of the production units has added value to them (value-added approach).
2 Alternatively, the total amount spent on the acquisition of goods and services can be estimated, which, after adding exports and subtracting imports, should correspond to the value of production and services (expenditure approach).
3 It is also possible to add up the value of total income from labour, capital, and government revenue, adjusted for the value of depreciation, on the assumption that what is earned is also spent (income approach).

Some countries (e.g., the United States) provide estimates separately for each approach. In the European Union, there is a Regulation No 549/2013 of the European Parliament and of the Council of 21 May 2013 on the European system of national and regional accounts, which implies a reconciliation of estimates from the generation side of GDP and from the distribution side of its components, taking into account the export balance. Community countries, therefore, count only one GDP according to a unified method, which is a composite of the two approaches. The estimation process itself, according to either of these approaches, is a complex statistical procedure that relies on a range of available data collected for various purposes, namely demographic data, labour force participation, unemployment, household budget surveys, production data, operating surplus of enterprises, imports, exports, price changes, etc. The complexity of this process and the quantity and quality of the available data mean that these estimates are far from being entirely objective and comparable, and they suffer from one of the fundamental problems resulting from complexity – structural instability. In other words, small changes in the initial data and the methods of their incorporation into the estimates lead to significant changes in the final result. These changes are made quite frequently. The revision of the EU's GDP estimation standard in 2013, which included a different treatment of research and development (R&D) expenditure (but also the inclusion of paid erotic services in GDP), led to a 2.4% revision of average GDP in the EU, and more than 4% in countries such as Sweden and Finland.[5] Even more radical may be the revisions of GDP in developing countries, such as the change in counting in Nigeria in 2014, which increased the country's GDP by 89%!

The problems with intertemporal comparisons of GDP were most vividly captured by the American economist and 2018 Nobel laureate in economics, William Nordhaus, using the example of the "price of light" (Nordhaus, 1998). In order to estimate it and compare it over time, one can, for example, count how much was spent on the purchase of light sources (from a candle to an electric bulb) in different periods. Such a comparison leads to the conclusion that this expenditure increased three to five times between 1800 and 1932. However, the juxtaposition of a candle with a 100 watts energy-saving bulb seems bizarre, to say the least. If, on the other hand, we were to approach these estimates from the efficiency side and convert the expenditure into lumen-hours, then the price would drop a hundredfold over the same period.

However, many more problems with GDP as a measure of output are well-known. First of all, it is pointed out that the measure captures too little. Historically, it was created during the period of industrialisation and was conceived as a measure of production.[6] It, therefore, does a poor job of estimating the services' value, especially if these services are unpaid, such as domestic work. The paradox of GDP is that it will be lower in a country where family members perform these jobs than where they are outsourced to hired maids. Paul Samuelson is credited with saying that GDP falls when a man marries his maid. The same is also true for unpaid public services. Paid education services increase GDP while universal, free education does not. In the digital age, a number of innovations have been added to this catalogue, which in their basic versions are available to all users free of charge: Facebook, YouTube, Airbnb, and Skype. The equivalents of these services in the past were highly charged. Paradoxically, the switch from analogue telephony to free Skype reduces GDP. Nor does this measure capture the benefits of the greater variety of products and services available. A million shoes in the same size and colour mean the same as a million shoes in different styles, colours, and sizes. Problems with inter-period comparisons also arise when completely new products enter the market, or when products that were goods until recently became services. CD (*compact disc*) and DVD (*digital video disc*) sales have turned into Spotify and VOD (*video on demand*) services. Instead of paper maps, we use services such as Google Maps or Navionics.[7]

GDP is even more problematic when we start using it as a measure of wealth. Although the index was originally designed as a measure of production, it was soon used to compare wealth between countries and their inhabitants. In order to make the data comparable, economists use the variable GDP *per capita* and GDP with respect to the purchasing power of money (PPP – *power purchase parity*). These two transformations themselves generate a number of additional problems. However, the essence of the inaccuracy lies elsewhere. This time, GDP seems to capture too much. GDP *per capita* in the United States is higher than in France, but in France, residents spend far less time at work and more time on leisure and entertainment. In such a case, it is difficult to say that the average well-being of the US resident is higher. GDP increases as industrial production increases. But this usually also means more pollution. GDP also increases with the growth of arms production, advertising services, and speculative financial services, which seem to have little to do with our well-being. Nor does GDP capture income inequality. As we already know from the chapter "Does wealth make us happier?", the link between well-being and happiness has limitations. Even if GDP were some representation of the individual income of the population, this does not necessarily mean that their subjective sense of well-being will be correlated with it in such a way that it increases as this variable increases. Easterlin's paradox, which we have written about, is a clear example of this.

The problem of devising the most appropriate measure of well-being is the subject of research by statisticians and economists (Kwarciński, 2019). So far, many have been proposed. Few, however, are actually used. Given their characteristics, two are worth noting. The HDI (*human development index*) is a hybrid measure developed by Pakistani economist Mahbub ul Haq in 1990 in collaboration with Nobel laureate in economics Amartya Sen (ul Haq, 1990). In addition to GDP, it also considers health and education. The former through life expectancy and the latter through the expected number of years of education. Although this measure adds values to income that we quite commonly recognise as significant to our well-being and tries to quantify them, its problem is, among other things, the arbitrary assignment of appropriate weights (equal in this case) to all components.

Therefore, someone has decided that we apply the same measure to education and income. Avoiding arbitrariness while taking into account components beyond income or consumption is possible within the framework of multivariate measures. Following a 2009 critique of GDP by three economists, Joseph Stiglitz, Amartya Sen, and Jean-Paul Fitoussi,[8] a set of 24 indicators grouped into 11 dimensions was developed under the aegis of the OECD (*Organisation for Economic Co-operation and Development*): housing, income, work, community, education, environment, social engagement, health, life satisfaction, security, and work-life balance. An aggregation is carried out within these dimensions, and a synthetic BLI (*Better Life Index*) is calculated. The peculiarity of this index is that everyone can generate an individual value for themselves by assigning weights to the individual dimensions according to their assessment.[9]

Operationalisation

As can be seen from the discussed example of GDP and HDI and BLI, the issue of measuring specific values in economics is immeasurably more complicated than measurement in physics. One of the imposing differences is that while in physics, we measure what we observe (some real entities or their representations), in social sciences, we have to construct these "virtual entities" for ourselves[10] (Wieczorkowska & Wierzbiński, 2011, p. 51). Such a constructed entity is usually referred to as a theoretical variable and the process of its construction, operationalisation. Thus, operationalisation is the determination of a sequence of procedures that allow the measurement of observable variables that are indicators of unobservable theoretical variables (Wieczorkowska & Wierzbiński, 2011, p. 33). Measuring observable variables can be done in very different ways. With some tolerable margin of error, we can determine visually whether someone is female or male (a bivalent variable). As in the examples at the beginning of the chapter, we can read the offered or transaction price or count the traffic volume. Or we can, as with the BLI index, conduct a survey that includes the weights assigned by respondents to specific elements of well-being. We evaluate such a construct/operationalisation according to a number of criteria:

1 The right conceptualisation of the measure. Suppose the object of our interest is the well-being of individuals. In that case, the key is a somewhat philosophical answer to the question of what should be included in this well-being, or in other words, what we consider to be good or not for individuals (or for whole societies). Certainly, a theological conception of well-being whose overriding value is the salvation of as many community members as possible will be quite different from a conception based on individual utility. Thus, underlying the conceptualisation are (often unnoticed or unconscious) choices of a moral nature.[11] The examples with GDP capturing too much or too little illustrate what the application of a measure improperly conceptualised to our idea of well-being can lead to.

2 The relevance of a measure to the adopted conceptualisation. A measure is accurate if the elements that, according to the adopted conceptualisation, make up the measure are adequately correlated with it. If, in relation to welfare, we consider its income component to be 1/3, then we expect that a twofold increase in income will translate into a 1/3 increase in welfare. In this way, the relevance of a measure will also determine the possibility of intertemporal (or interpersonal, international) comparisons.
3 Reliability of operationalisation. We can imagine the measurement process through the metaphor of shooting at a target.[12] Conceptualisation is responsible for determining the central point of the target. Accuracy will be determined by the proximity of the hit to the focal point. On the other hand, reliability is the concentration of the results of successive shots close together. The reliability of a measurement, i.e. obtaining similar results with each successive act of measurement, as long as the value of the measured variable does not change, depends on its operationalisation. Unreliably operationalised measures will require constant adjustments and modifications.
4 Empirical utility. The measure should be relatively easy to use practically and suitable for use in more complex models. A measure that is too operationally complex will be empirically unusable. One of the successes of GDP is that, while it is a poorly conceptualised measure, inaccurate, and requiring many retrospective revisions, it is also very useful empirically. Multivariate measures of well-being, which are much more accurate, are unlikely to have the same level of empirical utility.

Measures as mediating models

We have said that measures are theoretical constructs that allow us to express the unobservable by means of the observable. What we have here, therefore, is a kind of representation of some part of the economy, a useful simplification that we can use to study the relationships between different measures. In other words, what we are dealing with here is a model, and a special one at that, because it is iconic. We wrote about such models in the chapter " What models do economists use?", pointing out that a typical example of an iconic model is a map on which we present a number of different variables: distance, relative, and absolute altitude, location of certain objects, names of places, etc. A better comparison (especially with regard to GDP) would be the representation of a company in the form of financial statements (also indicated in this chapter). With such a comparison, GDP would correspond to the profit and loss account. Indeed, although GDP is used as a measure of wealth, in fact, as described above, it measures production or consumption in a given period, among other things, through the income generated in that period. A balance sheet approach to a country's wealth is possible, although practically unused, and would probably better reflect what we mean by wealth, although it would be unlikely to be suitable for determining quality of life or well-being.[13] In each of these cases, however, we are dealing with a model that mediates between observable phenomena and a directly unobservable quantity, transforming it in the process of operationalisation into an "observable" measure. Such a model is the input to the mathematical models constructed by economists. If we consider that it may be composed of many other mediating models, which are constructed sub-measures, and that these sub-measures are the result of a conceptualisation based on knowledge derived from mathematical models, then the world of economics appears as an infinite hierarchy of models, alternately iconic and mathematical. The peculiarity of these models that operationalise some economic variables is that they resemble old medieval measures more than physical SI measures (Chwalczyk, 2019).

1 They are meaningful by reflecting existing social relations. The example of unpaid domestic work, most often performed by women, not included in GDP illustrates this well. A similar function is also served by capitalising R&D expenditures according to EU standards, which reflects our approach to innovation and innovative economies.
2 They are subordinated to the function they perform. This feature seems the most obvious, and this subordination is essentially positive, as it indicates a correct conceptualisation. The trouble is that while physical measures have multifunctional value (the same measure can be successfully used for many different purposes), economic ones are most often not suitable for this. This is illustrated by the example of GDP, which leads to numerous paradoxes when used as a measure of well-being.
3 They are context-dependent. The measure changes its value depending on where and when we apply it. In addition to the examples of different types of revision of GDP identified in the text, the most glaring cases are those of "negotiating" its value for specific needs, as China did in 2000 for more favourable credit terms at the World Bank.
4 And they are at least partly anthropometric. The anthropometricity of a measure will become apparent wherever its component is subjective evaluations, such as the weights assigned to particular dimensions of the BLI or the valuation of an increase or decrease in income in the context of the valuer's current financial situation.[14] While this feature is removable in physical measures, its elimination in economic measures seems unattainable as long as economics remains a science with human actions at its core.

However, suppose we treat measures as iconic models that mediate between observable and unobservable economic reality. In that case, their conscious use in mathematical economic models, as well as their construction, becomes an incredibly important activity for economists. The quality of economic models and theories depends on how accurate, reliable, and empirically useful they are.

Notes

1 In Chapter 14 and the concluding chapter, Chapter 17.

2 Quetelet did not develop these accounts so much, but rather creatively applied already existing methods to the social sciences for very practical purposes. Among other things, astronomers used statistics to average out measurements. This is because it has been discovered that repeated observations give slightly different results each time due to measurement errors. The distribution of these results corresponds to the well-known Gaussian normal distribution, which allows the most accurate result to be calculated statistically. Quetelet applied these methods for practical purposes such as crime analysis, human body size, or the obesity index, now called BMI (body mass index).

3 Such a definition can be found in Wikipedia. However, many authors avoid defining statistics, being aware of how many issues are covered by this auxiliary science. Some distinguish between descriptive statistics (dealing with description and ordering of data), inductive statistics (dealing with statistical inference), and exploratory statistics (dealing with data analysis for hypothesis generation or data maining) (Polasek, 1994). But the authors of a popular Polish textbook write simply that it is "a tool to help answer interesting research questions" (Wieczorkowska & Wierzbiński, 2011).

4 https://ec.europa.eu/eurostat/statistics-explained/index.php?title=Glossary:Gross_domestic_product_(GDP) (Accessed: December 2024).

5 Of course, the decisive factor was not paid erotic services but R&D expenditure. Instead of treating them as so-called intermediate consumption, i.e. expenditure consumed entirely in a given period for the production process, it was decided to "capitalise" them, i.e. to consider them as acquired assets, and the cost that reduces production is their consumption over time, i.e. depreciation. As a result, the countries spending the most on research and development benefited the most from this operation, https://stat.gov.pl/download/gfx/portalinformacyjny/pl/defaultaktualnosci/5526/5/1/3/esa2010_pl.pdf (Accessed: December 2024).

6 The first estimate of national product was presented to the American Congress in 1934 by Simon Kuznets, an economist of Russian origin. A relatively standardised account was developed under the aegis of the UN by Richard Stone in 1950.

7 A popular online service that replaces nautical charts and facilitates cruise design, also available offline as part of a subscription.

8 The commission, chaired by Joseph Stiglitz, was set up by the French government in 2008 to determine how welfare and social progress should be measured without basing it on GDP. The final report was published in 2009 (Stiglitz et al. 2009).

9 To do so, you can visit the following: http://www.oecdbetterlifeindex.org/#/11111111111

10 This division seems intuitively accurate, but it is not evident to constructivists. For they may accuse it (not without reason) that concepts in the natural sciences also have the character of constructs, although perhaps made at a different level, and that their alleged observability is a cognitive illusion. In the philosophy of science, it is quite commonly accepted that observation is always "theorised" and that there is no such thing as pure facts uncontaminated by theoretical framing.

11 Unfortunately, the above may also lead to the inconclusive nature of certain conceptualisations that cannot be resolved by a simple survey of what people consider to be good. This is because, many times, what is perceived as good can lead to a deterioration in the well-being of a community, even if the same well-being criteria are maintained. In turn, what is perceived as a nuisance (e.g., having to adhere to some rigid legal and moral canon) can lead to an otherwise desirable cultural expansion of a community (Gorazda, 2017).

12 We have taken the liberty of borrowing this metaphor from Wieczorkowska and Wierzbiński (2011, p. 57).

13 This approach is used, among others, in the UN *Inclusive World Report 2012*, https://digitallibrary.un.org/record/784798, which distinguishes three types of assets: productive capital (machinery, equipment, buildings), social capital (education and skills), and natural capital (farmland, forests, natural resources).

14 We write about this in part in the chapter " Does wealth make us happier?". When we subjectively assess the change in our well-being with the gain of additional income or with the loss of it, our assessment will be different depending on what proportion that income represents in relation to our wealth. A £1,000 for a poor person and a rich person translates quite differently into their sense of satisfaction or loss.

References

Chwalczyk, F. (2019). Miary jako modele pośredniczące między gospodarką a ekonomią. In W. T. Kwarciński i & A. Wincewicz-Price (Eds.), *Metaekonomia II. Zgadnienie z filozofii makroekonomii* (pp. 253–286). Copernicus Center Press.

Gorazda, M. (2017). Law as a means to an end. Undecidability of the end problem. *Polish Law Review*, *3*(1), 63–79.

Kwarciński, T. (2019). Koncepcje pomiaru dobrobytu: założenia filozoficzne, kontrowersje metodologiczne i zastosowanie w polityce publicznej. In W. T. Kwarciński i & A. Wincewicz-Price (Eds.), *Metaekonomia II. Zagadnienia z filozofii makroekonomii* (pp. 373–404). Copernicus Center Press.

Nordhaus, W. D. (1998). Do real-output and real_wage measures capture reality? The history of lighting suggests not. Cowles Foundation Paper (957), pp. 28–66.

Nowak, A. W. (2014). Czy możliwa jest metrologiczna suwerenność? Metrologia i ekonomia polityczna miary. *Przegląd humanistyczny*, *5*(446), 19–32.

Polasek, W. (1994). EDA. Explorative datenanalyse. *Einführung in die deskriptive Statistik* (2nd ed.). Springer.

Quetelet, A. (1835). *Sur l'homme et le développement de ses facultés, ou Essai de physique sociale*. Bechelier, Imprimeur-Libraire.

Stiglitz, J., Sen, A., & Fitoussi, J.-P. (2009). The measurement of economic performance and social progress revisited. Reflections and Overview. Retrieved May 18, 2020, from https://web.archive.org/web/20140211022119/http://www.stiglitz-sen-fitoussi.fr/documents/overview-eng.pdf

ul Haq, M. (1990). *Human development report 1990*. Oxford University Press.

Wieczorkowska, G., & Wierzbiński, J. (2011). *Statystyka. Od teorii do praktyki*. Wydawnictwo Naukowe Scholar.

14

IS ECONOMICS AN EXPERIMENTAL SCIENCE?

I have just received £100 from a philanthropist – a stranger with an unusual sense of generosity. However, this gift comes with a condition: I must divide the amount between myself and you, dear reader. While I alone decide how much each of us will receive, it is you who will determine whether we receive anything at all. According to the philanthropist's terms, you have the power to either accept or reject my proposal. If you accept, we both receive the amounts I have allocated. If you reject, we both walk away with nothing.

Here is my proposal: £99.99 for me and £0.01 for you. Do you accept? It is almost certain that, disgusted or amused by my "generous" offer, you will reject it outright, leaving us both with nothing. What does this behaviour indicate? As usual, there are two messages – one optimistic and one less so. The good news is that your response aligns with that of most perfectly normal individuals. The bad news, however, is that you are behaving irrationally like them.

Econs versus humans

The ultimatum game we have just played is frequently employed in laboratory research on human rationality. According to the principles of rational choice theory, which will be discussed in greater detail in the chapter "Do humans think rationally?", rational agents always prefer more to less. Consequently, in seeking to maximise their payoff, the bidder should keep £99.99 and offer only £0.01 to the other player. Furthermore, a rational recipient should accept this offer, recognising that £0.01 is still preferable to nothing.

DOI: 10.4324/9781003469384-18

However, empirical studies reveal a different reality: most individuals tend to split the amount evenly. Offers of a 70–30% split are rejected in over half of cases. Similar findings have been replicated in hundreds of experiments conducted across numerous countries and diverse cultural contexts. As Ken Binmore, an economist specialising in game theory, notes, this result is not entirely universal, but one must venture to the remotest corners of the world to encounter significant deviations (Binmore, 2007).

If the majority of individuals are not hyper-rational "Econs" but rather emotion-driven, fairness-seeking "Humans", then this raises an important question: What is the utility of economic theories that rest on the assumption of rationality in market participants? This line of enquiry has inspired a body of experimental research pioneered by Daniel Kahneman and Amos Tversky, Israeli-American psychologists and economists, aimed at testing, and often challenging, the assumptions of mainstream economic theory. By employing behavioural experiments, this research has systematically identified cognitive biases (also referred to as heuristics or cognitive errors) that, if shown to be reproducible and consistent, could serve as the basis for revising these assumptions and refining economic models accordingly.

One such cognitive bias is the anchoring effect, introduced in the chapter "Is a state entitled to 'nudge' citizens?" The anchoring effect describes the tendency to rely excessively on the first piece of information encountered when making assessments or estimates. This initial reference point, or "anchor", influences subsequent judgements, even when the anchor is irrelevant to the issue at hand. In an experiment conducted by researchers at the University of Virginia, participants were asked to provide their national insurance number before estimating the number of physicians in New York. The results demonstrated a clear pattern: estimates were systematically influenced by the digits of the participants' insurance numbers. Participants with higher last five digits of their insurance number tended to overestimate, whereas those with lower last five digits underestimated the number of physicians (Wilson et al., 1996). This experiment underscores that such effects, if consistently reproducible, represent a significant departure from the principles of rational choice, thereby undermining the predictive accuracy of economic models.

Another experiment conducted by Kahneman and Tversky revealed a systematic cognitive bias caused by framing effects, which result in inconsistent preferences when identical options are presented differently. In the experiment, participants were asked to imagine a scenario in which the United States is preparing for an outbreak of an unusual Asian disease that could potentially kill 600 people. Two alternative treatment programmes were proposed:

- Program A: 200 people will be saved.
- Program B: There is a 1/3 probability that 600 people will be saved and a 2/3 probability that no one will be saved.

When presented with these options, the majority of respondents preferred Program A. However, a second group of participants was presented with the same problem, framed differently:

- Program C: 400 people will die.
- Program D: There is a 1/3 probability that no one will die and a 2/3 probability that 600 people will die.

In this case, the majority of respondents preferred Program D. Despite the fact that Programs A and C, as well as Programs B and D, are objectively identical, participants' choices were influenced by the way the outcomes were framed. Preferring Program A over B while simultaneously preferring Program D over C constitutes a violation of the consistency condition in rational choice theory. These findings highlight that individuals do not base decisions solely on "bare facts", such as the expected utility of different outcomes. Instead, decisions are shaped by the interpretation of facts, which is profoundly influenced by how the information is framed.

Kahneman and Tversky also explored the phenomenon of mental accounting through another experiment. Participants were asked to imagine attending the theatre, where a ticket costs $10. Two scenarios were presented to separate groups of respondents:

1 In the first scenario, while already inside the theatre building, participants discover that they have lost a $10 bill. When asked whether they would still pay another $10 for the ticket, 88% of respondents indicated they would do so, while only 12% said they would not.
2 In the second scenario, participants discover that they have lost their $10 ticket, which cannot be replaced. When asked if they would purchase a new ticket for $10, only 46% of respondents said they would, while 54% indicated they would not.

Although the monetary loss is identical in both scenarios, respondents exhibited significantly different preferences. According to rational choice theory, the decision to pay for a new ticket should remain the same in both cases. The inconsistency is attributed to mental accounting: in the first scenario, the $10 bill is treated as unrelated to the theatre budget, while in the second scenario, the lost ticket is perceived as a direct loss to the "theatre expense account". As a result, participants are more reluctant to pay for the same experience a second time (Kahneman & Tversky, 1981, pp. 453–458).

Undoubtedly, behavioural experiments have significantly deepened our understanding of how people make decisions. These experiments also challenge the fundamental assumptions underlying economic theory. However, does the fact that real, flesh-and-blood humans are not perfectly calculating "Econs" truly present a problem for economic theory, which seeks to explain market processes? This question, too, can be addressed through the design of an appropriate experiment.

A $30 billion experiment

An experiment demonstrating that individuals' lack of perfect rationality is not necessarily a barrier to market rationality was designed by Vernon Smith, the American economist who, along with Daniel Kahneman, was awarded the 2002 Nobel Prize in economics. This experiment, known as a double auction, involves a limited number of participants divided into sellers and buyers who engage in a bidding process. Sellers aim to sell hypothetical goods, while buyers bid to purchase them. Each seller knows the cost of producing each unit of their good (marginal cost), and each buyer is aware of the utility they derive from consuming each unit they purchase (marginal utility). However, this information remains private to each participant.

The purpose of the auction is to determine the selling price of each unit of the good offered. The seller's profit is calculated as the difference between the selling price and the marginal cost, while the buyer's advantage is the difference between the marginal utility and the negotiated price. This is termed a two-sided auction because sellers can propose prices for their goods, and buyers, responding to these bids, can submit counter-proposals for the prices they are willing to pay. The result of this dynamic process is a transaction price closely aligned with the price predicted by the perfectly competitive market model.

The final transactions in such experiments often occur at a price near the theoretical equilibrium price – the price that balances supply and demand in a perfectly competitive market. This equilibrium price is also referred to as the market-clearing price (Jaworski et al., 2010). Consequently, the experiment reveals that individual participants in the market do not need to be perfectly rational for the market as a whole to function efficiently. Even in the absence of complete information, with occasional miscalculations and relatively few participants, the market mechanism remains efficient, producing outcomes that align with theoretical predictions. This price mechanism spontaneously organises the decisions of buyers and sellers, harnessing their distributed knowledge. Such experiments, often referred to as market experiments, focus on the rationality and efficiency of the market itself, rather than on the rationality of individual participants, as is the case in behavioural experiments (Maas, 2014).

The practical importance of empirically testing whether markets operate efficiently under given conditions cannot be overstated. A particularly notable example of this, already mentioned in the chapter "Why can't economists predict future crises?", is the auction of third-generation (3G) telephony operator licences conducted by the UK government in April 2000. While the media speculated that the auction would generate revenues of £2–4 billion (US$3–6 billion), the actual revenue amounted to £22 billion (US$34 billion) – five to ten times the anticipated amount. This unprecedented success of the "biggest auction in history" raised the expectations of other European governments preparing to sell their own 3G licences. However, these subsequent auctions proved disappointing. For instance, in Italy, only €14 billion was raised compared to an expected €25 billion, while in the Netherlands, just €3 billion was generated against a projection of €10 billion (Klemperer, 2002).

Why did such stark differences occur? Ken Binmore and Paul Klemperer, the economists who designed the UK auction, attributed its success to meticulous planning, which included laboratory testing of alternative auction designs tailored to local conditions. For example, in the UK, five licences were auctioned, while the telecommunications market had four major players. This ensured that competition extended beyond the dominant players, as smaller companies also had an incentive to bid. Measures were also put in place to encourage competition and prevent collusion among bidders. Unfortunately, such careful preparation was lacking in other countries (Binmore & Klemperer, 2002). As Klemperer (2000) aptly stated, "European governments would be foolish not to imitate the UK in designing mobile frequency auctions but would act just as foolishly by blindly copying the UK design without paying attention to the specifics of local conditions". The disappointing outcomes of auctions in several countries underscore the importance of tailoring market designs to specific objectives and circumstances through experimentation.

Laboratory experiments allow researchers to observe human behaviour in controlled environments, enabling them to test whether participants act in accordance with economic theory (behavioural experiments) or whether specific market designs (e.g., particular types of auctions) ensure efficient outcomes (market experiments). The experimenter defines key parameters, such as participants' initial resources, the benefits and costs influencing their actions, and the institutional rules they must follow. These include the language of communication (e.g., offers, acceptances) and the methods by which information is exchanged among participants. Subsequently, the experimenter analyses participants' behaviour as a function of these environmental and institutional factors (Smith, 1994). In practice, behavioural and market experiments are usually conducted in purpose-built computer laboratories. Participants, seated in individual booths, begin by reviewing instructions, completing one or more trial rounds to clarify any uncertainties, and then proceeding to the main experiment.

Although both behavioural and market experiments share similar methodologies, as they are conducted in laboratory settings, their conclusions differ fundamentally. Behavioural experiments consistently reveal that human behaviour deviates systematically from the rational optimum. Individuals' current preferences often diverge from what they would choose if they were fully rational and informed. These findings provide a basis for justifying state interventions aimed at correcting irrational behaviour. The increasing adoption of so-called behavioural interventions (nudges) by governments worldwide, as discussed in the chapter "Is a state entitled to 'nudge' citizens?", reflects this perspective, portraying such measures as promoting citizens' well-being by addressing their irrational tendencies.

In contrast, market experiments highlight the inherent advantages of the free market system, demonstrating that market coordination mechanisms can function efficiently even when individual participants deviate from ideal rationality. This evidence forms the basis for advocating free market solutions over state intervention (Maas, 2014).

However, the relationship between state interventions and market functioning is far more complex than the general conclusions from laboratory experiments might suggest. In some cases, the need to address public policy challenges prompts economists to move beyond the controlled environment of the laboratory and conduct experiments in real-world settings.

How to combat poverty?

Although the number of people in the world living in extreme poverty (measured by an income of $1.90 a day) has decreased from nearly two billion in 1990 to just over 700 million in 2015, the issue of poverty remains unresolved in many regions. According to World Bank projections, the number of people living in extreme poverty is expected to continue increasing in African countries south of the Sahara, often referred to as Sub-Saharan Africa. It is estimated that by 2030, nine out of ten extremely poor people will reside in Africa. This raises fundamental questions: Why do poor countries remain poor? What are the ultimate causes of poverty? Can free market mechanisms effectively address poverty? Does the democratic system improve the plight of the poor? And is the development aid (commonly referred to as official development assistance) provided by highly developed countries truly effective?

Economists frequently attempt to answer these overarching questions about global poverty by analysing aggregate data for individual developing countries. Critics of development aid, for instance, argue that nations receiving substantial aid do not necessarily perform better economically than those that receive none. Does this argument provide a strong basis for discontinuing aid programmes? Not necessarily. It is plausible that countries where millions still live in extreme poverty would be in an even worse position without such aid. The truth is, we do not know for certain. In this regard, we can only speculate.

However, there is an alternative approach to tackling the global issue of poverty. Instead of focusing solely on the broad, theoretical questions about its causes, we can prioritise seeking practical solutions to the specific challenges faced by the poor. What actions are genuinely effective? This is the fundamental question being asked by economists affiliated with the Abdul Latif Jameel Poverty Action Lab (J-PAL), a global research centre co-founded by Esther Duflo and Abhijit Banerjee, the 2019 Nobel laureates in economics.

One example of a specific challenge facing impoverished countries is the persistent threat of malaria. According to the World Health Organization (WHO), approximately 249 million malaria cases were recorded worldwide in 2022, resulting in an estimated 608,000 deaths. Notably, about 95% of these deaths occurred in the WHO African Region, with children under five accounting for approximately 78% of the fatalities in that region.[1] Because malaria is transmitted through insect bites, one effective measure to combat the disease is the use of mosquito nets. As Banerjee and Duflo (2011) observe, for approximately $10, a mosquito net can be provided to a poor family, along with instructions on how to use it effectively. This raises important policy questions: Should governments or NGOs provide mosquito nets for free? Should individuals in malaria-prone areas purchase them themselves? Should the price of mosquito nets be subsidised, or should they be sold at market rates?

To answer such questions, properly designed field experiments are necessary. One notable example is the work of Together Against Malaria (TAMTAM), an organisation that provides mosquito nets free of charge to maternity clinics in Kenya. Over time, TAMTAM sought to determine whether their free distribution programme was still required by offering mosquito nets at varying prices to randomly selected clinics. The prices ranged from zero to the standard price charged by other NGOs distributing mosquito nets in the region. The results were striking: demand for mosquito nets was extremely sensitive to price. While people were eager to accept free mosquito nets, even a modest cost of 75 cents per net reduced demand to nearly zero (Banerjee & Duflo, 2011).

This type of study is referred to as a randomised control trial (RCT). In principle, the procedure mirrors that of drug efficacy trials, in which a test group of patients receives the drug being studied while a control group is given a placebo. Because patients are randomly assigned to each group, their individual characteristics (such as weight, height, and metabolism) are statistically balanced between the two groups. Consequently, any improvement in the health of the test group relative to the control group can be attributed to the effect of the drug being tested. A similar approach is employed when evaluating the pricing of mosquito nets. In this case, the control group consisted of individuals who received mosquito nets for free, while the test group comprised those offered mosquito nets at various prices. Since participants were randomly assigned to each group, their personal circumstances or life situations should not have influenced the overall results.

The key to any experiment lies in the researcher's ability to control the environment in which it is conducted. This involves determining the means of communication with participants, managing the resources available to them, and introducing a specific intervention – for instance, an offer to divide the money, an auction for goods, or the option to purchase a mosquito net. Such control is most easily achieved in a laboratory setting. In randomised field experiments, however, the random allocation of participants to test and control groups compensates for the lack of direct control over the environment.

In some cases, even this level of indirect control is unattainable. Nevertheless, through careful observation and fortuitous circumstances, economists can draw rigorous conclusions from experiments where "nature", rather than the researcher, assigns participants to test or control groups.

Does an increase in the minimum wage increase unemployment?

An example of an experiment that "nature" helped economists to carry out is the renowned study by David Card and Alan Krueger (a chief economic adviser in the Barack Obama administration), who sought to investigate the impact of the minimum wage on unemployment levels. It was widely assumed by economists that government intervention to establish a minimum wage below which workers' wages cannot fall distorts the labour market. Since the minimum wage is typically higher than the wage level that would naturally be set in the absence of such interference, two effects were believed to occur simultaneously. Firstly, there would be an increase in the number of people willing to work (labour supply rises), and secondly, employers would become less inclined to hire workers at the higher mandated wage (labour demand falls). The outcome of these two processes, a rise in supply and a fall in demand, is a surplus of workers willing to work at the minimum wage level but unable to secure employment, leading to unemployment. Such reasoning, usually presented without substantial empirical evidence, is familiar to students of introductory economics courses.

Unsurprisingly, therefore, the vast majority of the economics community accepted the link between minimum wage increases and rising unemployment as an established fact until the 1990s. This orthodoxy, however, was challenged by the research of Card and Krueger. The two economists capitalised on a unique opportunity created by the decision of authorities in the state of New Jersey to raise the minimum wage from $4.25 to $5.05 per hour on 1 April 1992. In contrast, the neighbouring state of Pennsylvania maintained its minimum wage at $4.25 per hour. Both states shared similar economic conditions prior to April 1992, making this a near-perfect natural experiment to examine the effects of a higher minimum wage on the labour market.

To investigate, Card and Krueger surveyed more than 400 fast-food restaurants – such as Burger King, Wendy's, Roy Rogers, and Kentucky Fried Chicken – in New Jersey and adjacent regions of eastern Pennsylvania. They collected data on staffing levels during two distinct periods: February and March, before the wage increase, and November and December, 1992, after the policy had taken effect and its impacts were expected to materialise. Given the similarity of business conditions in the two states, the researchers concluded that any observed changes in the labour market could be attributed to the minimum wage increase (Card & Krueger, 1994).

The results of this natural experiment were unexpected. Contrary to prevailing expectations, the findings did not support the conclusion that an increase in the minimum wage results in higher unemployment. On the contrary, the data revealed the opposite relationship: an increase in the minimum wage was associated with higher levels of employment in the surveyed restaurants. According to many economists, the research conducted by Card and Krueger was pioneering, not only for its challenge to established labour market theories but also for its methodological innovation. Their study served as a model for conducting natural experiments in economics and drawing rigorous, evidence-based conclusions.

Testing the "weirdos"

Although economists are constantly inventing new ways to experiment, the experimental method remains one of the less frequently utilised approaches in economics. A review of the popularity of various research methods employed in the social sciences, based on analyses of scientific articles from the late 1990s, reveals that only 6 out of 100 publications in economics used the experimental method (Saris & Gallhofer, 2014, p. 3). While this method affords economists considerable control over the entire research process, allowing them to generate the data used to test their hypotheses, it is an exceptionally challenging task to design and conduct an experiment in a robust and reliable manner. The growing awareness of this challenge, coupled with ongoing efforts to enhance research standards in empirical economics, has been referred to as the "credibility revolution" (Angrist & Pischke, 2010).

A well-designed experiment is primarily characterised by its ability to appropriately measure variables and accurately reflect the causal relationships between them, a feature known as internal validity. For example, in a behavioural experiment investigating the anchoring effect, one might question the rationale behind using digits from an insurance number – why use the last five digits rather than three or seven? Similarly, in the mosquito net experiment, concerns could arise about whether the design truly captured the effect of the price of mosquito nets on demand. Was the educational level of participants, for instance, adequately considered? It might have been the case that free mosquito nets were distributed to better-educated individuals who would have purchased them regardless, even at a higher price. Another example is the experiment conducted by Card and Krueger, which examined changes in employment in relation to the minimum wage. Here, one could ask whether the observed changes in employment were truly attributable to changes in the minimum wage or whether other factors were overlooked, such as the possibility that entrepreneurs had anticipated the legislative proposals for minimum wage adjustments and had pre-emptively altered their employment practices.

To address such concerns, experimenters typically attempt to mitigate potential biases through randomisation, where experimental groups are selected randomly. However, good experimental design and execution alone are not sufficient. Ideally, the conclusions drawn from laboratory or field experiments, such as those conducted in Kenya, should be applicable beyond the immediate context of the study. When the results of an experiment can be generalised to the broader population, the experiment is said to exhibit external validity.

Nevertheless, experiments, even those conducted in the field, inherently create somewhat artificial conditions, making it challenging to extrapolate findings to real-world interventions. In behavioural experiments, for instance, a common limitation has been the reliance on students, often from developed countries, as study participants. Critics have described such subjects as "WEIRD" (Western, Educated, Industrialised, Rich, and Democratic). This reliance on a narrow demographic raises questions about whether the conclusions of such studies can be generalised to entire populations. These limitations became evident when efforts to replicate certain behavioural experiments in social and cultural contexts different from the original often failed to yield comparable results.

Given these challenges in conducting experiments that focus on human behaviour, can economics truly be considered an experimental science? John Stuart Mill famously argued that, due to the complexity of social reality, only thought experiments are possible in economics and that empirical data must necessarily be limited to introspection. However, as the examples in this chapter demonstrate, this perspective has not stood the test of time. While the relatively limited scale of experimental research in economics makes it difficult to characterise the discipline as an experimental science, the growing prevalence of empirical approaches signals a clear "empirical turn" within economic research.

Note

1 https://www.who.int/news-room/fact-sheets/detail/malaria? (Accessed: December 2024).

References

Angrist, J. D., & Pischke, J.-S. (2010). The credibility revolution in empirical economics: How better research design is taking the con out of econometrics. *Journal of Economic Perspectives*, *24*(2), 3–30. https://doi.org/10.1257/jep.24.2.3

Banerjee, A. V., & Duflo, E. (2011). *Poor economics: A radical rethinking of the way to fight global poverty*. Public Affairs.

Binmore, K. (2007). *Game theory: A very short introduction*. Oxford University Press.

Binmore, K., & Klemperer, P. (2002). The biggest auction ever: The sale of the British 3G telecom licences. *The Economic Journal*, *112*(478), C74–C96. https://doi.org/10.1111/1468-0297.00020

Card, D., & Krueger, A. B. (1994). Minimum wages and employment: A case study of the fast-food industry in New Jersey and Pennsylvania. *American Economic Review*, *84*(4), 772–793.

Jaworski, T., Smith, V. L., & Wilson, B. J. (2010). Discovering economics in the classroom with experimental economics and the Scottish Enlightenment. *International Review of Economics Education*, *9*(2), 10–33. https://doi.org/10.1016/S1477-3880(15)30053-0

Kahneman, D., & Tversky, A. (1981). The framing of decisions and the psychology of choice. *Science*, *211*(4481), 453–458. https://doi.org/10.1126/science.7455683

Klemperer, P. (2000). What really matters in auction design (May 2000 version). *Economics Series Working Paper 2000-W26*. Oxford: Department of Economics, University of Oxford. https://econwpa.ub.uni-muenchen.de/econ-wp/mic/papers/0004/0004008.pdf
Klemperer, P. (2002). How (not) to run auctions: The European 3G telecom auctions. *European Economic Review*, *46*(4–5), 829–845. https://doi.org/10.1016/S0014-2921(01)00218-5
Maas, H. (2014). *Economic methodology: A historical introduction*. Routledge.
Saris, W. E., & Gallhofer, I. N. (2014). *Design, evaluation, and analysis of questionnaires for survey research* (2nd ed.). Wiley.
Smith, V. L. (1994). Economics in the laboratory. *Journal of Economic Perspectives*, *8*(1), 113–131. https://doi.org/10.1257/jep.8.1.113
Wilson, T. D., Houston, C. E., Etling, K. M., & Brekke, N. (1996). A new look at anchoring effects: Basic anchoring and its antecedents. *Journal of Experimental Psychology: General*, *125*(4), 387–402. https://doi.org/10.1037/0096-3445.125.4.387

15

WHO SHOULD CLEAN THE HOUSE?

The following story was posted on the online platform Quora, where users can ask any question and receive responses from others on the Internet. Someone posed the following question: "My wife-to-be earns 4.5 LPA and I draw 20 LPA. She expects me to help her. I told her 'marry a guy who earns 4.5 LPA, he will do whatever you demand.' Why should a husband share household chores if his wife doesn't earn even half of his salary?"

The Internet's reaction was immediate and emphatic. Many users posted accurate, albeit occasionally mischievous, responses. Some suggested the man should reflect on whether he needed a wife or a maid. Others pointed out that household duties should be shared because both partners share a home. One respondent stressed that a fair division of marital responsibilities is not about splitting them equally at 50/50 but about giving 100/100 effort from both sides.[1]

This raises an interesting question: What relevance could an economist possibly have to marital issues such as the division of household duties? Could a specialist in economic models or a careful observer of financial markets offer useful insights into the matter? As it turns out, the answer is yes.

In their book, *Spousonomics: Using Economics to Master Love, Marriage, and Dirty Dishes* (2011), Paula Szuchman and Jenny Anderson, economics journalists with experience at *The Wall Street Journal* and *The New York Times*, who are also wives and mothers, demonstrate how basic economic principles can be applied to enhance marital relationships. For instance, when addressing the division of household chores, they draw attention to the benefits of specialisation, a concept first championed by Adam Smith.

DOI: 10.4324/9781003469384-19

In *The Wealth of Nations*, Adam Smith used the example of a pin factory to demonstrate that the division of labour and task specialisation led to an enormous increase in productivity. In a factory with no division of labour, ten workers might produce only 20 pins a day. However, by specialising in individual tasks, those same ten workers could produce as many as 48,000 pins per day. The same logic can be applied to a marriage. When both spouses perform the same tasks, working professionally, washing the dishes, cleaning the house, mowing the lawn, etc., time is wasted. Efficiency can be greatly improved by dividing tasks and allowing each partner to specialise in what they do best.

But how, then, should household chores be divided? Should the division be based on fairness? One might be tempted to suggest that splitting household responsibilities 50/50 is the fairest approach. After all, as we saw in the previous chapter, humans tend to reject grossly unequal distributions of wealth in the ultimatum game and gravitate towards egalitarian proposals.

However, Szuchman and Anderson (2011) challenge the idea that an equal division of responsibilities is necessarily the most effective – or even the fairest – approach. Based on interviews with numerous couples, they argue that the pursuit of equality often results in poor time allocation and heightened feelings of frustration and dissatisfaction. This is unsurprising when one considers that an equal split forces both partners to undertake tasks they may strongly dislike (e.g., washing dishes) instead of focusing on tasks that come more naturally to them (e.g., cleaning the bathroom). Moreover, striving for an equal split often requires constant monitoring to ensure both parties are contributing equally, which can itself breed resentment.

The solution, they argue, lies in applying David Ricardo's model of comparative advantage, which was introduced in Chapter 11. Ricardo's principle, originally applied to trade between countries such as England and Portugal, can also be applied to married couples and the time they spend on household tasks. To illustrate, let us examine the following hypothetical scenario based on Szuchman and Anderson's analysis.

Let us assume the couple must complete two household chores: washing the dishes and cleaning the flat. According to Table 15.1, the wife is faster at both tasks, meaning she holds an absolute advantage. However, she understandably does not want to handle all the chores on her own. Additionally, both partners agree that their ultimate goal is to save time to engage in shared activities they enjoy, such as

TABLE 15.1 Marital Comparative Advantages

Task	*Wife: Time required*	*Husband: Time required*
Dishwashing	20 minutes	30 minutes
Cleaning the flat	10 minutes	60 minutes
Total	**30 minutes**	**90 minutes**

Source: Szuchman and Anderson (2011).

attending tango classes and participating in milongas (dance events). Does it then make sense to divide the household chores equally? The answer, as the comparative advantage model shows, is no.

If the couple splits the chores equally, each partner would spend three days a week washing dishes and three days cleaning the flat. With this arrangement, the husband would spend 270 minutes per week on household chores (3 × 30 minutes for dishwashing and 3 × 60 minutes for cleaning). The wife, on the other hand, would spend 90 minutes per week (3 × 20 minutes for dishwashing and 3 × 10 minutes for cleaning). In total, the couple would spend 360 minutes per week on household tasks.

However, if they divide the chores according to comparative advantage – where the husband focuses on dishwashing and the wife on cleaning – they can save significant time. The husband would spend 180 minutes per week washing dishes (6 × 30 minutes), while the wife would spend only 60 minutes per week cleaning the flat (6 × 10 minutes). Together, they would devote only 240 minutes to household chores, saving 120 minutes each week. This extra time could then be used for shared activities like their tango lessons.

Returning to the original question posed on Quora, does the above analysis provide a satisfactory answer? At first glance, yes. Considering the comparative advantages of each spouse, including income-generating capabilities that could allow them to hire external help, seems like a reasonable approach. However, something about this rationale feels unsatisfactory. Intuition tells us that neither the benefits of specialisation nor the exploitation of comparative advantages justifies one partner, such as the better-earning husband, neglecting household duties altogether. Even if one partner is better at domestic tasks, dumping all responsibilities on them is unlikely to lead to marital harmony. Resentment may manifest in other areas of the relationship.

Specialising in specific chores, whether it be washing dishes, cleaning the bathroom, doing laundry, or paying bills, requires effort, but it is not an insurmountable challenge. The allocation of tasks is not static and must be adaptable to changing circumstances. Life events such as moving house, the birth of a child, a career promotion, or a job loss may necessitate renegotiation and the building of new comparative advantages.

Should we, then, heed the advice of economists not only when they discuss gross domestic product (GDP), inflation, or unemployment but also when they venture into the realm of marriage? What accounts for the remarkable comprehensiveness of the economic approach?

Economical toolbox

As we noted in the first part of the book, in Chapter 2, the way in which economics is understood has evolved significantly as the discipline itself has developed. Over time, economists have shifted their focus from exclusively analysing the wealth of nations to examining human choices. This shift has changed the emphasis from explaining the broader functioning of economies to analysing the rational decisions of individuals wherever there is a distribution of scarce resources.

Economics began to distinguish itself from other social sciences not by the subject it analyses (e.g., the functioning of the economy) but by the tools and methods it employs. This remarkable generality of economic thinking allows economists to interpret a wide range of human behaviours through its analytical framework. For example, economists can view spouses as entrepreneurs and interpret their behaviour as analogous to market exchanges, in which each provides the other with goods and services by dividing household responsibilities. This perspective arises because it can be assumed that each spouse has specific preferences, meaning they prefer some tasks over others and order these preferences accordingly, thereby acting rationally. Furthermore, with limited time and resources, they aim to achieve their goals at the lowest possible cost (e.g., maintaining a clean home while preserving as much free time as possible). Consequently, they strive to make optimal decisions.

By employing economic concepts such as specialisation, optimisation, and comparative advantage, it appears possible not only to explain the behaviour of entrepreneurs but also that of spouses. For instance, one might conclude that inefficiencies in the division of labour within a household may underlie some marital disputes and disagreements.

But, surely people do not get married solely to provide services to one another? Perhaps it is love, rather than participation in market transactions, that brings spouses together. Or, could love itself be incorporated into such analyses? Nobel laureate in economics Gary S. Becker observed in one of his articles that the altruism of one spouse essentially consists of the fact that their utility function is partly dependent on the utility of the other. Put differently, the more satisfied one spouse is with the relationship, the more satisfied the other is as well. If we define love as a selfless concern for the well-being of the beloved, this factor, too, can be accounted for in economic terms (Becker, 1981).

Many readers may find economic analyses of marriage to be absurd because people generally do not think or behave as though they are guided by economic motives in their marital lives. As we explained in Chapter 11, the approach popularised by Milton Friedman, known as instrumentalism, does not place great importance on whether the assumptions underlying economic models are realistic or truthful. Even if people entering marriage are genuinely motivated by love (understood differently from the aforementioned interdependence of utility functions) and not by economic calculations, and even if they never consciously attempt to maximise benefits or minimise costs in their marital interactions, the assumption that they act *as if* they were rational enables economists to explain marital success or failure. It also provides a framework for proposing solutions to potential problems.

Advocates of applying economic reasoning to marital issues might suggest, for example, that instead of arguing persistently, couples should reconsider the division of household chores. Rather than focusing on perceived injustices, they might focus on rebuilding their comparative advantages.

Although Szuchman and Anderson (2011) have demonstrated that it is possible to write a marriage guide based on economic principles, economists typically apply their analytical frameworks to more fundamental issues, which are often already addressed by other social sciences.

From human capital to social capital

An example of the expansion of economics beyond its traditional areas of analysis is the development of the concept of human capital, spearheaded by the aforementioned American economist Gary S. Becker, who was awarded the Nobel Prize in economic sciences in 1992 for his work. Human capital refers to the idea that one can invest not in buildings, machines, stocks, or bonds but in human beings. The measure of these investments is the amount of future income earned by the person. We invest in human capital primarily by acquiring knowledge, developing skills, and maintaining our health. In many countries, this concept takes on a very tangible form when, for example, students take out loans to fund their desired degree programmes. However, it is worth noting that investing in higher education is not always cost-effective. For instance, while the return on investment (ROI) for a Stanford University graduate currently exceeds 8% annually, studying at the University of Montana-Western yields an annual loss of −12%.[2]

The distinctive feature of human capital is that it cannot be deposited in a bank or brokerage firm. Here, we become both the investor and the object of investment, a resource that is always with us. If external circumstances become unfavourable to our profession, we cannot simply transfer these assets to another city or country without relocating ourselves. By contrast, those who invest in financial capital may remain in Hong Kong after its transfer to Chinese jurisdiction or in London after Brexit while shifting portions of their assets to more favourable locations. Professionals whose principal capital lies in their knowledge and skills, however, are often compelled to move if the political or economic conditions of their workplace become untenable.

What determines the quality of human capital? The simplest answer is the amount of resources invested in it. An adult makes such investments by choosing an appropriate educational path, developing abilities, and maintaining physical and mental health. However, the quality of the capital with which an individual begins their adult life largely depends not on them but on the family into which they are born. Imagine that each family is akin to a small enterprise. Like a little factory, a family utilises market goods as well as the time, skills, and knowledge of its members to "produce" outcomes such as children, meals, healthcare, and skills, along with intangible outputs such as respect.[3] Yes, one might argue that children are "goods" produced within the family. The inputs spent on their education, health, nutrition, and developmental activities determine the quality of human capital they accumulate and will later deploy in life.

By examining family relationships through the tools of economic analysis and assuming that parents are rational actors with stable preferences who aim to maximise utility, Becker provides an economic framework to address questions such as the number of children, their quality, or the structure of society (e.g., monogamous or polygamous). In his economic model of the family, Becker posits that parents with limited resources face a trade-off: they can either raise a greater number of children with lower levels of human capital or focus their financial and temporal resources on fewer children, thereby increasing their quality through better nutrition, extracurricular activities, and higher education.

Yet, are the conclusions drawn from such analyses entirely accurate? Contemporary cultural anthropologists have criticised these models, arguing that they fail to explain phenomena such as the significant decline in female fertility in developed nations (Richerson & Boyd, 2005). Similarly, economists focused on developing countries highlight the apparent irrationality of the decisions made by extremely impoverished families regarding the number of children and their education. In such contexts, fewer children are not associated with increased per-child investment in education (as Becker's model predicts) but instead with the accumulation of greater savings to secure the family's old age in the absence of many offspring. Thus, the thesis that the quantity of children is interchangeable with the quality of their education has been shown to be flawed (Banerjee & Duflo, 2011). When analysing the rationality of specific choices, economists, particularly those with what might be termed an "imperialist" mindset, often overlook the myriad seemingly irrelevant factors that shape human preferences. Furthermore, classical rationality is not the sole factor governing decision-making. Many behavioural patterns conform instead to so-called ecological rationality, which eludes the frameworks of traditional economic analysis. This concept is discussed in greater detail in Chapter 17.

The family is not the only sphere Becker analysed through an economic lens. He also explored topics such as why people commit crimes and the decisions made by individuals addicted to drugs or alcohol under the assumption that they behave rationally, that is they are capable of formulating coherent plans and acting upon them. Other scholars expanded upon Becker's work, contributing to the development of economic analyses of law (e.g., Richard Posner) and the rational theory of addiction (e.g., Kevin Murphy). The former has even evolved into a distinct school within legal philosophy (Posner, 1972). For instance, why does a criminal commit a crime? According to this approach, the individual conducts an economic calculation of the expected utility derived from the act, factoring in the direct benefit of the crime, the probability of detection and punishment, and the severity of the punishment. Thus, a rational criminal justice system ought to be designed in such a way that the product of the probability of apprehension and the severity of punishment outweighs the benefit derived from the crime, resulting in a negative utility for the offender. Judges and officials applying such a system are similarly expected to act rationally, not guided by abstract notions of metaphysical justice but rather by considerations such as the likelihood of their decisions being overturned or the potential for career advancement.

The field of politics has likewise become a significant area of economic enquiry. Public choice theory, pioneered by James Buchanan (another Nobel laureate), examines how interest groups operate. For instance, Mancur Olson studied the phenomenon of rent-seeking, where individuals or groups lobby for desirable positions or resources that governments create specifically for them (Miklaszewska, 2005). All these analyses share a common foundation: they seek to apply the logic of economic thought, with its emphasis on rational actors, competitive markets, cost-benefit analysis, and optimisation of action, to issues traditionally explored by sociology, law, political science, anthropology, or history. By expanding into the territories of other social sciences, economists engage in what Uskali Mäki, a Finnish philosopher of economics, describes as "economics imperialism" (Mäki, 2009).

The concept of social capital represents another strategy for broadening the scope of economics. While primarily discussed by sociologists (e.g., Pierre Bourdieu, James Coleman, Robert Putnam), most scholars agree that social capital involves "an instantiated informal norm that promotes co-operation between two or more individuals" (Fukuyama, 2001). By sharing common values and ethical standards, individuals foster trust, which acts as a lubricant that enhances the performance of any social group.

Economists, often criticised for focusing narrowly on the decisions of individual agents (e.g., consumers, firms) and ignoring the broader social context, recognised in social capital an opportunity to incorporate the social dimension into their models. For them, social capital primarily refers to the network of social relationships within which an individual or entity operates, connections that can be leveraged to achieve personal or professional goals. In simplified terms, this economic understanding of social capital is well captured by the saying: "It's not what you know but whom you know that matters" (Fine & Milonakis, 2009). For example, a graduate of a prestigious university often begins their career not only with specialised knowledge but also with a network of contacts who can provide support and open up opportunities.

Recognition of the social dimension of economic relations coincided with increasing awareness of the imperfections inherent in markets. For instance, when a seller knows more about a car's condition than a prospective buyer (a case of information asymmetry), transactions may fail altogether. Similarly, when households use low-quality coal for heating, they harm not only themselves but also their neighbours through air pollution. Conversely, positive externalities arise when someone beautifies their home, benefiting others by enhancing the aesthetic quality of the neighbourhood. Classic examples of market failure, such as information asymmetry and externalities (Akerlof, 1970), underscore that markets do not always function efficiently. In such cases, customs, social norms, and mechanisms of social enforcement serve as corrective tools. For instance, mutual trust between a seller and buyer can reduce transaction costs, while shared norms may discourage harmful behaviours like burning low-quality fuel.

In this way, social norms are interpreted as institutions that mitigate market failures and unnecessary transaction costs by promoting cooperative behaviour. This approach characterises the "new institutional economics" championed by economists such as Ronald Coase, Oliver Williamson, and Douglass North, all Nobel laureates. It represents a more nuanced way of "colonising" the domains of other social sciences (Fine & Milonakis, 2009).

Ultimately, the belief that economics can explain not only market phenomena but also the family, crime, addiction, the usefulness of social norms, and values lead some to argue that economics provides the most fundamental understanding of social reality.

The economist in Plato's cave

One of the best-known philosophical allegories is Plato's depiction in Book VII of *The Republic* of the image of a cave with shackled individuals who, facing the rock wall, observe only the shadows cast upon it by real objects. This shadow play is, in fact, regarded by them as reality. It is only someone enlightened by philosophy who is able to break free from the shackles, turn towards the sun, and patiently wait until his eyesight adjusts to the light in order to finally see things as they truly are. However, when the philosopher attempts to share his knowledge with those still confined to the shadows of the cave, he is not met with gratitude but with hostility. The prisoners are unable to accept that what they perceive as reality is merely a pale reflection of the real world. Surprisingly, this ancient allegory aligns well with the beliefs of certain modern economists who extend the logic of economic thinking far beyond its original scope.

Steven Levitt and Stephen Dubner, authors of the bestselling book *Freakonomics: A Rogue Economist Explores the Hidden Side of Everythin*g (2005), offer an illustrative example of this approach. They propose that "…if morality represents how people would like the world to work, then economics shows how it actually does work". One of the intriguing issues they explore is the sudden and sharp decline in crime rates in the United States during the 1990s. Many possible explanations for this phenomenon have been proposed. Experts have attributed it to innovative policing strategies, an increase in the number of police officers, changes in the drug market, an ageing population, stricter gun ownership laws, or a strong economy. However, after analysing the data, Levitt and Dubner conclude that none of these hypotheses provides a convincing explanation. Instead, they propose a provocative link between the legalisation of abortion in the 1970s and the decline in crime observed two decades later.

After the legalisation of abortion, its costs dropped significantly, making it accessible to poor, poorly educated single women. Childhood poverty and single-parent upbringing are strong predictors of a child being at risk of a criminal future. However, these same factors (poverty and lack of support from a partner) also led many women in such circumstances to have abortions. In short, Levitt and Dubner argue that the widespread availability of abortion resulted in a significant reduction in the number of potential criminals being born. They acknowledge that this conclusion may provoke disbelief and moral outrage among many. Nevertheless, they argue that it is far more convenient for people to believe that better policing strategies or economic growth were the cause of the decline in crime, even if the data suggests otherwise. According to Levitt and Dubner, asking the right questions, collecting diverse data, and applying imaginative analysis leads to a clear conclusion: the reduction in crime was an unintended consequence of the legalisation of abortion.

This approach exemplifies what Levitt and Dubner refer to as *freakonomics*, or economics, for those who think differently. It also aligns with the economic marriage guide discussed earlier in the chapter, which can likewise be classified as part of the *freakonomics* approach. Proponents of this method emphasise the importance of data collection, bold hypothesis formation, and close observation of human behaviour in response to various stimuli, both financial and non-financial. For them, economics is no longer limited to the actions of hyper-rational actors (*homo oeconomicus*) within perfectly competitive markets. Instead, they are open to incorporating insights from fields such as behavioural economics into their analyses. What is particularly distinctive about this strategy, however, is the conviction that there is a "second bottom to everything" that a well-trained economist can uncover.

Like the philosopher in Plato's cave, the freakonomist is unafraid to turn his gaze towards the sun, in his case, collecting data and analysing it. Nor does he hesitate to draw radical conclusions, even when they challenge the widely held beliefs of the "quacks" – in other words, most of us – who see only shadows of the true reality. Similarly, like the philosopher in Plato's cave, the freakonomist often encounters misunderstanding or even hostility from those around him. Most importantly, however, he possesses a deep conviction that his economic perspective enables him to see the world as it truly is. But how should we regard this attitude?

While we share the belief that many important questions can be addressed through the careful collection and analysis of data, professional scepticism nevertheless urges us to approach such claims with caution and humility. Specifically, we must question the idea that there is always a "second bottom" to every phenomenon or that an economic answer is invariably the most reliable one. Morality, for instance, not only represents the world as we would like it to be but, as demonstrated in Chapter 4, plays a crucial role in shaping that world. Indeed, morality is, at times, more "real" than economic calculations, which, as in the case of the trade in human organs for transplantation, are unable to override the moral norms ingrained in communities.

Additionally, the philosophy of economics teaches us that economic models are not devoid of value judgements and that the way we select and measure data is largely shaped by conventions. Our patterns of decision-making, moreover, are heavily influenced by the legacies of biological and cultural evolution. These patterns are often driven by the imperatives of species or community survival and expansion rather than by individual calculations of costs and benefits. Thus, while empirical measurement and analysis are indispensable, we must reject the notion that they grant us access to absolute truth. In this sense, the scepticism of the so-called quacks and their resistance to the supposed enlightenment of freakonomists is, at times, justified.

Notes

1 https://www.quora.com/My-wife-to-be-earns-4-5-Lpa-and-I-draw-20-Lpa-She-expects-me-to-help-her-I-told-her-%E2%80%98marry-a-guy-who-earns-4-5-Lpa-he-will-do-whatever-you-demand-%E2%80%99-Why-should-a-husband-share-household-chores-if-his-wife-doesnt-earn-even-half-of-his-salary (accessed: December 2024).
2 https://www.payscale.com/college-roi/page/2 (accessed: December 2024).
3 With this comparison, the publisher of Becker's book, *A Treatise on the Family,* encourages the purchase of the publication, https://www.hup.harvard.edu/catalog.php?isbn=9780674906990 (accessed: December 2024).

References

Akerlof, G. A. (1970). The market for "lemons": Quality uncertainty and the market mechanism. *The Quarterly Journal of Economics*, *84*(3), 488–500. https://doi.org/10.2307/1879431

Banerjee, A. V., & Duflo, E. (2011). *Poor economics. A radical rethinking of the way to fight global poverty*. Public Affairs.

Becker, G. S. (1981, Feb). Altruism in the family and selfishness in the market place. *Economica*, *48*(189), 1–15. https://doi.org/10.2307/2552939

Fine, B., & Milonakis, D. (2009). *From economics imperialism to freakonomics: The shifting boundaries between economics and other social sciences*. Routledge.

Fukuyama, F. (2001). Social capital, civil society and development. *Third World Quarterly*, *22*(1), 7–20. https://doi.org/10.1080/713701144

Levitt, S. D., & Dubner, S. J. (2005). *Freakonomics: A rogue economist explores the hidden side of everything*. William Morrow.

Mäki, U. (2009). Economics imperialism: Concept and constraints. *Philosophy of the Social Sciences*, *39*(3), 351–380. https://doi.org/10.1177/0048393108319023

Miklaszewska, J. (2005). Public choice theory and the post-totalitarian state. In L. Koczanowicz, B. J. Singer, F. R. Kellogg, & Ł Nysler (Eds.), *Democracy and the post-totalitarian experience* (pp. 97–105). Brill. https://doi.org/10.1163/9789401201261_012

Posner, R. A. (1972). *Economic analysis of law*. Little, Brown.

Richerson, P. J., & Boyd, R. (2005). Not by genes alone. How culture transformed human evolution (Kindle ed.). The University of Chicago Press.

Szuchman, P., & Anderson, J. (2011). *Spousonomics: Using economics to master love, marriage, and dirty dishes*. Random House.

16

DO PROTESTANTS EARN MORE?

The origins of economics (later referred to as classical economics) are marked by two names and two key works in the development of this science: Scottish philosopher Adam Smith (1723–1790) and his "An Inquiry into the Nature and Causes of the Wealth of Nations by Adam Smith" (Smith 1776), and David Ricardo (1772–1823) and his "On the Principles of Political Economy and Taxation" (Ricardo, 1821). The former work was published in 1776, and the latter in 1817. In popular perception, the former was recognised as the eulogist of free trade and the author of the concept of the "invisible hand of the market", which creates global prosperity in an invisible way based on the individual, selfish preferences of the participants in that market. The latter laid the foundations for detailed theories and models of the market and international trade, such as the theory of land rents, wages, the quantity theory of money, and the model of comparative advantage. Although both used many examples from the concrete economic reality around them, classical economics by these two precursors was developed as an ahistorical science independent of the socio-geographical context. This does not mean, of course, that Smith or Ricardo did not notice differences in the economic development of individual countries. However, they nevertheless recognised that their economic principles were universal and applicable to all people and economic communities, regardless of their historical and geographical location. From their point of view, therefore, historical and social analyses were not necessary for understanding the economy as much as for making predictions about its future development. The problem was that the predictions they formulated did not work out, which gave rise to criticism of classical economics and the emergence of the historical school in Germany and the institutional school in the United States.

DOI: 10.4324/9781003469384-20

In the 19th century, social philosophy in Germany was steeped in historical thinking, with its origins in Hegel's Romantic philosophy. It is, therefore, not surprising that economists there took it for granted that abstracting from the "spirit of the nation" in analyses of the economy could not succeed. The key to understanding economic phenomena must be a holistic analysis, encompassing all aspects of society, particularly its causal, historical path to a given stage of socio-economic development. Such an analysis makes it possible to grasp the historical regularities expressed in successive stages of development, in which different economic laws may apply at each stage. A representative of this kind of thinking was Gustav von Schmoller (1838–1917), who at one stage even got into a sharp personal dispute with Carl Menger (1840–1921), a representative of the Austrian School, who continued the classical methodological approach in this respect. Thinking in terms of the specific historical path followed by different peoples was also combined with analyses of a sociological and demographic nature. Analyses intended to identify specific cultural patterns operating in a given society or social group, transmitted from one generation to the next, were crucial from the point of view of market functioning. As the spread of these patterns and their intergenerational transmission is important, demography, which examines trends in the spread or shrinkage of specific populations, also became involved in these analyses. Thus, somewhat younger sciences, originating in post-revolutionary France, began to enter economics. Indeed, the founding father of sociology (or social physics, as he called it) is considered to be Auguste Comte (1798–1857), a student at the Paris *École Polytechnique*, and the father of modern demography and statistics, the Belgian, Adolphe Quetelet (1796–1874).

This dispute, which began in the 19th century between classical economists and representatives of the historical school, continues to this day in varying degrees and intensity. On the one hand, it is represented by mainstream economists (mainly neoclassical) and, on the other, by institutional economists. Although these schools intermingle in various areas, they differ in their assumptions and research methods. According to institutionalists, agents' behaviour in the market is not universal but strongly dependent on the social and historical context. Local culture and history shape institutions understood as locally repeated and dominant patterns of behaviour. People's actions in the marketplace will depend on institutions understood in this way, including whether they tend to respect other people's property, want to work and save, or are more inclined to make risky investment decisions, including going into debt. Institutionalists are thus oriented towards the search for these local conditions using methods characteristic of history and sociology. Theoretical models, on the other hand, the search for linear, universal relationships between abstract variables, remain the domain of mainstream economics.

Protestant ethics

One of the first thinkers to draw on the work of sociologists in economic analyses, using research methods appropriate to this field, was Max Weber (1864–1920). Although his name is associated with sociology rather than economics, he devoted a significant part of his studies to the history of the economy since ancient times, including also Asian institutions (Weber, 1922, 2011). He became famous for his study of the influence of religion on the economic development of certain regions (Weber, 2002). The question he sought to answer was more or less the same as the one posed by Adam Smith: What makes some nations richer and others poorer? The answer he proposed on the basis of his research, however, was quite different from that given by Smith. Indeed, Weber's thesis was that the specific Protestant ethic, which boiled down to a work ethic, limiting consumption, and reinvesting accumulated resources, contributed to the significant enrichment of those German states where this religion predominated, while the states where Roman Catholicism predominated remained agricultural and less prosperous. It is worth noting at this point some characteristic elements of Weber's study:

1 By definition, it is very anti-classical. Any rational, wealth-seeking *homo oeconomicus* should, in effect, develop similar strategies of action. These might include diligent work, saving and investing capital surpluses. Classical economists did not assume that these strategies might differ depending on the environment in which the economic man operates. Differences in wealth could be determined by events independent of human action (e.g., natural disasters). In contrast, Weber came to the conclusion that not only our strategies are different but also this difference is due to religion.
2 The study is based on historical data and quantitative (statistical) methods. It is, therefore, empirical in nature and is not accompanied by any abstract mathematical model. However, Weber's conclusions actually lead to the formulation of a certain "loose" model of the causal relationships between variables characterising members of evangelical churches and their affluence. The model is "loose" as these variables do not lend themselves to quantification (they are difficult to describe numerically).
3 The study is, unfortunately, subordinated to Weber's prior ideological convictions. He made no secret of his nationalism (expressed, among other things, in his anti-Polonism) and his Hegelian conviction that the Protestant religion was somehow naturally compatible with the spirit of the German nation.

This last element has weighed on the results, which are widely questioned today. On the one hand, they are criticised by economic historians, drawing attention at the time to countries such as Catholic and rich Belgium and Protestant, as well as agricultural and poor Sweden (Hartwell, 2017). On the other hand, they are criticised by economists who, in a way, are repeating Weber's analyses from different historical periods but using contemporary statistical tools, either find no significant relationship between dominant religion and wealth (Cantoni, 2015) or argue that education, rather than religion, was the genuinely significant factor. Thus, education would constitute the common cause of both phenomena (wealth and Protestant denomination) mentioned in the chapter on causality,[1] often misleading researchers (Becker & Woessmann, 2009). Nonetheless, Weber's method and the thesis he formulated have made a permanent mark in economic thought. Their aftermath is the arguments that arise from time to time about the causes of significant differences in the wealth of certain countries or social groups. One example is the division of European countries, especially after the financial crisis of 2007/2008, into a rich (Protestant) north and a poor (Catholic or Orthodox) south, with rising unemployment and public debt. However, the boundaries may also run along wealth lines, e.g., through the recurrent hypothesis that extreme poverty (but also extreme wealth) is conditioned by particular, repetitive patterns of behaviour that make it hard for the poor to break out of the poverty trap (Banerjee & Duflo, 2011).

The reader expecting some kind of unambiguous answer here as to whether the individual qualities of the inhabitants of a certain region actually determine its economic development will be disappointed. Weber has been followed by other researchers who have tried to identify these determinants and whose research is not and will not be conclusive. The ambiguity, however, is not because we have a problem identifying specific social groups or nations that seem to get rich faster than others. Whether it be the already emblematic Protestants, Jewish diasporas in the United States, Episcopalians or Sikhs in India, their membership of a particular church is correlated with, but not necessarily a cause of, greater wealth. In other words, if one joins an Episcopalian church, one does not necessarily become wealthier because of it. Instead, causal factors may be a number of incidental circumstances loosely related to the religion adhered to, such as education, the socio-economic environment in which the adherents of that religion live, and particular practices that may be associated with the community. This socio-economic environment appears to be crucial in this regard. This is indicated, among other things, by the extensive research on the productivity growth of labour migrants once they have settled in a developed country. Referred to in Chapter 8, the "epidemiological" model, which assumes that the low productivity of labour migrants can "infect" the host country through the cultural factors they bring with them, is not empirically validated. Rather, historical episodes of mass migration have led to the opposite observation. Productivity *per capita* has increased (Clemens & Pritchett, 2019). Simplifying, we can say that it matters more where we are than what we are like.

Economy, evolution, and culture

These cultural determinants were also pointed out by the precursor of American institutionalism, Thorstein Veblen (1857–1929). The peculiarity of Veblen, who did not conduct any empirical research, was to describe the economy, particularly the agents operating in the market, in cultural-evolutionary terms. He analysed market behaviour, getting rich, capital accumulation, conspicuous consumption, and competition in terms of cultural evolution, social Darwinism, and actions subordinated to domination and procreation (Veblen, 1994). Economists still use the concept of the Veblen effect today to describe the particular characteristics of the demand curve in relation to so-called positional goods, for which demand does not fall but rises as the price increases. Such a strongly positional good is, for example, elite education, comprising the highest-ranked schools. The fact that there is little or no difference between the first-ranked school and the second-ranked one in terms of the quality of the education provided and its effects does not change the fact that the difference in tuition fees will be huge. The higher the tuition fees and the lower the number of graduates, the stronger the positioning or Veblen effect will be. According to some economists, however, this effect leads to a huge waste of social resources (Frank, 1985).

Particular forerunners of the historical and sociological approach in economics were Friedrich Engels and Karl Marx. The former became famous for his very sound sociological analysis of the situation of the working class in Manchester (Engels, 1993). He covered not only their economic situation but also the urban aspects of the neighbourhoods they inhabited, fostering *de facto* social exclusion and physical separation of social classes. In turn, the axis of Marx's reflections made the socio-economic transformations throughout history, resulting in different economic relations. In this respect, he remained faithful to the historical-dialectical method developed by Hegel. In modern economics, the research method which is based on the analysis of contradictions and conflicts between social classes and the search for a possible synthesis is rather a historical curiosity. However, the exploration and emphasis on the role of individual and collective social consciousness, which can significantly influence economic relations, has remained and is still present in today's considerations. In doing so, it is recognised that this consciousness is linked to a given historical moment, the degree of technological development, or the level of satisfaction of individuals' preferences. This is illustrated by Marx's well-known statement that "life is not determined by consciousness, but consciousness by life", which expresses the hypothesis that the current development of the so-called means of production determines our conception of the world and the relations within it (Marx, 1977). In Chapter 1, we referred to this hypothesis as "Marxist". In principle, it is shared by most economists, who are inclined to attribute certain social changes to technological progress. A different belief in this regard is presented by Deidre McCloskey, who argues that socio-cultural change is the precondition for technological change and not the other way around (McCloskey, 2016). The dispute is important insofar as in welfare economics, recommendations are made on, for example, the most effective ways to stimulate economic growth and, thus, prosperity. Trivialising, it then becomes crucial to decide whether to educate first, or perhaps hand out mobile phones, or build transport infrastructure. The dispute is also reflected in debates about how to measure well-being. Indeed, it is increasingly being related to local, individual, and historical circumstances. A particular example of this is the economics of Amartya Sen, the 1998 Nobel laureate in economics, who proposes to measure well-being through people's available *capabilities* and individually chosen ways of living and acting (*functionalities*). Both categories depend precisely on local socio-economic conditions (Kwarciński, 2011).

Poverty and wealth demographics

The links between economics and demography were noted relatively early on. In his work, Thomas Malthus drew attention to the relationship between the economic situation of the lowest-income social strata and their population (Malthus, 2000). In simple terms, the population of the poorest people was supposed to increase as income increased, resulting in an increase in the number of children to feed and a decrease in the *per capita* income of people in this social stratum, which in turn led to secondary impoverishment, increased mortality, and population decline. Such demographic changes were to be circular in nature, with a trend leading to increasing poverty. In our moral terms, the conclusions were somewhat striking, as they implied population control and a reduction in any charity that led only to a temporary improvement in the material situation of the poorest. Fortunately, these predictions did not materialise, but the analysis highlighted the strong correlation between population size, its social and age structure, and the economic situation. Malthus' pessimistic predictions failed, among other things, because he did not take into account the fact that each successive human being comes into the world not only as a consumer of limited resources but, above all, as their producer, with a creative mind and two hands to work. A similar argument is put forward against economic migrants as alleged consumers of social welfare, draining the welfare of developed countries. Empirical research, however, does not support such a scenario; on the contrary, more often than not, immigrants prove to be additional contributors to the economic success of host countries (The Economist, 2019).

Research on the relationship between a society's demographic structure and its economic situation has been carried out in various contexts, but two phenomena familiar to economists today are worth pointing out: demographic dividend and secular stagnation. The demographic dividend refers to a situation in which the age structure in society is dominated by people of working age or just before working age. In the 20th century, this demographic transition was associated with radical improvements in healthcare, resulting in falling infant mortality and increasing life expectancy, but also with improvements in education and gradually declining female fertility. These factors resulted in the formation of demographic waves that not only increased the population but, above all, changed its age structure so that in the first period, the structure is dominated by children, who are by definition passive consumers, and, in the later period, it becomes dominated by people of working age, who, having a shorter-lived generation ahead of them and at the same time choosing to have fewer offspring of their own, create the most favourable economic situation, precisely referred to as the demographic dividend. If this demographic effect hits the right socio-economic environment, it has the potential to result in a significant increase in prosperity. This prosperity results from three overlapping factors: the number of people able to work increases due to the age structure. Economists speak in this case of an increased labour supply. The working and earning generation is at the same time increasing its savings, accumulating capital for investment. In turn, improved education, particularly among women, increases their involvement in the labour market. Such an effect occurred between 1965 and 1990 in Ireland, which experienced an average annual growth rate of 6% in gross domestic product (GDP) *per capita* over this period, but especially in East Asia, where it is estimated that between ¼ and 3/5 of the Asian "economic miracle" can be attributed to it. However, demographic structure alone is not enough. A negative example is the Latin American countries, where protectionist economic policies and political instability have turned this demographic dividend into social conflict (Bloom et al., 2003).

Secular stagnation is at the other end of the demographic transition. As the baby boom generation enters the post-working age, leaving behind far fewer working people, the structure of wealth producers and consumers (i.e. pensioners, for example) changes. The latter are increasing in number and are becoming an economic burden. This effect is being offset in some countries by economic immigration, such as Ireland, Germany, Australia, and Canada. In the case of the latter two countries, one could even say that immigration openness is the source of their economic success. In economies closed to external labour inflows, this negative effect of an ageing population is particularly painful. A kind of testing ground for developed economies is Japan, which has been struggling for years with economic stagnation, growing public debt, and impoverishment, especially of the older part of the population. The stagnation of GDP has been associated with a decline in investment and over-accumulation of financial wealth (the elderly are more frugal and less willing to take investment risks) and the subsequent deflation associated with a decline in consumption (due to the different preferences of the elderly) (Müller, 2014).

It is better to be approximately right than precisely wrong[2]

The above examples highlight the rather difficult marriage between sociology, demography, and economics. These sciences stepped in, repeatedly demonstrating the weaknesses of economic models' assumptions but, above all, their completely inaccurate predictions. The criticism of economic models was on target. They usually gave (and still give) a very precise mathematical picture of economic reality, which is often inaccurate. Retrospectively, these sciences were able to identify the factors responsible for the failures and the likely other non-economic reasons why the development of economic reality took a different path from that implied by *mainstream* economic models. The limitations of the ability to formulate accurate predictions identified in Chapter 3 do not only extend to economics. Neither sociology, demography, nor all these sciences combined can produce accurate, workable models. They do, however, undoubtedly allow us to look at economic phenomena from different perspectives and thus to draw up alternative scenarios for their development, which in turn is an important instrument to help us make decisions that are important for our well-being. Sociological and demographic methods and the analyses that follow them are usually much less precise than economic models. Notwithstanding the increasing use of statistical analyses and *big data*, they cannot do without simple qualitative research – observation, interview, questionnaire – i.e. the so-called frog's perspective, which allows better research hypotheses from the point of view of identifying objective causal factors. The consequence of this approach is that the hypotheses are fuzzy and inaccurate, although they appear to be more accurate. And this is their strength.

Notes

1 Chapter 12.
2 This title is a frequently used quote by economists attributed to John Maynard Keynes. Wrongly so. Wikiquote states that the quote began to be attributed to Keynes after his death and originally comes from a work by Carveth Read, the 19th-century British philosopher and logician, *Logic: Deductive and Inductive.* This work is available in its entirety online and there is indeed this quote, on page 352, which in the original reads: *It is better to be vaguely right than exactly wrong.*

References

Banerjee, A., & Duflo, E. (2011). *Poor economics: A radical rethinking of the way to fight global poverty*. PublicAffairs.
Becker, S. O., & Woessmann, L. (2009, May). Was Weber Wrong? A Human Capital Theory of Protestant Economic History. *The Quarterly Journal of Economics*, *124*(2), pp. 531–596.
Bloom, D., Canning, D., & Sevilla, J. (2003). *The demographic dividend: A new perspective on the economic consequences of population change*. RAND Corporation.
Cantoni, D. (2015). The economic effects of the Protestant Reformation: Testing the Weber hypothesis in the German lands. *Journal of the European Economic Association*, *13*(4), 561–598. https://doi.org/10.1111/jeea.12117
Clemens, M. A., & Pritchett, L. (2019). The new economic case for migration restrictions: An assessment. *Journal of Development Economics*, *138*, 153–164. https://doi.org/10.1016/j.jdeveco.2018.12.003
Engels, F. (1993). *The condition of the working class in England* (D. McLellan, Red.). Oxford University Press.
Frank, R. H. (1985). *Choosing the right pond: Human behavior and the quest for status*. Oxford University Press.
Hartwell, R. M. (2017). *The industrial revolution and economic growth*. Routledge.
Kwarciński, T. (2011). *Równość i korzyść: Amartyi Kumar Sena koncepcja sprawiedliwości dystrybutywnej*. Wydawnictwo Uniwersytetu Ekonomicznego.
Malthus, T. R. (2000). An Essay on the Principle of Population. Retrieved 05 19, 2025, from Library of Economics and Liberty: http://www.econlib.org/library/Malthus/malPop3.html#VII.20
Marx, K. (1977). *A contribution to the critique of political economy*. Progress Publishers.
McCloskey, D. (2016). *Bourgeois equality. How ideas not capital or institutions, enriched the world*. The University of Chicago Press.

Müller, H. (2014). *Wirtschaftsirrtümer: 50 Denkfehler, die uns Kopf und Kragen kosten.* Frankfurt am Main.
Ricardo, D. (1821). On the Principles of Political Economy and Taxation. Pobrano 06.03.2013 z lokalizacji Library of Economics and Liberty: http://www.econlib.org/library/Ricardo/ricP1.html
Smith, A. (1776). *An inquiry into the nature and causes of the wealth of nations* (Cannan ed., Vol. 1). Methuen. https://oll.libertyfund.org/titles/smith-an-inquiry-into-the-nature-and-causes-of-the-wealth-of-nations-cannan-ed-vol-1
The Economist. (2019, November 16). Skilled migrants. Light bulb in their luggage. https://www.economist.com/special-report/2019/11/14/how-migration-makes-the-world-brainier
Veblen, T. (1994). *The theory of the leisure class.* Dover Publications Ltd.
Weber, M. (1922). *Wirtschaft und Gesellschaft.* Mohr.
Weber, M. (2002). *The protestant ethic and the spirit of capitalism: And other writings* (P. Baehr & G. C. Wells, Trans.). Penguin.
Weber, M. (2011). *Wirtschaftsgeschichte.* Duncker & Humblot GmbH.

17

DO HUMANS THINK RATIONALLY?

Rationality of the economic man

As seen from the previous chapters, the philosophy of economics is incredibly capacious. It is basically a bag into which philosophers and economists throw various issues that either do not fit into the economic mainstream or lie somewhere on the borderline between economics and philosophical or interdisciplinary reflection. Some focus on methodological issues (how to do economics for a better life), others on ontological issues (what does economics describe to us and does the subject of description exist, and if so, how), and still others on ethical issues (what does it mean to live better). Somewhat within the framework of the latter considerations is the issue of *homo oeconomicus* – the man of profit, disliked by ancient philosophers, who in popular literary narrative usually means some equivalent of the rich and miserly Ebenezer Scrooge from Charles Dickens' *A Christmas Carol*. Almost everyone abuses this poor economic man, humanists who see him as devoid of all human feelings (whatever those mean), psychologists who accuse him of empirical inadequacy (i.e. people are not like that) and sociologists who point out that the dominance of instrumental rationality in economic analysis leads to the "breeding" of a social class (economists) who see the world in these terms.

The key to understanding the economic man is precisely this instrumental rationality, which boils down, in some simplification, to the total subordination of the methods we choose to act, to the goals we set, or, in other words, to our preferences. It is the foundation of economic analysis. Suppose we understand economics as Lionel Robbins does,[1] i.e. "the science which studies human behaviour as a relationship between ends and scarce means which have alternative uses". In such case, the efficient management of these scarce resources will require instrumental rationality. There is no room here to assume an infinite or incalculable value of

DOI: 10.4324/9781003469384-21

human life, friendship, or love because the resources we could allocate to realise these values are neither infinite. At the same time, economists do not claim to create a complete and empirically adequate picture of human beings. Nevertheless, they make some simple assumptions (at least the classical ones and their successors), such as that people want something (they have certain preferences) and that if they want something, they communicate their needs through the decisions they make (they reveal their preferences) and that they are rational in the realisation of these preferences. This last assumption is the most problematic. For it turns out that there is no single "theory of rationality", but there may be many. They may differ in the scope of their application, but they may also differ in their approach and the results obtained from applying a given theory.

The simplest theory refers to a situation of certainty when we have a number of alternatives to choose from, and which one we implement depends solely on our choice. In such a case, for our choice to be rational, it is sufficient that we can rank all the alternatives (without exception) according to which we prefer more and which we are indifferent (or equivalent) to. Such an ordered set will fulfil two axioms: completeness (it includes all alternatives) and transitivity (if I prefer a car to a scooter and a scooter to a bicycle, I probably also prefer a car to a bicycle). According to this so-called ordinal utility theory, how much more I prefer a car to a scooter is irrelevant. I, therefore, do not need to assign any value to the alternatives. However, this most straightforward form of rationality (like the next two) has two aspects. Firstly, economists assume that people (at least in the vast majority of cases) exhibit such rationality. If they did not exhibit it (if their preferences were non-transitive), the first better rational profit man would pluck them from all resources. This is the so-called money-pump argument (Hausman et al., 2016). If one's preferences were non-transitive (i.e. even though he prefers a car to a scooter and a scooter to a bike, he still prefers a bike to a car), he might engage in a series of transactions that end in bankruptcy. This is because he will be willing to dispose of the scooter and acquire a car at a premium. Having a car available, he will be willing to incur the extra cost of swapping it for a bicycle. Preferring a scooter over a bicycle, he will be inclined to get rid of the bicycle and repurchase a scooter. This reasoning could continue indefinitely were it not for the limited budget of this irrational man. Secondly, utility theories have a normative dimension. They represent a certain ideal model according to which we should act if we want to satisfy our preferences to the greatest extent possible.

The problem gets more complicated when the alternatives we choose concern the future and uncertain states of affairs, e.g., whether one should play the lottery or spend the money on a cinema ticket. In the first case, there is some probability (albeit minimal) of a big win, and in the second case, if one likes the film, one has the chance to spend two hours pleasantly. According to the expected utility theory, one's choice will be rational if one makes it according to a pre-calculated value of this expected utility. To calculate the value, one needs to know (or estimate) the probability of achieving a certain outcome and the value (utility) that this outcome represents for her. We immediately run into problems here. While it is possible to calculate the probability of winning the lottery and to estimate the value of the win, how does one calculate the probability that she will enjoy a film and the value of the utility she will derive from watching it? Here, it is no longer enough to order preferences simply. One also has to assign specific values to them. This theory is much more complicated and entangled in all sorts of paradoxes. It also has more elaborate axiomatics, which, for example, makes an attempt to resolve the so-called Pascal's wager based on it problematic. Recall, this wager is about the expected utility from a virtuous life, which may be eternal salvation but which depends on the uncertain condition of the existence of God. The problem boils down to the fact that the value of utility on account of salvation is infinite, which violates one of the axioms of the theory. The necessity of the so-called cardinal ordering of preferences, i.e. assigning specific values to them to the exclusion of infinite values, inevitably pushes us towards Ebenezer Scrooge. In order to make rational choices, we must either restrict the application of the theory to monetisable preferences only (i.e. those whose value is by definition expressed in some currency) or monetise preferences that intuitively do not lend themselves to this, such as aesthetic experiences, health, life, love, family, and the like. We immediately point out that economists do not shy away from the latter strategy, either by proposing an "economy of the family" (as we discuss in more detail in Chapter 15) or monetising values from the point of view of assessing the implementation of a particular social policy. The latter way seems even inevitable. Imagine that the government could implement two alternative social programmes aimed at increasing the birth rate in a given society. One (e.g., 500+) costs EUR 20 billion a year and can result in 5000 more children being born. The other (e.g., Nursery+) costs EUR 5 billion and can result in 2000 more children being born. Which programme to choose? If anyone divides the amount of investment by the number of births, she has, in a way, made a valuation of the value of one additional life. However, if she assigns an infinite value to it, she cannot compare the two programmes.

Even the theory of expected utility is not enough when the choices (strategies) we make are conditioned by the choices made by other members of the community. In such a situation, in order to make a rational decision, one should calculate not only her expected utility but also the expected utility assumed by others and choose the optimal strategy, assuming that they are equally rational and will strive to maximise their utility. In this way, rational choice would amount to calculating the optimal strategy according to game theory. Here, however, we run into even more problems. This is because many games have more than one optimal strategy or no solution at all. Some indicate a different strategy when played once and another when played repeatedly. Among the flagship examples here is the so-called prisoner's dilemma. It takes its name from a popular story accompanying the game's matrix, according to which a prosecutor interrogates two arrested criminals from the same shaykh. He offers each of them a deal. He gets a lighter sentence if he agrees to testify incriminatingly for the other. If they both testify, the sentence is no longer so lenient. However, if neither testifies, there is a good chance that they will be acquitted, as the prosecutor has no other evidence. The solution to this game is an extremely selfish (non-cooperative) strategy, according to which it is always advantageous to testify. However, when the game is experimentally repeated, the adoption of the so-called tit-for-tat strategy leads to more cooperative choices, i.e. in this example, leading to a refusal to testify. This strategy involves starting with trust (in this story, refusal to testify) and, on subsequent iterations, repeating the opponent's previous choices. Thus, we will rat him out this time if he has previously ratted us out. This strategy is, therefore, educational. After a few attempts, each participant learns that incriminating their partner's testimony will end with someone else incriminating them. It is, therefore, better to remain silent.

Challenges to classical rationality

Are we rational in the sense of any of these three theories? If we were utterly irrational, then, as the example with the "money-pump" shows, it would be difficult in the course of our lives to realise any of our preferences, let alone increase the level of their satisfaction. Nevertheless, from the beginning of economics, the issue of this perfect instrumental rationality has raised several questions. Firstly, of an ethical nature. For if we assume that it is beyond the scope of economics to consider the content of these preferences and that it is not for us, economists to judge them, then we must treat equally the desire of a poor person to satisfy hunger and the desire of a rich person to own a chateau on the Loire. Such a comparison of preferences is clearly at odds with our moral intuitions and leads us to the intriguing considerations that are the subject of so-called welfare economics. The analysis of rationality, which boils down to different kinds of valuing and dealing with our preferences, has a particular assumption in the background: the more our preferences are satisfied, the better off we will be, the "richer" we will be, and implicitly also the happier we will be. If we assign monetary values to these preferences, we get a simplified recipe for public policies that make citizens happy: make them richer, and they will be happier. This is not always the case, as we know from Chapter 7. The chapter also hinted at certain paradoxes of happiness, in particular, one of the first discovered by Easterlin. In simple terms, it boiled down to the observation that, although there is a noticeable correlation between wealth and declared levels of happiness, with further increases in this wealth, this sense of happiness seems to be stuck at an unchanged level. One explanation for this paradox goes to the "treadmill of happiness", the relentless pursuit of fulfilling aspirations that increase as we get richer. Our level of happiness is not increasing, but we, like hamsters, are running faster and faster on the wheel. Such an explanation, however, leads to problems with our rationality. If we consider happiness to be an important goal we would like to pursue in the course of our lives, then getting richer and richer beyond the threshold of increasing happiness is irrational, as it does not lead to an increase in our happiness. We can only speak of irrationality if we fill our preferences with content (e.g., the desire for subjective happiness). However, if we consider that whatever an individual chooses, he does so in accordance with his preferences and, therefore, rationally, then there is no problem. The concept of utility based on revealed preferences, which is usually accompanied by the inadmissibility of so-called interpersonal utility comparisons, leads, according to Amartya Sen, to tautologies and to choices that are clearly contrary to our moral intuitions (as in the example with the Chateau de la Loire) (Bruni & Porta, 2005, p. 16).

Behavioural and cognitive psychologists presented a second set of objections to classical conceptions of rationality. Starting with Nobel laureates in economics, Herbert Simon (1916–2001), Daniel Kahneman, and Amos Tversky (1937–1996), they began to draw attention to systemic deviations from classical rationality occurring at the level of individuals, based on numerous experiments. Kahneman and Tversky even formulated a theory of these deviations, called prospect theory (Kahneman i Tversky, 1979). One of the first deviations revealed was the so-called Ellsberg paradox. In 1961, Ellsberg described an experiment whose essence consisted of presenting participants with two games with the possibility of winning (Ellsberg, 1961). Although, according to expected utility theory, the outcome was the same in both cases, participants were statistically more likely to reject the game in which the payoff calculation was more ambiguous. This paradox revealed one of the first recognised effects of cognitive bias – an aversion to ambiguity and risk. Over time, it has been shown to accurately describe much of the behaviour of investors in the market, who make choices with a lower expected value when in doubt about the quantification of risk.

The aforementioned prospect theory was a real breakthrough in the study of our rationality. Two Israeli psychologists confirmed in their research the existence of ambiguity and risk aversion and revealed a number of further deviations, including the following:

1 Certainty effect – Individuals tend to overestimate outcomes that are certain compared to those that are only probable (better a certain but smaller gain than a higher but uncertain one);
2 Reflection effect – Risk aversion mainly operates when risk-taking involves a potential loss. However, when its taking involves a significant reward, it will be prioritised over a lower but certain reward;
3 Isolation effect – In order to make choices between different alternatives, individuals often overlook the importance of the components common to the alternatives they choose, focusing only on those that seem to distinguish them.

In Chapter 14, we also described the so-called framing effect revealed by the same Nobel laureates, which leads to inconsistent choices when the same situation is described in a different way. Further research in this direction revealed more and more effects that, from the point of view of the principles of rationality described above or from the point of view of the commonly accepted rules of inference, seemed problematic, to say the least. Even before the promulgation of prospect theory, Kahneman and Tversky drew attention to a heuristic (simplified decision-making strategy) often used by skilled researchers, which they called the "law of small numbers" or, somewhat more broadly, "representativeness". Its essence lies in drawing far-reaching conclusions from a very limited (non-representative) set of data (Tversky & Kahneman, 1971). Further research by their disciples revealed further biases such as "probability sampling" (which consists of choosing alternatives with a low probability of success under conditions of risk that are inconsistent with expected utility theory), *status quo* bias (preferring the existing state over a more favourable future state), anchoring effect (e.g., estimation of numerical value based on unrelated, random but previously presented numbers), mental accounting (separate estimation of utility for related alternatives without comparing them), endowment effect (assigning greater value to owned goods over potentially acquired goods), sunk cost fallacy (assigning to owned goods a value increased by the costs incurred to acquire or possessing them), hyperbolic discounting (assigning to future goods a value that decreases hyperbolically with increasing time distance), and a number of others.

Ecological rationality

Does the above mean that we are irrational in our choices, or perhaps, as Sen noted, is the characterisation of rationality in economic theory inconsistent with actual human rationality? Perhaps we are guided in our choices by a different kind of rationality, a collective one – an ecological one. When making life decisions of various kinds, we rarely make complex utility calculations according to any of the concepts described above. Instead, we are most often guided by certain heuristics developed over several million years of the biological and cultural evolution of humans and their ancestors. Since at least the 1970s, economists have been researching and discovering further heuristics (or cognitive biases) that make our decisions appear irrational from the point of view of classical theories. In the case of the prisoner's dilemma, experiments show that participants, even when confident that the game is a one-off, irrationally often choose strategies based on trust and cooperation. This cooperative pattern of behaviour is therefore likely to be in the nature of such an evolutionarily developed heuristic that, even if it does not increase the utility of the decision-maker in a particular case, so proves adaptive in the long run for the species *homo sapiens*. How is this possible? The basic mechanisms of evolution are random genetic mutations, natural selection (individuals unsuited to the environment die out more quickly, leading to the extinction of maladaptive traits), and sexual selection (more "attractive" individuals are more often chosen as sexual partners, leading to the spread of their genetic material). However, Charles Darwin had already drawn attention to the possibility of group selection within a species. If, within a species, different social groups compete with each other for the same limited resources, then a group consisting of mutually supportive "altruists", sacrificing themselves for the group as a whole, is likely to dominate groups consisting of instrumentally rational "egoists", maximising individual utility. In that case, the "egoists" will be eliminated. One of the first economists to draw attention to the evolutionary (i.e. spontaneous) formation of competing social orders was Friedrich A. Hayek (1983). In this sense, ecological rationality is not only about individual heuristics but also about the astonishing effectiveness of institutions of spontaneous order, such as private property or the liberal freedom to trade and express oneself. Such rationality, while creating space for the improvement of individual well-being, no longer has much in common with the selfish man of profit.

Understanding the mechanisms of this ecological rationality is used by contemporary evolutionary economists (who, however, still represent a certain exotic in the discipline) to explain the specific behaviour of financial markets leading to speculative bubbles and economic crises. Following one of them (Lo, 2017) we cite the intriguing example of fictional creatures, the Tribbles, who, over the course of their lives, must make one crucial decision: should they settle and beget offspring in a valley or on a plain? In sunny weather, the valley provides shade and access to water, which maximises the number of offspring, while the plain is drought-ridden, which limits the number of offspring. However, in wet weather, the rising water in the valley floods the nests, and most Tribbles die, whereas in plain conditions are ideal. Let us assume that the ratio of sunny and rainy days is 75/25. The probability of the valley being flooded is, therefore, ¼. According to expected utility theory, the rational individual choice of each Tribble should always fall on the valley. However, the entire population will become extinct in that case at the first flood. A simulation analysis of the different strategies leads to an interesting conclusion: from the point of view of the entire population, the most optimal strategy is to distribute the habitat between the valley and the plain in the same proportion as sunny and rainy days remain in relation to each other. Thus, a population of individuals employing just such a seemingly irrational heuristic has the best chance of spreading.

How does this apply to financial markets? One of the interesting cognitive biases discovered by experimental economists is people's inability to estimate probabilities when making decisions under risk. Imagine a very simple "one-armed bandit" type game where only two letters, A and B, alternate on the screen at each draw. The ratio of occurrences of A and B is 75/25. Which letter should one bet on in the next iteration to maximise her chances of winning? The answer seems obvious. It should always be the letter A. However, the players in the experiment, making such bets repeatedly, "irrationally" occasionally bet on the letter B. Interestingly, the frequency of betting on the letter B corresponds to the frequency of its falling on the screen, which in this case would be 25/100. Such heuristics have no "ecological" justification. It serves neither the player nor the population. It is the application of a pattern developed over the course of evolution, which took into account extraordinary events in nature, to a situation for which the pattern is not suitable. According to Andrew Lo, a lot of behaviour in the market is of precisely this, sometimes dangerous, nature.

Ecological rationality has several interesting features that clearly distinguish it from 'classical' rationality. Firstly, it is a collective rationality that often diminishes the utility of the individual subject applying it. If we return to the example with the "treadmill of happiness", the interpretation of the behaviour of continually getting rich, even though it does not lead to increasing our sense of happiness and therefore does not seem rational, is of a completely different nature. This is because our social and cultural context determines our aspirations. The higher the aspirations of our reference group, the higher ours will be, too, but not in order to be happier, but in order to stand out. The best way to do this is through the demonstrative acquisition of so-called positional goods, which are more valuable, rarer, and more expensive. This differentiation acts as a peacock's tail. It is a burden but increases the chances of procreative success (Frank, 1985). Secondly, by analysing certain patterns from hindsight, we can reconstruct them from the point of view of their adaptation to a particular environment. However, just as it is impossible to predict the direction of the evolution of certain species in the future, it is impossible to predict what patterns of behaviour will develop in the market (e.g., patterns of consumer or investment behaviour). This is the bane of evolutionary economists and evolutionarily oriented cultural anthropologists, who are unable to construct effective predictive models. Thirdly, classical rationality has a strong normative dimension. In concrete situations, it allows us to create decision-making matrices that, however imperfect, are helpful for individual and political decision-making. Ecological rationality has almost no normative dimension. Almost, because from the point of view of the development and enrichment of society, it allows for a weak postulate of diversity of behaviour patterns (which increases the chance that at least some of them will prove adaptive). From the point of view of the stability of the normative system, on the other hand, it postulates an "early warning system" against spreading patterns of market behaviour that could lead to another financial crisis.

Note

1 Robbins' views are presented in more detail in Chapter 2.

References

Bruni, L., & Porta, P. L. (Eds.). (2005). *Economics and happiness: Framing the analysis*. Oxford University Press.

Ellsberg, D. (1961). Risk, ambiguity, and the savage axioms. *The Quarterly Journal of Economics*, *75*(4), 643–669. https://doi.org/10.2307/1884324

Frank, R. H. (1985). *Choosing the right pond: Human behavior and the quest for status*. Oxford University Press.

Hausman, D., McPherson, M., & Satz, D. (2016). *Economic analysis, moral philosophy, and public policy*. Cambridge University Press.
Hayek, F. A. (1983). *Law, legislation and liberty, Volume I: Rules and order.* The University of Chicago Press.
Kahneman, D., & Tversky, A. (1979). Prospect theory: An analysis of decision under risk. *Econometrica*, *47*(2), 263–291. https://doi.org/10.2307/1914185
Lo, A. W. (2017). *Adaptive market: Financial evolution at the speed of thought*. Princeton University Press.
Tversky, A., & Kahneman, D. (1971). Belief in the Law of Small Numbers. *Psychological Bulletin*, *76*(2), 106–110. https://doi.org/10.1037/h0031322

Kolibri 360 GmbH
Ferdinand-Jühlke-Straße 7
99095 Erfurt, Deutschland
produktsicherheit@kolibri360.de